THE
OFFICIAL
theory
test for car drivers and
motorcyclists

VALID FOR TESTS TAKEN FROM 2 AUGUST 1999

London: The Stationery Office

Written and compiled by the Publications Unit of the Driving Standards Agency (DSA)

Questions and answers are compiled by the Question Development Team of the DSA with support from the National Foundation for Educational Research

Published by The Stationery Office with the permission of the Controller of Her Majesty's Stationery Office on behalf of the Driving Standards Agency.

© Crown Copyright 1999

First published 1996

ISBN 0 11 552017 1

A CIP catalogue record for this book is available from the British Library

Other titles in the Driving Skills series

The Official Theory Test for Drivers of Large Vehicles
The Official Motorcycling Manual
The Official Driving Manual
The Official Guide to Compulsory Basic Training for Motorcyclists
The Official DSA Guide for Driving Instructors
The Official Bus and Coach Driving Manual
The Official Goods Vehicle Driving Manual
The Official Theory Test and Beyond (CD-ROM)
The Official Guide to Tractor and Specialist Vehicle Driving Tests

Acknowledgements

The Driving Standards Agency would like to thank their staff and the following organisations for their contribution to the production of this publication.

National Foundation for Educational Research

Transport Research Laboratory

Department of Environment, Transport and the Regions

Driver & Vehicle Testing Agency, Northern Ireland

Important Information

At the time of writing, the way in which theory tests are taken is under review. DSA plans to introduce a new, multi-media computerised theory test from January 2000. The new test will be easy to use, provide candidates with a more interesting test and give better help for people with reading or language difficulties. Candidates will get their test result before leaving the test centre.

The information in this book about how the test is taken and the address for correspondence are correct only until 31 December 1999.

Full details of the new test arrangements are not yet available. However, information about the new test, and changes to any addresses will be publicised nearer the time and will be available from the DSA Theory Test Unit at 56 Talbot Street, Nottingham, NG1 5GU; Tel: **0115 901 2500.**

The Driving Standards Agency (DSA) is an executive agency of the Department of Environment, Transport and the Regions (DETR).

You'll see its logo at test centres.

The aim of DSA is to promote road safety through the advancement of driving standards.

DSA

- conducts practical driving tests for drivers or riders of cars, mopeds, motorcycles, lorries, buses and other vehicles
- plans, maintains and supervises the theory test for drivers or riders of cars, mopeds, motorcycles, lorries and buses
- controls the register of Approved Driving Instructors (ADIs)
- controls the voluntary register of Large Goods Vehicle (LGV) instructors
- supervises Compulsory Basic Training (CBT) courses for motorcyclists
- aims to provide a high-quality service to its customers.

DVTA

The Driver & Vehicle Testing Agency (DVTA) is an executive agency within the Department of the Environment for Northern Ireland. Its primary aim is to promote and improve road safety through the advancement of driving standards and implementation of the Government's policies for improving the mechanical standards of vehicles.

CONTENTS

DSA THEORY TEST for car drivers and motorcyclists

With the ever-increasing volume of traffic on the roads today, it's important to make sure that new drivers have a broad spread of driving knowledge. New car drivers and motorcycle riders are required to pass a separate theory test before obtaining a full driving licence. This is a major step towards improving road safety in the UK.

This book is intended to help new drivers prepare for the theory test. An extensive knowledge of driving theory will help towards a better understanding of practical driving skills. This is necessary to become a safe and confident driver.

The performance of all aspects of the theory test is continually monitored and, as a result, the question bank has been updated. This book contains the theory test question bank, set out in an easy-to-read style with plenty of illustrations. To assist preparation for the test it explains why the answers are correct and identifies good driving practice.

There are other books in the Driving Skills series that will help you to develop your skills:

The Official Driving Manual
The Official Motorcycling Manual
The Official Driving Test
The Official Guide to Compulsory Basic Training for Motorcyclists

All are published by The Stationery Office.

The Stationery Office also publishes a range of videos, which are designed to explain what to expect during the test and to dispel some of the myths associated with them. An interactive CD-ROM, *The Official Theory Test and Beyond* is also available to help you to develop your knowledge using this modern approach to learning. However it does not contain all of the current theory test questions.

Robin Cummins

Robin Cummins
The Chief Driving Examiner
Driving Standards Agency

This book will help you to

- study for your theory test
- prepare and be successful.

Part One gives you information on how to get started.

Part Two tells you about the question paper and how to answer it.

Part Three shows you the questions that may be used in your test. Don't worry, you won't have to answer all of them. Your paper will have 35 questions.

Books for study

Although this book helps to explain the answers, you should study other publications that cover the subjects in more detail. The DSA recommends that you buy and study *The Highway Code*, *The Official Driving Manual* and *The Official Motorcycling Manual* (which explain driving and riding skills in more detail), and *Know Your Traffic Signs*. Practice theory test papers are also available. All these are published by The Stationery Office.

These books will help you to answer the questions correctly and will also guide you when studying for your practical test. Keep them so that you can refer to them throughout your driving life. You can find them in most booksellers, together with relevant books from other publishers.

It's important that you study – not just to pass the test but to become a safe driver.

To ensure that all candidates are tested fairly, questions used in the theory test are under continuous review. *Some of the questions used will be changed periodically to reflect changes in legislation, or as a result of customer feedback. If you take the theory test you may find questions that don't appear in this book.*

The information needed to answer them is readily available in the books recommended for study.

Driving is a life skill.

Your tests are just the beginning.

When you pass your test you will be given a certificate. **This has a life of two years from the date of your test.** You will have to take and pass your practical test within this two-year period. If you don't, you will have to take and pass the theory test again before a booking for a practical test can be accepted.

Some of the questions in this book will not be used on question papers in Northern Ireland.

 These are marked with NI.

If you're a motorcycle rider there will be some specific questions on motorcycling.

 In this book those questions are marked with a motorcycle symbol.

If you want to drive a car

DSA in Great Britain, and DVTA in Northern Ireland, approve instructors to teach learner drivers for payment. These instructors have their standards checked regularly.

Approved Driving Instructors (ADIs) must

- pass a series of difficult examinations
- reach a high standard of instruction
- be registered with DSA or DVTA
- display an Approved Driving Instructor's certificate (except in Northern Ireland).

These professional instructors will give you guidance on

- what books to read
- your practical skills
- how to study and practise
- when you're ready for your tests
- further training after passing your practical test.

DSA and the main bodies representing ADIs place great emphasis on professional standards and business ethics. A code of practice has been created, setting a framework within which all instructors should operate. Details of this can be obtained from DSA headquarters:
Tel: **0115 901 2500**.

Videos and a CD-ROMs are available to help you study. The CD-ROM *The Official Theory Test and Beyond* helps you to learn interactively and goes beyond the theory test, teaching you driving skills for life. Visit your local bookshop or ask your driving instructor about relevant material.

If you want to ride a motorcycle

Before you take your practical motorcycle test you must attend and successfully complete a Compulsory Basic Training (CBT) course (except in Northern Ireland). CBT courses can only be given by training bodies approved by DSA. Frequent checks are made to ensure a high standard of instruction.

The course will include

- classroom training
- practical skills training.

You can find out about CBT courses from

- your local Road Safety Officer
- your motorcycle dealer
- DSA Tel: **0115 901 2500.**

DSA also produces *The Official Guide to Compulsory Basic Training for Motorcyclists*, which will give you details about the course.

You'll have to answer specific questions on motorcycling in the theory test. DSA's *The Official Motorcycling Manual* tells you about motorcycling skills in more detail. Books from other publishers are also available. In addition, you should buy and study a copy of *The Highway Code.*

Keep it and refer to it after you've passed your tests. Make sure that you have the latest copy as it's updated periodically.

All these books are available from The Stationery Office.

Applying for your licence

You'll need to apply for a provisional driving licence, as you must produce it at the theory test centre. An application form (D1, or DL1 in Northern Ireland) can be obtained from any post office.

When you receive your provisional licence, sign it immediately. Don't drive until you've done so.

Residency requirements

You can't take a test or obtain a full licence unless you are normally resident in this country. Normal residence means the place where you reside because of personal or occupational ties. However, if you moved to the United Kingdom (UK) having recently been permanently resident in another state of the EC/EEA (European Economic Area), you must have been normally resident in the UK for 185 days in the 12 months prior to your application for a driving test or full driving licence.

About the theory test

The actual delivery of the test is undertaken by a contractor, although DSA (DVTA in Northern Ireland) has overall responsibility for managing the theory test operation.

Note.

From January 2000 a new contractor will deliver a computerised theory test. The source material and question bank will remain the same. In time, when the question bank is reviewed, a new edition of this book will be published.

The theory test is straightforward and you'll pass if you're well prepared. You need to have a knowledge of *The Highway Code* and understand the principles of road safety.

Does everyone have to take the theory test?

Foreign licence holders:

If you hold a foreign driving licence issued outside the EEA first check with the Driver Vehicle Licencing Authority (Tel: **01792 772151**) whether you can exchange your driving licence. If you cannot exchange your licence you will need to take a driving test.

UK licence holders:

Holders of a full car licence who wish to obtain a motorcycle licence don't have to take the theory test. Nor will holders of a full motorcycle licence who require a full car licence. If you passed a theory test and then a practical moped test, then you won't have to take the theory test again in order to upgrade to a car or motorcycle licence.

Any particular enquiries about whether a theory test is required should be addressed to the Theory Test Unit, Driving Standards Agency, Stanley House, 56 Talbot Street, Nottingham, NG1 5GU; Tel: **0115 901 2500.**

Can I take my practical test first?

No. You have to take and pass your theory test before a booking for the practical test is accepted.

Will I be asked to do lots of writing?

No. The question paper is designed so that you only have to put a cross against the answers you think are correct.

How many questions are there?

There are 35 questions in the paper. You should try to answer all of them

How long do I have to complete the test?

Each test session lasts for 40 minutes. You can take all this time if you need to, and there will be a clock in the room to remind you of the time. The invigilator will also tell you when there are five minutes left.

Where do I have to go to take the test?

There are over 150 test centres throughout England, Scotland, Wales and Northern Ireland. Most people have a test centre within 20 miles of their home, but this will vary depending on the density of the population in your area. You can find a list of test centres at the back of this book or telephone the information line on **0870 01 01 372.**

Candidates wishing to take a test in Northern Ireland should telephone **0645 000 555.**

When are the test centres open?

Sessions are provided on weekdays, evenings and on Saturdays. However, where demand is less than 100 tests per year test sessions may be less frequent.

Will I know the result straight away?

Not straight away, but you'll be informed in about seven to ten days.

Some centres provide a facility for results while you wait, at a premium fee. You can ask about this service when you book your test.

When a computerised service is offered, the test result will be available before leaving the test centre. This will usually be offered within 30 minutes of completing the test.

If I don't pass, when can I take the test again?

You will have to wait a minimum of three days before you take the test again. If you fail your test you've shown that you aren't fully prepared. Good preparation will save you time and money.

Is the test only available in English?

No. The test is currently available in the following languages

English	Chinese
Gujarati	Welsh
Hindi	Bengali
Punjabi	Urdu

The range of languages in which test papers are provided may change. To check the latest list of languages available please telephone **0870 01 01 372**.

If you can *speak* English but can't read in any of the languages provided, a member of staff will be available to read through the test on a one-to-one basis. State this on your application form or ask the operator when you call to book your test.

Can I bring a translator with me?

Yes. If you can't read or write any of the languages available you're allowed to bring a translator with you when you take your test. The Theory Test Unit can provide a list of approved bodies who provide translators. You can only bring a translator who's approved by DSA or DVTA. You should tell the booking office that you intend to bring a translator with you.

Are there any provisions for special needs?

Every effort has been made to ensure that the theory test can be taken by all candidates. It's important that you state your needs when booking so that the necessary arrangements can be made.

If you're dyslexic or have difficulty with reading, don't worry. You may be allowed double the normal time to take the test or have the test read to you, if necessary. In order that DSA can provide you with these additional services, we will require a letter from a teacher or educationalist, a psychologist or a doctor (if appropriate) which confirms your special needs. If it isn't possible to get this confirmation from a relevant professional, DSA will consider a statement from an independent person who knows something about your reading ability. This could be your employer, but if you're unsure about who to ask, telephone **0870 01 01 372**.

Candidates in Northern Ireland should telephone **0645 000 555**

Post or fax your documentation as soon as possible, along with your booking reference number or driving licence number, to the address opposite.

Special Needs

DSA
PO Box 445
Coventry
CV1 2ZZ

Fax: **0870 01 04 372**.

DSA is unable to take responsibility for the safe return of any original documentation sent, so it is advisable to send copies only.

If you're deaf and also have difficulty reading, a British Sign Language signer or lip-speaker can be provided. If you have any physical disability that could prevent you marking the boxes on the test paper, help will be available for you.

If you require wheelchair access and your nearest test centre doesn't provide this, DSA will arrange for you to take the test at a suitable location, such as a library or job centre, or take you to another test centre where the facilities are provided. For details telephone **0870 01 01 372**.

How do I book a test?

Application forms are available from

* theory test centres
* driving test centres
* your Approved Driving Instructor.

The easiest way to book a test is by telephone, using your credit or debit card. The person who books the test must be the card-holder.
If you book by this method you'll be given the date and time of your test immediately. You can do this by calling **0870 01 01 372** or **0645 000 555** for Northern Ireland at any time between 8 am and 6 pm Monday to Friday. When you phone you should have ready your

* DVLA/DVLNI driving licence number
* credit or debit card details.

If you're deaf and need a minicom machine telephone **0870 01 06 372**.

Welsh speakers can telephone **0870 01 00 372**.

You'll be given a booking number, and sent an appointment letter that you should expect to receive within four days of your call. Take this, together with your signed driving licence and photo identity, or both parts of your signed photocard licence, if you have one, when you attend your theory test.

For information about cancelling a test please refer to page 429.

At the test centre

Make sure that you have all the necessary documents with you. You'll need

- your signed driving licence and photo identity, or
- both parts of your signed photocard licence, and
- your apointment card or booking number.

The form of photographic identification acceptable at both theory and practical tests is as follows

- **your passport**, which doesn't have to be a British passport
- ***cheque guarantee card or credit card** bearing your photograph and signature
- **an employer's identity or workplace pass** bearing your photograph and name or signature or both
- **Trade Union Card** bearing your photograph and signature
- **Student Union Card** with reference to either the NUS or an education establishment/course reference number. The card must bear your photograph and name or signature or both
- **School Bus Pass** bearing the name of the issuing authority and your photograph and signature

- ***card issued in connection with sale and purchase of reduced-price railway tickets** bearing the name of the issuing authority and your photograph and signature. This is a card issued by a Railway Authority or other authorised body to purchase a reduced-price railway ticket (e.g. a Young Persons Railcard)
- ***Gun Licence**, including a Firearm or Shotgun Certificate, which bears your photograph and signature
- ***Proof of Age Card** issued by the Portman Group bearing your photograph and signature
- ***Standard Acknowledgement Letter (SAL)** issued by the Home Office bearing your photograph and signature.

*Not valid in Northern Ireland.

Remember...

No photo
No licence
No test

If you don't have any of these you can bring a signed photograph, together with a statement like the one shown below, that it's a true likeness of you. Both the statement, and the back of the photograph must be signed by the same person. This can be any of the following

- *Approved Driving Instructor, but not a trainee (pink licence) holder
- *DSA-certified motorcycle instructor
- Member of Parliament
- medical practitioner
- *local authority councillor
- teacher (qualified)
- Justice of the Peace
- civil servant (established)
- police officer
- bank official
- minister of religion
- barrister or solicitor
- *Commissioned Officer in Her Majesty's Forces
- *LGV Trainers on the DSA Voluntary Register of LGV Instructors.
  *Not valid in Northern Ireland.

If you don't bring these documents on the day, you won't be able to take your test and you'll lose your fee. If you have any queries about what photographic evidence we will accept, contact the enquiry line on **0870 01 01 372** or **0645 000 555** in Northern Ireland.

Arrive in plenty of time so that you aren't rushed. The test centre staff will check your documents and ensure that you have the right category test paper to complete. If you arrive after the session has started you will not be allowed to sit the test.

I (name of certifier), certify that this is a true likeness of , who has been known to me for (number) months / years in my capacity as

Signed

Dated

Daytime phone no.

ADI/CBT Instructor no.

THEORY TEST FOR DRIVERS

PRACTICE QUESTIONS

Surname

First Names

Booking Ref. 88

Pro. Licence No.

ENGLISH M.V.

Centre No.

Date D D M M Y Y Y Y

Time H H M M

GENERAL INSTRUCTIONS

1. For each question you must find the right answer(s) and mark an X in the box next to it.
2. Do not write any comments on your test paper.
3. Two examples have been done to show you how to mark your answers.
4. If you make a mistake cross out your original choice completely and mark your other choice as shown.

EXAMPLES

E1 You are invited to a pub lunch. You know that you will have to drive in the evening. You are advised to

Mark one answer

a ☒ avoid mixing your alcoholic drinks

b ☒ not drink any alcohol at all

c ☒ have some milk before drinking alcohol

d ☒ eat a hot meal with your alcoholic drinks

E2 You are approaching a roundabout. There are horses just ahead of you. You should

Mark two answers

a ☒ treat them like any other vehicle

b ☒ be prepared to stop

c ☒ give them plenty of room

d ☒ accelerate past them as quickly as possible

e ☒ sound your horn as a warning

P1 The pictured vehicle is 'Environmentally Friendly' because it

Mark three answers

a ☒ reduces noise pollution

b ☒ use diesel fuel

c ☒ uses electricity

d ☒ uses unleaded fuel

e ☒ reduces parking spaces

f ☒ reduces town traffic

P2 You see an elderly pedestrian about to cross the road ahead. You should

Mark one answer

a ☒ expect them to wait for you to pass

b ☒ speed up to get past them quickly

c ☒ stop and wave them across the road

d ☒ be careful, they may misjudge your speed

P3 Motorcyclists are more at risk from other road users because they

Mark one answer

a ☒ are less experienced then other drivers

b ☒ are more likely to break down than other motorists

c ☒ are always faster than other drivers

d ☒ are more difficult to see than other vehicles

P4 You are approaching this cyclist. You should

Mark one answer

a ☒ overtake before the cyclist gets to the junction

b ☒ flash your headlights at the cyclist

c ☒ slow down and allow the cyclist to turn

d ☒ overtake the cyclist on the left hand side

11 A vehicle has a flashing green light. What does this mean?

Mark one answer

a ☒ A doctor is answering an emergency call

b ☒ The vehicle is slow moving

c ☒ It is a motorway police patrol vehicle

d ☒ A vehicle is carrying hazardous chemicals

12 You MUST obey signs giving orders. These signs are mostly in

Mark one answer

a ☒ blue rectangles

b ☒ green rectangles

c ☒ red triangles

d ☒ red circles

13 Another driver does something that upsets you. You should

Mark one answer

a ☒ try not to react

b ☒ let them know how you feel

c ☒ flash your headlamps several times

d ☒ sound your horn

14 You are driving behind a cyclist. You wish to turn left just ahead. You should

Mark one answer

a ☒ overtake the cyclist before the junction

b ☒ pull alongside the cyclist and stay level until after the junction

c ☒ hold back until the cyclist has passed the junction

d ☒ go around the cyclist on the junction

15 Which TWO of the following are correct? When overtaking at night you should

Mark two answers

a ☒ wait until a bend so you can see the oncoming headlights

b ☒ sound your horn twice before moving out

c ☒ be careful because you can see less

d ☒ beware of bends in the road ahead

e ☒ put headlights on full beam

1 Which sign means no overtaking?

Mark one answer

a ☒
b ☒
c ☒
d ☒

2 You are turning left into a side road. Pedestrians are crossing the road near the junction. You must

Mark one answer

a ☒ wave them on
b ☒ sound your horn
c ☒ wait for them to cross
d ☒ switch on your hazard lights

3 As a car driver, which THREE lanes must you NOT use?

Mark three answers

a ☒ Crawler lane
b ☒ Bus lane at the times shown
c ☒ Overtaking lane
d ☒ Acceleration lane
e ☒ Cycle lane
f ☒ Tram lane

4 You are driving at night and are dazzled by the headlights of an oncoming car. You should

Mark one answer

a ☒ slow down or stop
b ☒ close your eyes
c ☒ flash your headlights
d ☒ pull down the sun visor

5 What does this sign mean?

Mark one answer

a ☒ Through traffic use left lane
b ☒ Right-hand lane T junction only
c ☒ Right-hand lane closed ahead
d ☒ 11 ton weight limit

At the start of the test you'll be asked to complete some practice questions.

There will be different types of questions in the paper. Most of them will ask you to mark ONE correct answer from four. Other questions will ask for TWO OR MORE correct answers from a selection. Some of the questions will show you a picture. This is to test your knowledge of traffic signs or your ability to spot a hazard. Look at the question carefully.

The questions will cover a variety of topics relating to road safety. Mark the box alongside the answers you think are correct.

Some questions will take longer to answer than others. There are no trick questions. If you're well prepared you won't find them difficult.

Take your time and read the questions carefully. You're given plenty of time, so relax and don't rush. Try to answer all 35 questions.

When you think you've finished, read through your test again and check your answers before you hand the paper in.

If you're taking a motorcycle theory test

As well as questions which apply to all road users, you'll be asked some specific questions on motorcycling matters.

The topics covered in the test

Alertness

The need to be alert and attentive when driving or riding. You must consider

- **Observation**
  look all around for other road users and pedestrians.

- **Anticipation**
  look ahead and giving yourself enough time to react to hazards.

- **Concentration**
  be alert at all times when driving or riding.

- **Awareness**
  understand the actions of other road users.

- **Distraction**
  don't become distracted whilst driving or riding. Your attention must be on the road.

- **Boredom**
  could make you feel sleepy. Keep your mind on your driving.

Attitude

Your attitude will affect your driving. Attitude consists of

- **Consideration**
  consider other road users. Be positive but treat them as you would wish to be treated.

- **Close following**
  don't follow too closely. As well as being dangerous, it can feel threatening to the driver in front.

- **Courtesy**
  treat other road users as colleagues or team members. They too are trying to complete their journey safely.

- **Priority**
  be aware that all rules on priority won't always be followed by other road users. Try to be calm and tolerant if other drivers or riders break the rules.

Safety and your vehicle

To prevent your vehicle endangering lives you must ensure that it's in good condition. You should be aware of

- **Fault detection**
  be able to detect minor faults on your vehicle.

- **Defects and their effects on safety**
  be aware that an unroadworthy vehicle might endanger your passengers or other road users.

- **Use of safety equipment**
  make sure you have any necessary training

- **Emissions**
  make sure your vehicle complies with correct emissions regulations.

- **Noise**
  be aware that vehicles are noisy. Prevent excessive noise, especially at night.

Safety Margins

You must be aware of the safety margins when driving in all conditions. You should consider

- **Stopping distances**
  leave enough room to stop in all conditions.

- **Road surfaces**
  be aware of uneven or slippery surfaces.

- **Skidding**
  be aware that preventing a skid is most important, but you should also know how to react should you lose control of your vehicle.

- **Weather conditions**
  be aware that weather conditions will have an effect on how your vehicle behaves.

Hazard Awareness

Your good judgement and perception of the road ahead will lessen the risk of an accident. You should keep in mind

- **Anticipation**
  plan ahead to prevent last-second reactions.

- **Hazard awareness**
  recognise a hazard ahead and preparing yourself for it.

- **Attention**
  look out for problems ahead when you're driving or riding.

- **Speed and distance**
  be aware of the correct speed for the situation, leaving enough space to react.

- **Reaction time**
  be aware that you need time to react.

- **The effects of alcohol and drugs**
  understand how these will affect your reaction time.

- **Tiredness**
  don't drive or ride if you're tired. You need to be alert at all times.

Vulnerable Road Users

Others on the road may need more time or room. Potential hazards to consider are

- **Pedestrians**
  be aware of their actions as they cross the road.

- **Children**
  be aware that they are particularly unpredictable on and around roads.

- **Elderly drivers**
  be aware that they may be slower to make decisions.

- **Disabled people**
  be aware that they might not be able to react to danger as quickly or easily as the able-bodied.

- **Cyclists**
  be aware that they may swerve to avoid obstructions and are often affected by weather conditions.

- **Motorcyclists**
  be aware of their presence on the road.

- **Animals**
  be aware that animals can be unpredictable and may move slowly.

- **New drivers**
  be aware that they may be more hesitant, allow for this and be patient. They lack experience and are, therefore, more vulnerable.

Other types of vehicle

Other vehicles might behave differently on the road. You should consider

- **Motorcycles**
  be aware that they may need as much room as a car.

- **Lorries**
  are larger and need more room on the road.

- **Buses**
  are usually large and might make frequent stops.

Vehicle Handling

You need to adapt your driving or riding to the different conditions on the road. You should consider

- **Weather conditions**
  be aware of how wet or icy roads will affect the handling of your vehicle.

- **Road conditions**
  be aware of how the road surface may affect your vehicle.

- **Time of day**
  be aware of hazards when driving or riding at night.

- **Speed**
  be aware that it's more difficult to control your vehicle at high speeds.

- **Traffic calming**
  be aware of measures used to slow down traffic where there are pedestrians.

Motorway rules

You must know the rules that apply to you and your vehicle on the motorway. Factors to consider are

- **Speed limits**
  be aware of the speed restrictions on the motorway.

- **Lane discipline**
  keep to the left unless overtaking.

- **Stopping**
  know when and where you can stop on the motorway.

- **Lighting**
  be aware of the importance of being seen.

- **Parking**
  don't park on the motorway unless in an emergency.

Rules of the road

You should know the rules of the road. Aspects include

- **Speed limits**
  be aware of the speed limits for different types of vehicle.

- **Lane discipline**
  be sure you select the correct lane for the direction you wish to take.

- **Parking**
  choose a sensible place to park.

- **Lighting**
  don't let your vehicle become a hazard.

Road and traffic signs

Traffic signs are a means of giving messages to road users. You should know what they mean. You should consider

- **Road signs**
  these tell you about the road ahead.

- **Speed limits**
  recognise signs showing speed limits.

- **Road markings**
  be aware that directions might be painted on the road surface.

- **Regulations**
  these can be shown to you by means of a road sign.

Documents

You and your vehicle must be licensed to be on the road. The documents you'll need include

- **Licences**
  you must know what the law requires.

- **Insurance**
  you must have the cover you need to drive or ride.

- **MOT test certificate**
  you should be aware of the safety checks your vehicle must undergo to gain an MOT certificate.

Accidents

You should know what to do if you arrive at or are involved in an accident.

You should be aware of

- **First Aid**
  if you have the knowledge, your fast, effective action might save a life.

- **Warning devices**
  know how to warn other road users of an accident.

- **Reporting procedures**
  know where and when to report an accident.

- **Safety regulations**
  know what to do if a vehicle carrying hazardous loads is involved in an accident.

Vehicle loading

You should be aware of the importance of secure loads. You should consider

- **Stability**
  make sure that your load doesn't affect the stability of your vehicle.

- **Towing regulations**
  be aware of the effects of towing a trailer and the rules that apply.

About Part Three

In this part of the book you'll find questions that might be used in your theory test. The answers have been provided to help you to study.

For easy reference and to help you to study, the questions have been divided into topics and put into sections. Although this isn't how you'll find them in your test it's helpful if you want to refer to particular subjects.

The questions are in the left-hand column with a choice of answers beneath. On the right-hand side of the page you'll find the correct answers and a brief explanation of why they are correct. There will also be some advice on correct driving procedures.

DON'T JUST LEARN THE ANSWERS. It's important that you know **why** the answers are correct. This will help you with your practical skills and prepare you to become a safe and confident driver.

Taking exams or tests is rarely a pleasant experience, but you can make your test less stressful by being confident that you have the knowledge to answer the questions correctly.

Make studying more fun by involving friends and relations. Take part in a question-and-answer game. Test those 'experienced' drivers who've had their licence a while: they might learn something too!

If you're taking a motorcycle theory test

In this part of the book the specific questions for motorcyclists are marked with a motorcycle symbol.

Most of the other questions refer to all road users, so you should study these too. Some will appear in your test with slight changes, for example 'rider' instead of 'driver' or 'headlight' instead of 'headlights'.

This section looks at alertness and attention when you're driving.

The questions will ask you about

- observation
- anticipation
- concentration
- awareness
- distraction
- boredom.

Question 1.1

When turning your car in the road, you should always

Mark one answer

☒ overhang the kerb

☒ use a driveway

☒ check all around for other road users

☒ keep your hand on the handbrake

Answer

 check all around for other road users

There might be an occasion when you need to turn your car around to face the opposite way. Ensure that you're fully aware of other road users by practising good observation. The road you intend to turn around in shouldn't be busy. If it is, find a quiet side road to turn in.

Question 1.2

Before you make a U-turn in the road, you should

Mark one answer

☒ give an arm signal as well as using your indicators

☒ signal so that other drivers can slow down for you

☒ look over your shoulder for a final check

☒ select a higher gear than normal

Answer

 look over your shoulder for a final check

If you want to make a U-turn, slow down and ensure that the road is clear in both directions. Make sure that the road is wide enough to carry out the manoeuvre safely.

Question 1.3

To move off safely from a parked position you should

Mark one answer

☒ signal if other drivers will need to slow down

☒ leave your motorcycle on its stand until the road is clear

☒ give an arm signal as well as using your indicators

☒ look over your shoulder for a final check

Answer

X look over your shoulder for a final check

If you're intending to move off from the side of the road on a motorcycle you should take a final look around over your shoulder. There may be another road user not visible in your mirrors.

Question 1.4

As a driver what does the term 'Blind Spot' mean?

Mark one answer

- [ ] An area covered by your right hand mirror
- [ ] An area not covered by your headlights
- [ ] An area covered by your left hand mirror
- [ ] An area not seen in your mirrors

Answer

- [X] **An area not seen in your mirrors**

Modern vehicles provide the driver with well positioned mirrors which are essential for safe driving. However, they cannot show every aspect of the scene behind. It is essential you are aware of this and check over your shoulder for any dangers not reflected in your mirrors.

Question 1.5

Objects hanging from your interior mirror may

Mark two answers

- [ ] restrict your view
- [ ] improve your driving
- [ ] distract your attention
- [ ] help your concentration

Answers

- [X] **restrict your view**
- [X] **distract your attention**

Ensure that you can see clearly through the windscreen of your vehicle. Stickers or hanging objects could affect your field of vision or draw you eyes away from the road.

Question 1.6

You are most likely to lose concentration when driving if you

Mark two answers

- [ ] use a mobile phone
- [ ] listen to very loud music
- [ ] switch on the heated rear window
- [ ] look at the door mirrors

Answers

- [X] **use a mobile phone**
- [X] **listen to very loud music**

Distractions, especially those which cause you to take your hands from the steering wheel, are dangerous. You should be in full control of your vehicle at all times.

DSA THEORY TEST for car drivers and motorcyclists

Question 1.7

Which FOUR are most likely to cause you to lose concentration while you are driving?

Mark four answers

- Using a mobile phone
- Talking into a microphone
- Tuning your car radio
- Looking at a map
- Checking the mirrors
- Using the demisters

Answers

- ❌ **Using a mobile phone**
- ❌ **Talking into a microphone**
- ❌ **Tuning your car radio**
- ❌ **Looking at a map**

Planning your journey is important. With sensible preparation before moving off you can

- tune your radio into frequencies in your areas of travel
- plan your breaks (which can be used for phone calls)
- plan your route (make notes of road numbers and junction numbers if necessary). This will mean you don't need to look at maps while driving.

Question 1.8

When riding, your shoulders obstruct the view in your mirrors. To overcome this you should

Mark one answer

- indicate earlier than normal
- fit smaller mirrors
- extend the mirror arms
- brake earlier than normal

Answer

- ❌ **extend the mirror arms**

It's essential that you have a clear view all around. Check the position of the mirrors before you move off.

Question 1.9

You want to change lanes in busy, moving traffic. Why could looking over your shoulder help?

Mark two answers

☒ Mirrors may not cover blind spots

☒ To avoid having to give a signal

☒ So traffic ahead will make room for you

☒ So your balance will not be affected

☒ Following motorists would be warned

Answers

☒ **Mirrors may not cover blind spots**

☒ **Following motorists would be warned**

Before you change lanes you need to know that there's a safe gap to move into. Looking over your shoulder

- allows you to see into the area not covered by the mirrors and which could hide another vehicle
- warns following motorists that you want to change lanes.

Question 1.10

You are about to turn right. What should you do just before you turn?

Mark one answer

☒ Give the correct signal

☒ Take a 'lifesaver' glance over your shoulder

☒ Select the correct gear

☒ Get in position ready for the turn

Answer

☒ **Take a 'lifesaver' glance over your shoulder**

When you're turning right, plan your approach to the junction. Signal and select the correct gear in good time. Just before you turn give a 'lifesaver' glance for a final check behind and alongside.

Question 1.11

What, according to *The Driving Manual*, do the letters MSM mean?

Mark one answer

☒ Mirror, signal, manoeuvre

☒ Manoeuvre, signal, mirror

☒ Mirror, speed, manoeuvre

☒ Manoeuvre, speed, mirror

Answer

☒ **Mirror, signal, manoeuvre**

Always use the MSM routine when you're approaching a hazard. Use your mirrors to check the position of traffic around you. Signal your intention to change course or slow down. Do this in good time. A 'manoeuvre' is any change of speed or position, from slowing or stopping the car to turning off a busy main road.

Question 1.12

What is the 'lifesaver' when riding a motorcycle?

Mark one answer

- [ ] A certificate every motorcyclist must have
- [ ] A final, rearward glance before changing direction
- [ ] A part of the motorcycle tool kit
- [ ] A mirror fitted to check blind spots

Answer

❌ **A final, rearward glance before changing direction**

This action makes you aware of what's happening behind and alongside. It should be timed so that you are still able to react if it isn't safe to perform the manoeuvre.

Question 1.13

You are driving on a wet road. You have to stop your vehicle in an emergency. You should

Mark one answer

- [ ] apply the handbrake and footbrake together
- [ ] keep both hands on the wheel
- [ ] select reverse gear
- [ ] give an arm signal

Answer

❌ **keep both hands on the wheel**

As you drive look well ahead and all around so that you're ready for any hazards that might occur. There may be occasions when you have to stop in an emergency. React as quickly as you can whilst keeping control of the vehicle.

Question 1.14

You see road signs showing a sharp bend ahead. What should you do?

Mark one answer

- [ ] Continue at the same speed
- [ ] Slow down as you go around the bend
- [ ] Slow down as you come out of the bend
- [ ] Slow down before the bend

Answer

❌ **Slow down before the bend**

Road signs might give you advance warning of a hazard. Always look and plan well ahead. This will avoid the need for late, harsh braking. Your motorcycle should be upright and moving in a straight line when you brake. This will ensure maximum control when dealing with the hazard.

Question 1.15

As you approach this bridge you should

Mark three answers

- [x] move into the middle of the road to get a better view
- [x] slow down
- [x] get over the bridge as quickly as possible
- [x] consider using your horn
- [x] find another route
- [x] beware of pedestrians

Question 1.16

When following a large vehicle you should keep well back because

Mark one answer

- [x] it allows you to corner more quickly
- [x] it helps the large vehicle to stop more easily
- [x] it allows the driver to see you in the mirrors
- [x] it helps you to keep out of the wind

Answers

- [x] **slow down**
- [x] **consider using your horn**
- [x] **beware of pedestrians**

This signs gives you a warning. You can't see over the bridge for oncoming traffic, so you must be cautious; slow right down. Consider the hidden hazards and be ready to react if necessary.

Answer

- [x] **it allows the driver to see you in the mirrors**

You also need to keep well back so that you get the best view of the road ahead.

DSA THEORY TEST for car drivers and motorcyclists

Question 1.17

In which of these situations should you avoid overtaking?

Mark one answer

- [X] Just after a bend
- [X] In a one-way street
- [X] On a 30 mph road
- [X] Approaching a dip in the road

Answer

[X] **Approaching a dip in the road**

As you begin to think about overtaking, ask yourself if it's really necessary. If you can't see well down the road, stay back and wait for a safer place to pull out.

Question 1.18

Which of the following may cause loss of concentration on a long journey?

Mark four answers

- [X] Loud music
- [X] Arguing with a passenger
- [X] Using a mobile phone
- [X] Putting in a cassette tape
- [X] Stopping regularly to rest
- [X] Pulling up to tune the radio

Answers

[X] **Loud music**
[X] **Arguing with a passenger**
[X] **Using a mobile phone**
[X] **Putting in a cassette tape**

You should not allow other factors to distract you from driving. You need to concentrate fully to ensure you are safe on the road. Loud music could mask other sounds, such as the audible warning of an emergency vehicle. Any distraction which causes you to take your hands off the steering wheel unnecessarily is dangerous.

Question 1.19

You should not use a mobile phone whilst driving

Mark one answer

- [X] until you are satisfied that no other traffic is near
- [X] unless you are able to drive one handed
- [X] because it might distract your attention from the road ahead
- [X] because reception is poor when the engine is running

Answer

[X] **because it might distract your attention from the road ahead**

Driving requires all your attention and concentration at all times. Don't be distracted by unnecessary mobile phone calls. Be safe, switch off your phone while driving.

Question 1.20

Your vehicle is fitted with a hands-free phone system. Using this equipment whilst driving

Mark one answer

- [x] is quite safe as long as you slow down
- [x] could distract your attention from the road
- [x] is recommended by *The Highway Code*
- [x] could be very good for road safety

Answer

 could distract your attention from the road

Having a hands-free system doesn't mean that you can safely drive and use a mobile phone. This type of mobile phone doesn't lessen your responsibility to keep yourself and other road users safe at all times.

Question 1.21

Using a hands-free phone is likely to

Mark one answer

- [x] improve your safety
- [x] increase your concentration
- [x] reduce your view
- [x] divert your attention

Answer

 divert your attention

Unlike someone in the car with you, the person on the other end of the line is unable to see the traffic situations you are dealing with. They will not stop speaking to you even if you are approaching a hazardous situation. You need to be concentrating on your driving all of the time, but especially so when dealing with a hazard.

Question 1.22

Using a mobile phone while you are driving

Mark one answer

- [x] is acceptable in a vehicle with power steering
- [x] will reduce your field of vision
- [x] could distract your attention from the road
- [x] will affect your vehicle's electronic systems

Answer

could distract your attention from the road

Driving today requires all of your attention, all of the time. Any distraction, however brief, is dangerous.

Question 1.23

The white arrow means that you should not plan to

Mark one answer

- ☒ slow down
- ☒ turn right
- ☒ overtake
- ☒ turn left

Answer

 overtake

Look out for road signs and markings as you drive. The arrow on the road surface means that it is not safe to pull out to overtake.

Question 1.24

This road marking warns

Mark one answer

- ☒ drivers to use the hard shoulder
- ☒ overtaking drivers there is a bend to the left
- ☒ overtaking drivers to move back to the left
- ☒ drivers that it is safe to overtake

Answer

 overtaking drivers to move back to the left

You should plan your overtaking to take account of any hazards ahead. In this picture the markings indicate that you are approaching a junction. You will not have time to overtake and move back to the left safely.

Question 1.25

You are driving along this narrow country road. When passing the cyclist you should drive

Answer

 slowly, leaving plenty of room

Look well ahead and only pull out if it is safe. You will need to use all of the road to pass the cyclist, so be extra cautious. Look out for entrances to fields, where there could be tractors or equipment pulling out.

Mark one answer

- slowly, sounding the horn as you pass
- quickly, leaving plenty of room
- slowly, leaving plenty of room
- quickly, sounding the horn as you pass

Question 1.26

You are driving a vehicle fitted with a hand-held telephone. To use the telephone you should

Mark one answer

- reduce your speed
- find a safe place to stop
- steer the vehicle with one hand
- be particularly careful at junctions

Answer

 find a safe place to stop

Your attention should be on your driving at all times. Never attempt to dial or reach out for your phone whilst on the move. It could mean taking your eyes off the road, and in only a second your vehicle will travel about 27 metres if you are travelling at 60 mph.

Question 1.27

Your mobile phone rings while you are driving on the motorway. Before answering you should

Mark one answer

☒ reduce your speed to 50 mph

☒ pull up on the hard shoulder

☒ move into the left hand lane

☒ stop in a safe place

Answer

 stop in a safe place

Plan your journey, and take breaks to keep in touch if necessary. When driving on motorways, you can't just pull up to answer the mobile phone. Be safe, switch it off and use the mail retrieval service to get any messages when you are parked in a safe and proper place.

Question 1.28

To answer a call on your mobile phone when driving, you should

Mark one answer

☒ reduce your speed wherever you are

☒ stop in a proper and convenient place

☒ keep the call time to a minimum

☒ slow down and allow others to overtake

Answer

 stop in a proper and convenient place

No phone call is important enough to endanger someone's life. If you must be contactable when driving, plan your route to include breaks where you can catch up on telephone messages in safety. Always choose a safe and convenient place to take a break.

Question 1.29

You want to use a mobile phone whilst driving. You should only use the phone

Mark one answer

☒ after stopping in a suitable place

☒ when driving on quiet, minor roads

☒ if you are driving on a motorway

☒ if you feel your driving will be unaffected

Answer

 after stopping in a suitable place

Always choose a safe and convenient place to stop and use a mobile phone. Safe and convenient means using a proper, legal parking place.

Your mobile phone rings while you are travelling. You should

Mark one answer

☒ stop immediately

☒ answer it immediately

☒ pull up in a suitable place

☒ pull up at the nearest kerb

Answer

✗ **pull up in a suitable place**

Always use the safe option. It is not worth taking the risk of endangering others. Make sure that you pull up in a place that does not obstruct other road users. The use of a message service can enable you to complete your journey without interruptions, and you can catch up with your calls when you take your rest breaks.

Question 1.31

You should ONLY use a mobile phone when

Mark one answer

☒ receiving a call

☒ suitably parked

☒ driving at less than 30 mph

☒ driving an automatic vehicle

Answer

✗ **suitably parked**

It it far more convenient for you, as well as being safer, if you are properly parked when receiving or making a call. You will be free to take notes or refer to papers, which is not possible whilst driving.

Question 1.32

What is the safest way to use a mobile phone in your vehicle?

Mark one answer

☒ Use hands-free equipment

☒ Find a suitable place to stop

☒ Drive slowly on a quiet road

☒ Direct your call through the operator

Answer

✗ **Find a suitable place to stop**

If the use of mobile phone causes you to drive in a careless or dangerous manner, you could be prosecuted for those offences. The penalties include an unlimited fine, disqualification and up to two years imprisonment.

Question 1.33

Why should you be parked safely before using a mobile phone?

Mark one answer

- [ ] Because reception is better when stopped
- [ ] So control of your vehicle is not affected
- [ ] So a proper conversation can be held
- [ ] Because the car electrics will be affected

Answer

✗ So control of your vehicle is not affected

Responsibility for the safe control of your vehicle always rests with you. A mobile phone can be a valuable asset, but you must not let it distract your attention from the road. Always stop in a safe place before using it. Use a message service and take regular breaks if you are expecting calls.

Question 1.34

You are riding at night. You have your headlight on main beam. Another vehicle is overtaking you. When should you dip your headlight?

Mark one answer

- [ ] When the other vehicle signals to overtake
- [ ] As soon as the other vehicle moves out to overtake
- [ ] As soon as the other vehicle passes you
- [ ] After the other vehicle pulls in front of you

Answer

✗ As soon as the other vehicle passes you

At night you should dip your headlight to avoid dazzling

- oncoming drivers
- drivers in front.

If you're being overtaken, dip your headlight as the other vehicle comes past. When you dip you'll see less of the road, so look ahead for hazards on your side of the road before dipping.

Question 1.35

On a motorcycle you should only use a mobile telephone when you

Mark one answer

- [ ] have a pillion passenger to help
- [ ] have parked in a safe place
- [ ] have a motorcycle with automatic gears
- [ ] are traveling on a quiet road

Answer

 have parked in a safe place

It's important that you're in full control of your machine at all times. If you need to use a hand-held phone, you should stop in a safe place before you do so.

Question 1.36

On a long motorway journey boredom can cause you to feel sleepy. You should

Mark two answers

- [ ] leave the motorway and find a safe place to stop
- [ ] keep looking around at the surrounding landscape
- [ ] drive faster to complete your journey sooner
- [ ] ensure a supply of fresh air into your vehicle
- [ ] stop on the hard shoulder for a rest

Answers

✗ **leave the motorway and find a safe place to stop**

✗ **ensure a supply of fresh air into your vehicle**

Plan your journey to include suitable rest stops. You should take all precautions against feeling sleepy whilst driving. Any lapse of concentration could have dire consequences.

DSA THEORY TEST for car drivers and motorcyclists

Question 1.37

You are driving at night and are dazzled by the headlights of an oncoming car. You should

Mark one answer

- slow down or stop
- close your eyes
- flash your headlights
- pull down the sun visor

Answer

✗ **slow down or stop**

If you're driving at night there will be extra hazards. Speeds and distances can be more difficult to judge. If the darkness makes you feel drowsy then take a rest. The lights of oncoming vehicles can often distract. If you're dazzled by them don't

- close your eyes
- flash your headlights. This will only distract the oncoming driver too.

Question 1.38

You are riding at night and are dazzled by the headlights of an oncoming car. You should

Mark one answer

- slow down or stop
- close your eyes
- flash your headlight
- turn your head away

Answer

✗ **slow down or stop**

If you're riding a motorcycle, taking a hand off the handlebars to adjust your visor might lead to loss of control. A dirty or scratched visor could cause dazzle and impair vision further. Whether riding or driving, slow down or stop until your eyes have adjusted.

Question 1.39

You are driving at dusk. You should switch your lights on

Mark two answers

- even when street lights are not lit
- so others can see you
- only when others have done so
- only when street lights are lit

Answers

✗ **even when street lights are not lit**
✗ **so others can see you**

Your lights are there to help others on the road see you. It may be necessary to turn on your lights during the day due to bad light or heavy rain. In these conditions the light might fade before the street lights are timed to switch on. Be seen to be safe.

Why are these yellow lines painted across the road?

Mark one answer

 To help you choose the correct lane

 To help you keep the correct separation distance

 To make you aware of your speed

 To tell you the distance to the roundabout

Answer

✖ To make you aware of your speed

These lines are often found on an approach to a roundabout or a dangerous junction. They give you extra warning to reduce your speed. Look well ahead and do so in good time.

To overtake safely, which of the following applies?

Mark one answer

 Check the speed and position of following traffic

 Cut back in sharply when you have passed the vehicle

 Get in close behind before signalling to move out

 Steer round the vehicle sharply

Answer

✖ Check the speed and position of following traffic

You should do this as part of your MSM routine. There might be a vehicle about to overtake you, so assess the situation before you commit yourself to changing speed or direction.

Question 1.42

You are riding along a motorway. You see an accident on the other side of the road. Your lane is clear. You should

Mark one answer

 assist the emergency services

⊠ stop, and cross the road to help

⊠ concentrate on what is happening ahead

⊠ place a warning triangle in the road

Answer

✗ **concentrate on what is happening ahead**

Always concentrate on the road ahead. If you become distracted you may not see a hazard ahead until it's too late to avoid it.

Question 1.43

You leave a brightly lit building at night. Before riding off, you should

Mark one answer

⊠ put on tinted glasses

⊠ wait until your eyes adjust to darkness

⊠ use your sidelights only

⊠ use a tinted visor

Answer

 ✗ **wait until your eyes adjust to darkness**

Your eyes take a minute or two to adjust to sudden changes in lighting conditions. While your eyes are adjusting you could clean your lights, mirrors and visor.

This section looks at your attitude to other road users.

The questions will ask you about

- consideration
- close following
- courtesy
- priority.

Question 2.1

A pelican crossing that crosses the road in a STRAIGHT line and has a central island MUST be treated as

Mark one answer

- [ ] one crossing in daylight only
- [ ] one complete crossing
- [ ] two separate crossings
- [ ] two crossings during darkness

Answer

✗ one complete crossing

The lights that control the crossing show to both directions of traffic. If a pedestrian from either side is still crossing when the amber light is flashing, you must wait.

Question 2.2

At a pelican crossing the flashing amber light means you MUST

Mark one answer

- [ ] stop and wait for the green light
- [ ] stop and wait for the red light
- [ ] give way to pedestrians waiting to cross
- [ ] give way to pedestrians already on the crossing

Answer

✗ give way to pedestrians already on the crossing

Pelican crossings are light-controlled crossings where pedestrians use push-button controls to change the signals. Pelican crossings have no red-and-amber stage before green. Instead, they have a flashing amber light, which means you must give way to pedestrians on the crossing. If it's clear, you may go on.

Question 2.3

You are approaching a pelican crossing. The amber light is flashing. You MUST

Mark one answer

- [ ] give way to pedestrians who are crossing
- [ ] encourage pedestrians to cross
- [ ] not move until the green light appears
- [ ] stop even if the crossing is clear

Answer

✗ give way to pedestrians who are crossing

While the pedestrians are crossing don't

- encourage people to cross by waving or flashing your headlights – others may misunderstand your signal
- rev your engine impatiently.

You are driving towards a zebra crossing. Pedestrians are waiting to cross. You should

Mark one answer

- ☒ give way to the elderly and infirm only
- ☒ slow down and prepare to stop
- ☒ use your headlights to indicate they can cross
- ☒ wave at them to cross the road

Answer

☒ **slow down and prepare to stop**

Zebra crossings have

- flashing amber beacons on both sides of the road
- black and white stripes on the crossing
- white zigzag markings on both sides of the crossing.

Where pedestrians are waiting to cross, slow down and prepare to stop.

You have stopped at a pedestrian crossing to allow pedestrians to cross. You should

Mark one answer

- ☒ wait until they have crossed
- ☒ edge your vehicle forward slowly
- ☒ wait, revving your engine
- ☒ signal to pedestrians to cross

Answer

☒ **wait until they have crossed**

Be patient, especially if they are elderly or disabled. Don't rev your engine or sound your horn.

You should never wave people across at pedestrian crossings because

Mark one answer

- ☒ there may be another vehicle coming
- ☒ they may not be looking
- ☒ it is safer for you to carry on
- ☒ they may not be ready to cross

Answer

☒ **there may be another vehicle coming**

If it's safe you should always stop for pedestrians waiting at pedestrian crossings. Don't wave them to cross the road since another driver may not

- have seen them
- have seen your signal
- be able to stop safely.

Question 2.7

You are riding towards a zebra crossing. Pedestrians are waiting to cross. You should

Mark one answer

- ☒ give way to the elderly and infirm only
- ☒ slow down and prepare to stop
- ☒ use your headlight to indicate they can cross
- ☒ wave at them to cross the road

Answer

☒ **slow down and prepare to stop**

It's courteous to stop if you can do so safely, especially if

- anyone is waiting on the pavement with a pram or pushchair
- children or the elderly are hesitating to cross because of heavy traffic.

Question 2.8

Why should you give an arm signal on approach to a zebra crossing?

Mark three answers

- ☒ To warn following traffic
- ☒ To let pedestrians know you are not stopping
- ☒ To let pedestrians know you are slowing down
- ☒ To warn oncoming traffic
- ☒ To warn traffic you intend to turn

Answers

☒ **To warn following traffic**
☒ **To let pedestrians know you are slowing down**
☒ **To warn oncoming traffic**

By giving clear correct signals you will alert other road users to your intentions. Be aware that a pedestrian may step out onto the crossing before you have stopped.

Question 2.9

At zebra crossings you should

Mark one answer

- ☒ rev your engine to encourage pedestrians to cross quickly
- ☒ park only on the zigzag lines on the left
- ☒ always leave it clear in traffic queues
- ☒ wave pedestrians to cross if you intend to wait for them

Answer

☒ **always leave it clear in traffic queues**

Look well down the line of traffic ahead so that you don't stop over the crossing. This should be left clear so that pedestrians are able to cross.

Question 2.10

You stop for pedestrians waiting to cross at a zebra crossing. They do not start to cross. What should you do?

Mark one answer

- [X] Be patient and wait
- [X] Sound your horn
- [X] Drive on
- [X] Wave them to cross

Answer

[X] Be patient and wait

If you stop for pedestrians and they don't start to cross don't

- wave them across
- sound your horn.

This could be dangerous if another vehicle is approaching and hasn't seen or heard your signal.

Question 2.11

At puffin crossings which light will not show to a driver?

Mark one answer

- [X] Flashing amber
- [X] Red
- [X] Steady amber
- [X] Green

Answer

[X] Flashing amber

A flashing amber light is shown at pelican crossings, but puffin crossings are different. They are controlled electronically and automatically detect when pedestrians are on the crossing. The phase is shortened or lengthened according to the position of the pedestrians.

Question 2.12

You are approaching a red light at a puffin crossing. Pedestrians are on the crossing. The red light will stay on until

Mark one answer

- [X] you start to edge forward on to the crossing
- [X] the pedestrians have reached a safe position
- [X] the pedestrians are clear of the front of your vehicle
- [X] a driver from the opposite direction reaches the crossing

Answer

[X] the pedestrians have reached a safe position

The electronic device will automatically detect that the pedestrians have reached a safe position. Don't proceed until the green light shows it is safe to do so.

DSA THEORY TEST for car drivers and motorcyclists

Question 2.13

At a puffin crossing what colour follows the green signal?

Mark one answer

☒ Steady red

☒ Flashing amber

☒ Steady amber

☒ Flashing green

Answer

✖ **Steady amber**

Puffin crossings have infra-red sensors which detect when pedestrians are crossing and hold the red traffic signal until the crossing is clear. The use of a sensor means there is no flashing amber phase as there is with a pelican crossing.

Question 2.14

You could use the 'Two-Second Rule'

Mark one answer

☒ before restarting the engine after it has stalled

☒ to keep a safe gap from the vehicle in front

☒ before using the 'Mirror–Signal–Manoeuvre' routine

☒ when emerging on wet roads

Answer

✖ **to keep a safe gap from the vehicle in front**

To measure this, choose a reference point such as a bridge, sign or tree. When the vehicle ahead passes the object say to yourself 'Only a fool breaks the two-second rule.' If you reach the object before you finish saying this you're TOO CLOSE.

Question 2.15

A two-second gap between yourself and the car in front is sufficient when conditions are

Mark one answer

☒ wet

☒ good

☒ damp

☒ foggy

Answer

✖ **good**

In good, dry conditions an alert driver who's driving a vehicle with tyres and brakes in good condition needs a distance of at least two seconds from the car in front.

Question 2.16

In fast traffic a two-second gap may be enough only when conditions are

Mark one answer

- [ ] dry
- [ ] wet
- [ ] damp
- [ ] foggy

Answer

❌ **dry**

You must be aware that when the weather is bad, you will have to keep a greater distance from the vehicle in front. It will take you further to stop. In wet weather it will take twice as far, in icy weather it could increase by ten times.

Question 2.17

'Tailgating' means

Mark one answer

- [ ] using the rear door of a hatchback car
- [ ] reversing into a parking space
- [ ] following another vehicle too closely
- [ ] driving with rear fog lights on

Answer

❌ **following another vehicle too closely**

'Tailgating' is used to describe this dangerous practice, often seen in fast-moving traffic and on motorways. Following the vehicle in front too closely will

- restrict your view of the road ahead
- leave you no safety margin if the vehicle in front stops suddenly.

Question 2.18

You are driving on a clear night. There is a steady stream of oncoming traffic. The national speed limit applies. Which lights should you use?

Mark one answer

- [ ] Full beam headlights
- [ ] Sidelights
- [ ] Dipped headlights
- [ ] Fog lights

Answer

❌ **Dipped headlights**

You should always be sure that you can be seen by other traffic. Use the main beam of your headlights only when you can be sure that you won't dazzle other road users.

Question 2.19

Following this vehicle too closely is unwise because

Mark one answer

☒ your brakes will overheat

☒ your view ahead is increased

☒ your engine will overheat

☒ your view ahead is reduced

Answer

 your view ahead is reduced

Staying back will increase your view of the road ahead. This will help you to see any hazards and allow you more time to react.

Question 2.20

You are following this lorry. You should keep well back from it to

Mark one answer

☒ give you a good view of the road ahead

☒ stop following traffic from rushing through the junction

☒ prevent traffic behind you from overtaking

☒ allow you to hurry through the traffic lights if they change

Answer

 give you a good view of the road ahead

By keeping well back you will increase your vision around the rear of the lorry. This will allow you to see further down the road and be prepared for any hazards.

You are driving behind a large goods vehicle. It signals left but steers to the right. You should

Mark one answer

 slow down and let the vehicle turn

 drive on, keeping to the left

 overtake on the right of it

 hold your speed and sound your horn

Answer

❌ **slow down and let the vehicle turn**

Large long vehicles need extra room when making turns at junctions. They may move out to the right in order to make a left turn. Keep well back, and don't attempt to pass on the left.

You are following a vehicle on a wet road. You should leave a time gap of at least

Mark one answer

 one second

 two seconds

 three seconds

 four seconds

Answer

❌ **four seconds**

Wet roads will increase the time it will take you to stop. The 'two-second rule' will double to AT LEAST FOUR SECONDS.

You are driving along this road. The red van cuts in close in front of you. What should you do?

Mark one answer

 Accelerate to get closer to the red van

Give a long blast on the horn

Drop back to leave the correct separation distance

Flash your headlights several times

Answer

❌ **Drop back to leave the correct separation distance**

There are times when other drivers make incorrect or ill-judged decisions. Be tolerant and try not to react aggressively or retaliate. Always consider the safety of other road users, your passengers and yourself.

Question 2.24

You are in a line of traffic. The driver behind you is following very closely. What action should you take?

Mark one answer

 Ignore the following driver and continue to drive within the speed limit

 Slow down, gradually increasing the gap between you and the vehicle in front

 Signal left and wave the following driver past

 Move over to a position just left of the centre line of the road

Answer

X **Slow down, gradually increasing the gap between you and the vehicle in front**

It can be worrying to see that the car behind is following you too closely. If you ease back from the vehicle in front you'll give yourself a greater safety margin.

Question 2.25

You are driving at the legal speed limit. A vehicle comes up quickly behind, flashing its headlights. You should

Mark one answer

 accelerate to make a gap behind you

 touch the brakes to show your brake lights

 maintain your speed to prevent the vehicle from overtaking

 allow the vehicle to overtake

Answer

X **allow the vehicle to overtake**

Don't enforce the speed limit by blocking another vehicle's progress. This will only lead to the other driver becoming more frustrated. Allow the other vehicle to pass when you can do so safely.

Question 2.26

You are waiting in a traffic queue at night. To avoid dazzling following drivers you should

Mark one answer

 apply the handbrake only

 apply the footbrake only

 switch off your headlights

 use both the handbrake and footbrake

Answer

X **apply the handbrake only**

You should consider the driver behind; brake lights can dazzle.

Question 2.27

When are you allowed to exceed the maximum speed limit?

Mark one answer

- [ ] Between midnight and 6 am
- [ ] At no time
- [ ] When overtaking
- [ ] When the road is clear

Answer

 At no time

Speed limits are set for a reason. There are many aspects taken into consideration when the limit is set. It may depend on

- junctions
- schools
- pedestrians
- bends
- narrow roads.

Travelling at the correct speed will allow you more time to deal with potential hazards.

Question 2.28

You are driving at the legal speed limit. A vehicle behind wants to overtake. Should you try to prevent the driver overtaking?

Mark one answer

- [ ] No, unless it is safe to do so
- [ ] Yes, because the other driver is acting dangerously
- [ ] No, not at any time
- [ ] Yes, because the other driver is breaking the law

Answer

No, not at any time

Don't enforce the speed limit by blocking other road users' progress. If they wish to overtake and it means they break the law, it's their risk.

Question 2.29

You are driving in traffic at the speed limit for the road. The driver behind is trying to overtake. You should

Mark one answer

 move closer to the car ahead, so the driver behind has no room to overtake

 wave the driver behind to overtake when it is safe

 keep a steady course and allow the driver behind to overtake

 accelerate to get away from the driver behind

Answer

 keep a steady course and allow the driver behind to overtake

Keep a steady course to give the driver behind an opportunity to overtake safely. If necessary, slow down. Reacting incorrectly to another's impatience will only lead to danger.

Question 2.30

You are driving at night on an unlit road following a slower moving vehicle. You should

Mark one answer

 flash your headlights

 use dipped beam headlights

 switch off your headlights

 use full beam headlights

Answer

 use dipped beam headlights

If you follow another vehicle with your headlights on full beam it could dazzle the driver by reflecting in the interior mirror. Leave a safe distance. Your dipped headlight beam should fall short of the vehicle in front.

Question 2.31

A long, heavily-laden lorry is taking a long time to overtake you. What should you do?

Mark one answer

 Speed up

 Slow down

 Hold your speed

 Change direction

Answer

 Slow down

A long lorry with a heavy load will need more time to pass you than a car. It won't be able to accelerate to pass you quickly, especially on an uphill stretch of road. Ease off the accelerator and allow the lorry to pass.

Question 2.32

You are driving a slow-moving vehicle on a narrow winding road. You should

Mark one answer

- ☒ keep well out to stop vehicles overtaking dangerously
- ☒ wave following vehicles past you if you think they can overtake quickly
- ☒ pull in safely when you can, to let following vehicles overtake
- ☒ give a left signal when it is safe for vehicles to overtake you

Answer

☒ **pull in safely when you can, to let following vehicles overtake**

Don't

- wave the other traffic on – other drivers may not have seen your signal
- show discourtesy by not pulling in at a safe place.

Try to be courteous and considerate to other road users. Imagine how you would feel if you were the following driver or rider.

Question 2.33

You are driving a slow-moving vehicle on a narrow road. When traffic wishes to overtake you should

Mark one answer

- ☒ take no action
- ☒ put your hazard warning lights on
- ☒ stop immediately and wave it on
- ☒ pull in safely as soon as you can do so

Answer

☒ **pull in safely as soon as you can do so**

Try not to hold up a queue of traffic. This might lead to other road users becoming impatient. If you're driving a slow-moving vehicle and the road is narrow look out for a safe place to pull in.

Question 2.34

You are driving a slow-moving vehicle on a narrow winding road. In order to let other vehicles overtake you should

Mark one answer

- ☒ wave to them to pass
- ☒ pull in safely when you can
- ☒ show a left turn signal
- ☒ keep left and hold your speed

Answer

☒ **pull in safely when you can**

Don't frustrate other road users by driving for long distances with a queue of traffic behind you. This could lead them into losing concentration or making ill-judged decisions.

Question 2.35

You are riding a motorcycle and following a large vehicle at 40 mph. You should position yourself

Mark one answer

- [ ] close behind to make it easier to overtake the vehicle
- [ ] to the left of the road to make it easier to be seen
- [ ] close behind the vehicle to keep out of the wind
- [ ] well back so that you can see past the vehicle

Answer

- ☒ **well back so that you can see past the vehicle**

You need to be able to see well down the road and be ready for any hazards that occur. Staying too close to the vehicle will leave you insufficient separation distance and also reduce your view of the road ahead.

Question 2.36

Which of the following vehicles will use blue flashing beacons?

Mark three answers

- [ ] Motorway maintenance
- [ ] Bomb disposal
- [ ] Blood transfusion
- [ ] Police patrol
- [ ] Breakdown recovery

Answers

- ☒ **Bomb disposal**
- ☒ **Blood transfusion**
- ☒ **Police patrol**

Try to move out of the way of emergency vehicles with blue flashing beacons. Do so safely and without delay.

Question 2.37

Which THREE of these emergency services might have blue flashing beacons?

Mark three answers

- [ ] Coastguard
- [ ] Bomb disposal
- [ ] Gritting lorries
- [ ] Animal ambulances
- [ ] Mountain rescue
- [ ] Doctors' cars

Answers

- ☒ **Coastguard**
- ☒ **Bomb disposal**
- ☒ **Mountain rescue**

These vehicles will be travelling at speed. You should help their progress by pulling over and allowing them to pass. Do so safely. Don't stop suddenly or in a dangerous position.

When being followed by an ambulance showing a flashing blue beacon you should

Mark one answer

☒ pull over as soon as safely possible to let it pass

☒ accelerate hard to get away from it

☒ maintain your speed and course

☒ brake harshly and immediately stop in the road

Answer

❌ **pull over as soon as safely possible to let it pass**

Pull over where the ambulance can pass safely. Check that there are no bollards or obstructions in the road that will prevent it from doing so.

Question 2.39

You see a car showing a flashing green beacon. Should you give way to it?

Mark one answer

☒ Yes, it is a doctor going to an emergency

☒ Yes, it is a fire crew support vehicle

☒ No, it is a slow-moving vehicle

☒ No, it is a breakdown vehicle

Answer

❌ **Yes, it is a doctor going to an emergency**

Give way by pulling over and letting the vehicle pass. Don't just stop suddenly. Choose a safe place as soon as you can to allow the doctor's vehicle to pass.

Question 2.40

What type of emergency vehicle is fitted with a green flashing beacon?

Mark one answer

☒ Fire engine

☒ Road gritter

☒ Ambulance

☒ Doctor's car

Answer

❌ **Doctor's car**

A green flashing beacon on a vehicle means the driver or passenger is a doctor on an emergency call. Give way to them if it's safe to do so. Be aware that the vehicle may be travelling quickly or may stop in a hurry.

Question 2.41

A flashing green beacon on a vehicle means

Mark one answer

- [ ] police on non-urgent duties
- [ ] doctor on an emergency call
- [ ] road safety patrol operating
- [ ] gritting in progress

Answer

 doctor on an emergency call

If you see such a vehicle in your mirrors, allow it to pass if you can. Be aware that someone's life could depend on the driver making good progress through traffic.

Question 2.42

A vehicle has a flashing green beacon. What does this mean?

Mark one answer

- [ ] A doctor is answering an emergency call
- [ ] The vehicle is slow-moving
- [ ] It is a motorway police patrol vehicle
- [ ] A vehicle is carrying hazardous chemicals

Answer

 A doctor is answering an emergency call

A doctor attending an emergency might show a green flashing beacon on his or her vehicle. Give way to them as they will need to reach their destination quickly. Be aware that they might pull over suddenly.

Question 2.43

Diamond-shaped signs give instructions to

Mark one answer

- [ ] tram drivers
- [ ] bus drivers
- [ ] lorry drivers
- [ ] taxi drivers

Answer

 tram drivers

These signs apply to trams only. They are directed at tram drivers, but you should know their meaning so that you're aware of the priorities and are able to anticipate the actions of the driver.

Question 2.44

Scooter riders should be especially careful when crossing tram lines because scooters have

Mark one answer

- [ ] small engines
- [ ] wide panniers
- [ ] automatic gear boxes
- [ ] narrow tyres

Answer

 narrow tyres

Tram rails can affect steering and braking, especially when wet. If you ride a small motorcycle with narrow tyres, you can be affected more than riders on larger machines which have wider tyres.

Question 2.45

On a road where trams operate, which of these vehicles will be most at risk from the tram rails?

Mark one answer

- [ ] Cars
- [ ] Cycles
- [ ] Buses
- [ ] Lorries

Answer

 Cycles

The narrow tyres of a cycle can become stuck in the tram rails. This could cause the cyclist to wobble or even lose balance altogether. The tram lines are also slippery and this could cause a cyclist to slide or fall off.

Question 2.46

At unmarked junctions where tram lines cross over roads, who has priority?

Mark one answer

- [ ] Cars
- [ ] Motorcycles
- [ ] Trams
- [ ] Buses

Answer

❌ Trams

Be on the lookout and cross the junction with caution. Trams can often approach silently giving you no audible warning of their presence.

Question 2.47

A bus is stopped at a bus stop ahead of you. Its right-hand indicator is flashing. You should

Mark one answer

☒ flash your headlights and slow down

☒ slow down and give way if it is safe to do so

☒ sound your horn and keep going

☒ slow down and then sound your horn

Answer

☒ **slow down and give way if it is safe to do so**

Give way to buses whenever you can do so safely, especially when they signal to pull away from bus stops. Look out for people leaving the bus and crossing the road.

Question 2.48

A bus lane on your left shows no times of operation. This means it is

Mark one answer

☒ not in operation at all

☒ only in operation at peak times

☒ in operation 24 hours a day

☒ only in operation in daylight hours

Answer

☒ **in operation 24 hours a day**

Don't drive or park in a bus lane when it's in operation. This can cause disruption and spoil the efficiency of public transport.

Question 2.49

You should ONLY flash your headlights to other road users

Mark one answer

- ☒ to show that you are giving way
- ☒ to show that you are about to reverse
- ☒ to tell them that you have right of way
- ☒ to let them know that you are there

Answer

☒ to let them know that you are there

You should only flash your headlights to warn others of your presence. Don't use them to

- greet others
- show impatience
- give up your priority.

Question 2.50

What should you use your horn for?

Mark one answer

- ☒ To alert others to your presence
- ☒ To allow you right of way
- ☒ To greet other road users
- ☒ To signal your annoyance

Answer

☒ To alert others to your presence

Don't use it to

- greet others
- show impatience
- give priority.

Your horn shouldn't be used between 11.30 pm and 7 am in a built-up area or when your vehicle's stationary – unless a moving vehicle poses a danger.

Question 2.51

A vehicle pulls out in front of you at a junction. What should you do?

Mark one answer

- ☒ Swerve past it and blow your horn
- ☒ Flash your headlights and drive up close behind
- ☒ Slow down and be ready to stop
- ☒ Accelerate past it immediately

Answer

☒ Slow down and be ready to stop

Try to be ready for the unexpected. Plan ahead and learn to anticipate hazards. You'll then give yourself more time to react to any problems that might occur. Be tolerant of the behaviour of other road users who don't behave correctly.

Question 2.52

When riding a motorcycle your normal road position should allow

Mark two answers

- [ ] other vehicles to overtake on your left
- [ ] the driver ahead to see you in the mirrors
- [ ] you to prevent following vehicles from overtaking
- [ ] you to be seen by traffic that is emerging from junctions ahead
- [ ] you to ride within half a metre (1 foot 8 ins) of the kerb

Answers

❌ **the driver ahead to see you in the mirrors**

❌ **you to be seen by traffic that is emerging from junctions ahead**

You should ask yourself: can I see and be seen?

When following another vehicle, don't get too close.

Question 2.53

You are in a one-way street and want to turn right. You should position yourself

Mark one answer

- [ ] in the right-hand lane
- [ ] in the left-hand lane
- [ ] in either lane, depending on the traffic
- [ ] just left of the centre line

Answer

❌ **in the right-hand lane**

If you're travelling in a one-way street and wish to turn right, you should take up a position in the right-hand lane. This will enable other road users not wishing to turn to proceed on the left. Indicate your intention and take up your position in good time.

Question 2.54

You wish to turn right ahead. Why should you take up the correct position in good time?

Mark one answer

- [ ] To allow other drivers to pull out in front of you
- [ ] To give a better view into the road that you're joining
- [ ] To help other road users know what you intend to do
- [ ] To allow drivers to pass you on the right

Answer

❌ **To help other road users know what you intend to do**

If you wish to turn right into a side road take up your position in good time. Move to the centre of the road when it's safe to do so. This will allow vehicles to pass you on the left. Early planning will show other traffic what you intend to do.

You are driving along a country road. A horse and rider are approaching. What should you do?

Mark two answers

- [ ] Increase your speed
- [ ] Sound your horn
- [ ] Flash your headlights
- [ ] Drive slowly past
- [ ] Give plenty of room
- [ ] Rev your engine

Answers

✗ Drive slowly past
✗ Give plenty of room

It's important that you reduce your speed. Passing too closely, or at speed, could startle the horse and unseat the rider.

A person herding sheep asks you to stop. You should

Mark one answer

- [ ] ignore them as they have no authority
- [ ] stop and switch off your engine
- [ ] continue on but drive slowly
- [ ] try and get past quickly

Answer

✗ stop and switch off your engine

Allow the animals to clear the road before you proceed. Animals are unpredictable and startle easily; they could turn and run into your path.

When overtaking a horse and rider you should

Mark one answer

- [ ] sound your horn as a warning
- [ ] go past as quickly as possible
- [ ] flash your headlights as a warning
- [ ] go past slowly and carefully

Answer

✗ go past slowly and carefully

Horses can become startled by the sound of a car engine or the rush of air caused by passing too closely. Keep well back, and only pass when it is safe; leave them plenty of room. Consider that you may have to use the other side of the road to pass.

Question 2.58

Which of the following are at greatest risk from other road users?

Mark one answer

 Motorcyclists

☒ Lorry drivers

☒ Learner car drivers

☒ Busy bus drivers

Question 2.59

You are riding on a country road. Two horses with riders are in the distance. You should

Mark one answer

☒ continue at your normal speed

☒ change down the gears quickly

☒ slow down and be ready to stop

☒ flash your headlight to warn them

Answer

 Motorcyclists

Motorcycles tend to

• be small and more difficult to see than most other vehicles

• have little or no protective bodywork.

These factors make motorcyclists amongst the most vulnerable of all road users.

Answer

 slow down and be ready to stop

Animals are easily frightened by moving motor vehicles. If you're approaching horses keep your speed down and watch to see if the rider has any difficulty keeping control. Always be ready to stop if necessary.

This section looks at safety and your vehicle.

The questions will ask you about

- fault detection
- defects and their effect on safety
- use of safety equipment
- emissions
- noise.

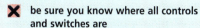

Question 3.1

When riding a different motorcycle you should

Mark one answer

- [ ] ask someone to ride with you for the first time
- [ ] ride as soon as possible as all controls and switches are the same
- [ ] leave your gloves behind so switches can be operated easier at first
- [ ] be sure you know where all controls and switches are

Answer

✗ be sure you know where all controls and switches are

Before you ride any motorcycle make sure you're familiar with the layout of all the controls and switches. While control layouts are generally similar, there may be differences in their feel and method of operation.

Question 3.2

When should you especially check the engine oil level?

Mark one answer

- [ ] Before a long journey
- [ ] When the engine is hot
- [ ] Early in the morning
- [ ] Every 6000 miles

Answer

✗ Before a long journey

Also make checks on

- fuel
- water
- tyres.

Question 3.3

Which of these, if allowed to get low, could cause an accident?

Mark one answer

- [ ] Antifreeze level
- [ ] Brake fluid level
- [ ] Battery water level
- [ ] Radiator coolant level

Answer

✗ Brake fluid level

In order to keep your vehicle in good working order you should carry out frequent checks. As a driver or rider you must ensure that you're using a safe vehicle or machine that won't endanger other road users.

Question 3.4

Which FOUR of these MUST be in good working order for your car to be roadworthy?

Mark four answers

- ☒ Temperature gauge
- ☒ Speedometer
- ☒ Windscreen washers
- ☒ Windscreen wiper
- ☒ Oil warning light
- ☒ Horn

Answers

- ☒ **Speedometer**
- ☒ **Windscreen washers**
- ☒ **Windscreen wiper**
- ☒ **Horn**

Also check the

- lights – get someone to help you check the brake lights
- indicators
- battery – this may be maintenance-free and not need topping up
- steering – check for 'play' in the steering
- oil
- water
- suspension.

Question 3.5

A loose drive chain on a motorcycle could cause

Mark one answer

- ☒ the front wheel to wobble
- ☒ the ignition to cut out
- ☒ the brakes to fail
- ☒ the rear wheel to lock

Answer

- ☒ **the rear wheel to lock**

Drive chains are subject to wear and require frequent adjustment and lubrication. If the chain is worn or slack it can jump off the sprocket and lock the rear wheel.

 DSA THEORY TEST for car drivers and motorcyclists

Question 3.6

A wrongly adjusted drive chain can

Mark three answers

☒ cause an accident

☒ make wheels wobble

☒ create a noisy rattle

☒ affect gear changing

☒ cause a suspension fault

Answers

☒ **cause an accident**

☒ **create a noisy rattle**

☒ **affect gear changing**

A motorcycle drive chain will stretch as it wears and needs adjusting to keep the tension correct. If the chain is wrongly adjusted it can

- jump off the sprocket and lock the rear wheel causing loss of control
- rattle as it flaps loosely
- cause problems selecting gears.

Question 3.7

Which THREE does the law require you to keep in good condition?

Mark three answers

☒ Gears

☒ Transmission

☒ Headlights

☒ Windscreen

☒ Seat belts

Answers

☒ **Headlights**

☒ **Windscreen**

☒ **Seat belts**

Also check the

- lights – get someone to help you check the brake lights
- indicators
- battery – this may be maintenance-free and not need topping up
- steering – check for 'play' in the steering
- oil
- water
- suspension.

Whether driving or riding, check that the speedometer is working once you've moved off.

Question 3.8

New petrol-engined cars must be fitted with catalytic converters. The reason for this is to

Mark one answer

- [ ] control exhaust noise levels
- [ ] prolong the life of the exhaust system
- [ ] allow the exhaust system to be recycled
- [ ] reduce harmful exhaust emissions

Answer

✗ reduce harmful exhaust emissions

We should all be concerned by the effect traffic has on our environment. Fumes from vehicles are causing damage to the air around us. Catalytic converters act like a filter, removing some of the toxic waste.

Question 3.9

Which TWO are badly affected if the tyres are under-inflated?

Mark two answers

- [ ] Braking
- [ ] Steering
- [ ] Changing gear
- [ ] Parking

Answers

✗ Braking

✗ Steering

Your tyres are your only contact with the road and therefore very important to your safety. Incorrect tyre pressures will affect steering and braking, so it's very important that you take the time to attend to them. Correct tyre pressures can reduce the risk of skidding and will provide a more comfortable ride.

Question 3.10

What can cause heavy steering?

Mark one answer

- [ ] Driving on ice
- [ ] Badly worn brakes
- [ ] Over-inflated tyres
- [ ] Under-inflated tyres

Answer

✗ Under-inflated tyres

If your tyres don't have enough air in them they'll drag against the surface of the road. This makes the steering feel heavy.

Question 3.11

Your car is fitted with power assisted steering. This will make the steering seem

Mark one answer

 lighter

 heavier

 quieter

 noisier

Answer

❌ **lighter**

Some modern vehicles are fitted with power steering to help manoeuvring at low speeds. It lightens the steering, enabling the driver to steer with less effort. This is especially useful when parking or steering into tight corners.

Question 3.12

What is the most important reason why you should keep your motorcycle regularly maintained?

Mark one answer

 To accelerate faster than other traffic

 So the motorcycle can carry panniers

 To keep the machine roadworthy

 So the motorcycle can carry a passenger

Answer

❌ **To keep the machine roadworthy**

Whenever you use any vehicle on the road it must be in a roadworthy condition. Regular maintenance will help to identify any faults at an early stage and help avoid more serious problems.

Question 3.13

It is essential that tyre pressures are checked regularly. When should this be done?

Mark one answer

 After any lengthy journey

 After driving at high speed

 When tyres are hot

 When tyres are cold

Answer

❌ **When tyres are cold**

When you check the tyre pressures, do so when the tyres are cold. This will give you a more accurate reading. The heat generated from a long journey will raise the pressure inside the tyre.

Question 3.14

It is important that tyre pressures are correct. They should be checked at least

Mark one answer

 every time the vehicle is serviced

once a week

once a month

every time the vehicle has an MOT test

Answer

❌ **once a week**

Regular checks of the pressure should also highlight any tyre wear or damage.

Question 3.15

How often should motorcycle tyre pressures be checked?

Mark one answer

Only during each regular service

After each long journey

At least monthly

At least weekly

Answer

❌ **At least weekly**

As a motorcyclist your tyres are vital to your safety. Make sure that you check the pressure in your tyres at least once a week. Don't ride your machine if the tyres are incorrectly inflated.

Question 3.16

Driving with under-inflated tyres can affect

Mark two answers

- ☒ engine temperature
- ☒ fuel consumption
- ☒ braking
- ☒ oil pressure

Answers

- ☒ **fuel consumption**
- ☒ **braking**

Regular checks of tyre pressures can prevent adverse effects.

Question 3.17

The legal minimum depth of tread for motorcycle tyres is

Mark one answer

- ☒ 1 mm
- ☒ 1.6 mm
- ☒ 2.5 mm
- ☒ 4 mm

Answer

- ☒ **1 mm**

The entire original tread should be continuous. Don't ride a machine with worn tyres. Your tyres are your only contact with the road, so it's very important that they're in good condition.

Question 3.18

A police officer orders you to stop. He finds you have a faulty tyre. Who is responsible for the tyre?

Mark one answer

- ☒ The previous owner
- ☒ Whoever services the car
- ☒ You, the driver
- ☒ Whoever issued the MOT certificate

Answer

- ☒ **You, the driver**

You should check the condition of your tyres as a matter of routine. A worn or damaged tyre can have an affect on the handling of your vehicle. It can also have extremely dangerous consequences if the tyre bursts while you are driving.

Question 3.19

Your motorcycle has tubed tyres fitted as standard. When replacing a tyre you should

Mark one answer

 replace the tube if it is 6 months old

 replace the tube if it has covered 6,000 miles

 replace the tube only if replacing the rear tyre

 replace the tube with each change of tyre

Answer

☒ **replace the tube with each change of tyre**

It isn't worth taking risks to save money. Your life could depend on the condition of your machine.

Question 3.20

You are riding a machine of more than 50cc. Which FOUR would make a tyre illegal?

Mark four answers

 Tread less than 1.6 mm deep

 Tread less than 1 mm deep

 A large bulge in the wall

 A recut tread

 Exposed ply or cord

 A stone wedged in the tread

Answers

☒ **Tread less than 1 mm deep**
☒ **A large bulge in the wall**
☒ **A recut tread**
☒ **Exposed ply or cord**

When checking tyres make sure there are no bulges or cuts in the side walls. Always buy your tyres from a reputable dealer to ensure quality and value for money.

Question 3.21

It is illegal to drive with tyres that

Mark one answer

 have been bought second-hand

 have a large deep cut in the side wall

 are of different makes

 are of different tread patterns

Answer

☒ **have a large deep cut in the side wall**

When checking your tyres for cuts and bulges in the side walls, don't forget the inner walls (i.e., those facing each other under the vehicle).

Question 3.22

The legal minimum depth of tread for car tyres over three quarters of the breadth is

Mark one answer

- [ ] 1 mm
- [ ] 1.6 mm
- [ ] 2.5 mm
- [ ] 4 mm

Answer

- **1.6 mm**

Tyres must have a good depth of tread. The legal limit for cars is a minimum of 1.6 mm. This depth should be throughout the central three-quarters of the breadth of the tyre and around the entire circumference.

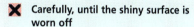

Question 3.23

How should you ride a motorcycle when NEW tyres have just been fitted?

Mark one answer

- [ ] Carefully, until the shiny surface is worn off
- [ ] By braking hard especially into bends
- [ ] Through normal riding with higher air pressures
- [ ] By riding at faster than normal speeds

Answer

- **Carefully, until the shiny surface is worn off**

New tyres have a shiny finish which needs to be worn off before the tyre will give the best grip, especially if the roads are wet.

Question 3.24

Excessive or uneven tyre wear can be caused by faults in the

Mark two answers

- [ ] gearbox
- [ ] braking system
- [ ] suspension
- [ ] exhaust system

Answers

- **braking system**
- **suspension**

Uneven wear on your tyres can be caused by the condition of your vehicle. Have it serviced regularly so that the brakes, steering and wheel alignment are checked.

Question 3.25

There is vibration on your steering wheel as you drive. You should check that the

Mark one answer

- [ ] doors are closed
- [ ] wheels are balanced
- [ ] exhaust is not loose
- [ ] engine oil level is correct

Answer

✗ wheels are balanced

It could also mean that you have a badly worn or damaged tyre. Have the vehicle checked as soon as possible.

Question 3.26

Your vehicle pulls to one side when braking. You should

Mark one answer

- [ ] change the tyres around
- [ ] consult your garage as soon as possible
- [ ] pump the pedal when braking
- [ ] use your handbrake at the same time

Answer

✗ consult your garage as soon as possible

The brakes on your vehicle or machine must be effective and properly adjusted. If your vehicle pulls to one side when braking, take it to be checked by a qualified mechanic. Don't take risks.

Question 3.27

The main cause of brake fade is

Mark one answer

- [ ] the brakes overheating
- [ ] air in the brake fluid
- [ ] oil on the brakes
- [ ] the brakes out of adjustment

Answer

✗ the brakes overheating

If your vehicle is fitted with drum brakes, they can get hot and may lose a lot of their effect. This happens when they're continually used, such as on a long, steep downhill stretch of road. Using a lower gear will assist the braking and prevent the vehicle gaining momentum.

Your anti-lock brakes warning light stays on. You should

Mark one answer

- [ ] check the brake fluid level
- [ ] check the footbrake free play
- [ ] check that the handbrake is released
- [ ] have the brakes checked immediately

Answer

- [✗] **have the brakes checked immediately**

It is advisable to call out a mechanic to check. Your brakes may be defective.

You should maintain cable operated brakes

Mark two answers

- [ ] by regular adjustment when necessary
- [ ] at normal service times only
- [ ] yearly, before taking the machine for its MoT
- [ ] by oiling cables and pivots regularly

Answers

- [✗] **by regular adjustment when necessary**
- [✗] **by oiling cables and pivots regularly**

Keeping your brakes in good working order is vital for road safety. With cable operated brakes the cables need

- adjustment because they will stretch with use
- lubrication to prevent friction and wear of the cables and pivots.

If you notice a strong smell of petrol as you drive along you should

Mark one answer

- [ ] not worry, as it is only exhaust fumes
- [ ] carry on at a reduced speed
- [ ] expect it to stop in a few miles
- [ ] stop and investigate the problem

Answer

- [✗] **stop and investigate the problem**

Don't smoke or put naked lights anywhere near the leakage. Have it checked by a qualified mechanic as soon as possible. Your vehicle could be a fire hazard.

Question 3.31

What does this instrument panel light mean when lit?

Mark one answer

 Gear lever in park

Gear lever in neutral

Handbrake on

Handbrake off

Answer

❌ **Handbrake on**

If you are not sure about any lights or switches, check the vehicle manual. You should be aware that a light on the instrument panel could be a warning about the condition of your vehicle.

Question 3.32

When MUST you use dipped headlights during the day?

Mark one answer

All the time

Along narrow streets

In poor visibility

When parking

Answer

❌ **In poor visibility**

This will allow other road users to see you. You MUST use them in heavy rain, mist, or in foggy conditions.

Question 3.33

Which instrument panel warning light would show that headlights are on full beam?

Mark one answer

Answer

❌

You should be aware of where all the warning lights and visual aids are on the vehicle you are driving. If you are driving a vehicle for the first time you should take time to check all the controls.

Question 3.34

While driving, this warning light on your dashboard comes on. It means

Mark one answer

- [ ] a fault in the braking system
- [ ] the engine oil is low
- [ ] a rear light has failed
- [ ] your seat belt is not fastened

Answer

☒ **a fault in the braking system**

Don't ignore this warning light; it could have dangerous consequences.

Question 3.35

You are driving on a motorway. The traffic ahead is braking sharply because of an accident. How could you warn following traffic?

Mark one answer

- [ ] Briefly use the hazard warning lights
- [ ] Switch on the hazard warning lights continuously
- [ ] Briefly use the rear fog lights
- [ ] Switch on the headlights continuously

Answer

☒ **Briefly use the hazard warning lights**

This situation (and on dual carriageways) is the only time you are permitted to use your hazard warning lights on the move. Only use them just long enough to ensure that your warning has been observed.

Question 3.36

When may you use hazard warning lights?

Mark one answer

- [ ] To park alongside another car
- [ ] To park on double yellow lines
- [ ] When you are being towed
- [ ] When you have broken down

Answer

☒ **When you have broken down**

Hazard warning lights may be used to warn other road users when you

- have broken down and are causing an obstruction
- are on a motorway and want to warn the traffic behind you of a hazard ahead. Don't use them when being towed.

Question 3.37

Hazard warning lights should be used when vehicles are

Mark one answer

- [ ] broken down and causing an obstruction
- [ ] faulty and moving slowly
- [ ] being towed along a road
- [ ] reversing into a side road

Answer

✗ broken down and causing an obstruction

Don't use hazard lights as an excuse for illegal parking. If you do use them, don't forget to switch them off when you move off. There must be a warning light on the control panel to show when the hazard lights are in operation.

Question 3.38

It is important to wear suitable shoes when you are driving. Why is this?

Mark one answer

- [ ] To prevent wear on the pedals
- [ ] To maintain control of the pedals
- [ ] To enable you to adjust your seat
- [ ] To enable you to walk for assistance if you break down

Answer

✗ To maintain control of the pedals

When you're driving or riding ensure that you're wearing comfortable clothing. It is essential that you have proper control of your vehicle.

Question 3.39

A properly adjusted head restraint will

Mark one answer

- [ ] make you more comfortable
- [ ] help you to avoid neck injury
- [ ] help you to relax
- [ ] help you to maintain your driving position

Answer

✗ help you to avoid neck injury

The restraint should be adjusted so that it gives maximum protection to the head. This will help in the event of a rear-end collision.

Question 3.40

What will reduce the risk of neck injury resulting from a collision?

Mark one answer

- [ ] An air-sprung seat
- [ ] Anti-lock brakes
- [ ] A collapsible steering wheel
- [ ] A properly adjusted head restraint

Answer

- [x] **A properly adjusted head restraint**

Head restraints will reduce the risk of neck injury if you're involved in a collision. They must be properly adjusted. Make sure they aren't positioned too low, or in an accident they could cause damage to the neck.

Question 3.41

How can you, as a driver, help the environment?

Mark three answers

- [ ] By reducing your speed
- [ ] By gentle acceleration
- [ ] By using leaded fuel
- [ ] By driving faster
- [ ] By harsh acceleration
- [ ] By servicing your vehicle properly

Answers

- [x] **By reducing your speed**
- [x] **By gentle acceleration**
- [x] **By servicing your vehicle properly**

Plan ahead and watch the traffic flow. Constant late braking will mean that you have to accelerate again, when perhaps a gentle easing off the accelerator is all you need.

Cleaner oil means your engine is not only more efficient in it's power output, but it will produce cleaner emissions and have a longer life.

Question 3.42

To help the environment, you can avoid wasting fuel by

Mark three answers

- [ ] having your vehicle properly serviced
- [ ] making sure your tyres are correctly inflated
- [ ] not over-revving in the lower gears
- [ ] driving at higher speeds where possible
- [ ] keeping an empty roof rack properly fitted
- [ ] servicing your vehicle less regularly

Answers

- ☒ **having your vehicle properly serviced**
- ☒ **making sure your tyres are correctly inflated**
- ☒ **not over-revving in the lower gears**

If you don't have your vehicle serviced regularly, the engine will not burn all the fuel efficiently. This will cause excess toxic gases to be discharged into the atmosphere.

Question 3.43

Why do MOT tests include a strict exhaust emission test?

Mark one answer

- [ ] To recover the cost of expensive garage equipment
- [ ] To help protect the environment against pollution
- [ ] To discover which fuel supplier is used the most
- [ ] To make sure diesel and petrol engines emit the same fumes

Answer

- ☒ **To help protect the environment against pollution**

Emission tests are carried out to ensure your vehicle is not polluting the atmosphere. If your vehicle is not serviced regularly, it may fail the annual MOT test.

Question 3.44

Which THREE things can you, as a road user, do to help the environment?

Mark three answers

☒ Cycle when possible

☒ Drive on under-inflated tyres

☒ Use the choke for as long as possible on a cold engine

☒ Have your vehicle properly tuned and serviced

☒ Watch the traffic and plan ahead

☒ Brake as late as possible without skidding

Answers

✖ **Cycle when possible**

✖ **Have your vehicle properly tuned and serviced**

✖ **Watch the traffic and plan ahead**

The car is a very convenient mode of transport. We can travel directly from our homes, in the dry and often with in-car entertainment. However, we all have an obligation to protect the environment from damage caused by excessive use of the internal combustion engine. Think about the journeys you make. Public transport can often be even more convenient, quicker and less stressful.

Question 3.45

As a driver you can cause more damage to the environment by

Mark three answers

☒ choosing a fuel efficient vehicle

☒ making a lot of short journeys

☒ driving in as high a gear as possible

☒ accelerating as quickly as possible

☒ having your vehicle regularly serviced

☒ using leaded fuel

Answers

✖ **making a lot of short journeys**

✖ **accelerating as quickly as possible**

✖ **using leaded fuel**

For short journeys it may be quicker to walk, and it's far better for your health too. In built-up areas just think about the time you are stationary in traffic with the engine running. This is damaging and expensive.

Question 3.46

Motor vehicles can harm the environment. This has resulted in

Mark three answers

- ☒ air pollution
- ☒ damage to buildings
- ☒ reduced health risks
- ☒ improved public transport
- ☒ less use of electrical vehicles
- ☒ using up natural resources

Answers

- ☒ **air pollution**
- ☒ **damage to buildings**
- ☒ **using up natural resources**

Exhaust emissions cause buildings to discolour and erode. Millions of pounds have been spent restoring old buildings to their original state. Constant vibration caused by heavy traffic also damages buildings.

Question 3.47

To reduce the damage your vehicle causes to the environment you should

Mark three answers

- ☒ use narrow side streets
- ☒ avoid harsh acceleration
- ☒ brake in good time
- ☒ anticipate well ahead
- ☒ use busy routes

Answers

- ☒ **avoid harsh acceleration**
- ☒ **brake in good time**
- ☒ **anticipate well ahead**

By looking well ahead and recognising hazards early you can avoid last minute harsh braking. Watch the traffic flow and judge your speed accordingly. Avoid over-revving the engine and accelerating harshly

Question 3.48

You will help the environment if you

Mark one answer

- ☒ reduce the tyre pressures
- ☒ drive continually using full choke
- ☒ accelerate and brake sharply
- ☒ walk or cycle when you can

Answer

- ☒ **walk or cycle when you can**

Walking and cycling are better for you. Keep your car for longer trips, although it could still be cheaper to use public transport. Do some research to find out if this is the case.

DSA THEORY TEST for car drivers and motorcyclists

Question 3.49

To help protect the environment you should NOT

Mark one answer

- [ ] remove your roof rack when unloaded
- [ ] use your car for very short journeys
- [ ] walk, cycle, or use public transport
- [ ] empty the boot of unnecessary weight

Answer

❌ **use your car for very short journeys**

Try not always to use your car as a matter of routine, whatever the length of your journey. Consider walking or cycling; it's much better for both you and the environment. Make use of the increasing number of cycle lanes.

Question 3.50

You service your own vehicle. How should you get rid of the old engine oil?

Mark one answer

- [ ] Take it to a local authority site
- [ ] Pour it down a drain
- [ ] Tip it into a hole in the ground
- [ ] Put it into your dustbin

Answer

❌ **Take it to a local authority site**

Never pour the oil down any drain. The oil is highly pollutant and could harm wildlife. Put it in a closed container and dispose of it sensibly at an authorised site.

Question 3.51

Waste engine oil should be disposed of

Mark one answer

- [ ] at the local demolition site
- [ ] down a water drain
- [ ] at the local authority site
- [ ] on nearby waste land

Answer

❌ **at the local authority site**

When taking oil to a disposal site ensure that it is safely contained and there is no danger of spillage.

Question 3.52

Which of the following would NOT make you more visible in daylight?

Mark one answer

- [ ] A black helmet
- [ ] A white helmet
- [ ] Switching on your dipped headlamp
- [ ] Wearing a fluorescent jacket

Answer

❌ **A black helmet**

Wearing bright or fluorescent clothes will help other road users to see you. Wearing a white helmet can also make you more visible.

Question 3.53

When riding and wearing brightly coloured clothing you will

Mark one answer

☒	dazzle other motorists on the road
☒	be seen more easily by other motorists
☒	create a hazard by distracting other drivers
☒	be able to ride on unlit roads at night with sidelights

Answer

 be seen more easily by other motorists

For safety you want other road users to see you easily. One way of achieving this is to wear brightly coloured or fluorescent clothing during daylight. At night, reflective clothing is the best material to help others to see you.

Question 3.54

You are riding a motorcycle in very hot weather. You should

Mark one answer

☒	ride with your visor fully open
☒	continue to wear protective clothing
☒	wear trainers instead of boots
☒	slacken your helmet strap

Answer

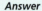 **continue to wear protective clothing**

In very hot weather it's tempting to ride in light summer clothes. Don't do this. If you fall from your machine you'll have no protection from the hard road surface. Always wear your protective clothing, whatever the weather.

Reflective

Reflective

Question 3.55

Why should you wear fluorescent clothing when riding in daylight?

Mark one answer

- [ ] It reduces wind resistance
- [ ] It prevents injury if you come off the machine
- [ ] It helps other road users to see you
- [ ] It keeps you cool in hot weather

Answer

✗ It helps other road users to see you

When riding a motorcycle it's very important that other road users are able to see you clearly. Fluorescent clothing will help towards this, reducing the risk of an accident. You must be visible from all directions.

Question 3.56

Why should riders wear reflective clothing?

Mark one answer

- [ ] To protect them from the cold
- [ ] To protect them from direct sunlight
- [ ] To be seen better in daylight
- [ ] To be seen better at night

Answer

✗ To be seen better at night

Fluorescent clothing will help others to see you during the day. At night, however, you should wear clothing that reflects the light. This allows other road users to see you with their headlights. Ask your local motorcycle dealer about the correct clothing.

Question 3.57

Which of the following makes it easier for motorcyclists to be seen?

Mark three answers

- [ ] Using a dipped headlight
- [ ] Wearing a fluorescent jacket
- [ ] Wearing a white helmet
- [ ] Wearing a grey helmet
- [ ] Wearing black leathers
- [ ] Using a tinted visor

Answers

✗ Using a dipped headlight
✗ Wearing a fluorescent jacket
✗ Wearing a white helmet

Many road accidents involving motorcyclists occur because another road user didn't see them. Using some form of visibility aid will help others to see you. Be aware that you're vulnerable, and ride defensively.

You are carrying two 13-year-old children and their parents in your car. Who is responsible for seeing that the children wear seat belts?

Mark one answer

☒ The children's parents

☒ You, the driver

☒ The front seat passenger

☒ The children

Answer

✖ **You, the driver**

Seat belts save lives and reduce the risk of injury. You MUST wear a seat belt unless you're exempt. There are also legal requirements for your passengers. Make sure that you know the rules for wearing seat belts. Check the chart below.

	FRONT SEAT	REAR SEAT	RESPONSIBILITY
Driver	Seat belt must be worn if fitted		Driver
Child under 3 years	Appropriate child restraint must be worn	Appropriate child restraint must be worn if fitted	Driver
Child aged 3 to 11 and under 1.5 metres (about 5 feet)	Appropriate child restraint must be worn if available. If not, an adult seat belt must be worn if fitted.	Appropriate child restraint must be worn if available. If not, an adult seat belt must be worn if fitted.	Driver
Child aged 12 or 13 or a younger child 1.5 metres in height (about 5 feet) or more	Adult seat belt must be worn if fitted	Adult seat belt must be worn if fitted	Driver
Adult passengers	Seat belt must be worn if fitted	Seat belt must be worn if fitted	Passenger

Question 3.59

You are driving a friend's children home from school. They are both under 14 years old. Who is responsible for making sure they wear a seat belt?

Mark one answer

☒ An adult passenger

☒ The children

☒ You, the driver

☒ Your friend

Answer

☒ **You, the driver**

Children should always be secured and safe. They should be encouraged to fasten their seat belts themselves from an early age so that it becomes a matter of routine. As the driver you must check that the seat belts are fastened securely; it's *your* responsibility.

Question 3.60

Car passengers MUST wear a seat belt, if one is available, unless they are

Mark one answer

☒ under 14 years old

☒ under 1.5 metres (5 feet) in height

☒ sitting in the rear seat

☒ exempt for medical reasons

Answer

☒ **exempt for medical reasons**

Although it's your adult passengers' responsibility to wear a seat belt, remind them to put them on as they get in the car.

Question 3.61

Excessive or uneven tyre wear can be caused by faults in which THREE?

Mark three answers

☒ The gearbox

☒ The braking system

☒ The accelerator

☒ The exhaust system

☒ Wheel alignment

☒ The suspension

Answers

☒ **The braking system**

☒ **Wheel alignment**

☒ **The suspension**

Regular servicing will help to detect faults at an early stage, and help prevent minor faults becoming serious or even dangerous.

Question 3.62

Which of the following fairings would give you the best weather protection?

Mark one answer

 Handlebar

Sports

Touring

Windscreen

Answer

✖ Touring

Fairings give protection to the hands, legs and feet. They also make riding more comfortable by keeping you out of the wind.

Question 3.63

It would be illegal to ride WITH a helmet on when

Mark one answer

the helmet is not fastened correctly

the helmet is more than four years old

you have borrowed someone else's helmet

the helmet does not have chin protection

Answer

✖ the helmet is not fastened correctly

In an accident a motorcycle helmet which is incorrectly fastened is liable to come off and provide little or no protection. The law requires that when you ride on the road your helmet must be correctly fastened.

Question 3.64

Your safety helmet has a small crack. You should

Mark one answer

get a new one before riding

ride at low speeds only

ask the police to inspect it

have it repaired by an expert

Answer

✖ get a new one before riding

If you damage your motorcycle helmet, even slightly, buy a new one. The smallest damage can make a helmet unreliable. A little expense now may save your life later.

Question 3.65

Your visor becomes badly scratched. You should

Mark one answer

- [ ] polish it with a fine abrasive
- [ ] replace it
- [ ] wash it in soapy water
- [ ] clean it with petrol

Answer

✗ replace it

Your visor protects your eyes from wind, rain, insects and road dirt. It's therefore important to keep it clean and in good repair. A badly scratched visor will

- obscure your view
- cause dazzle from lights of oncoming vehicles.

Question 3.66

You want to ride your motorcycle in the dark. What could you wear to be seen more easily?

Mark two answers

- [ ] Fluorescent clothing
- [ ] Reflective clothing
- [ ] A white helmet
- [ ] A red helmet
- [ ] A black leather jacket

Answers

✗ Reflective clothing
✗ A white helmet

When riding in the dark you will be more easy to see if you wear

- reflective clothing
- a white helmet.

A white helmet contrasts starkly with the surrounding darkness, while reflective clothing reflects the light from other vehicles and makes the rider much more visible.

Question 3.67

You are testing your suspension. You notice that your vehicle keeps bouncing when you press down on the front wing. What does this mean?

Mark one answer

- [ ] Worn tyres
- [ ] Tyres under-inflated
- [ ] Steering wheel not located centrally
- [ ] Worn shock absorbers

Answer

✗ Worn shock absorbers

If you find that your vehicle bounces as you drive around a corner or bend the shock absorbers might be worn. Press down on the front wing, and if the vehicle continues to bounce when you release the pressure, take it to be checked by a qualified mechanic.

Question 3.68

Which of the following will improve fuel consumption?

Mark two answers

- ☒ Reducing your road speed
- ☒ Planning well ahead
- ☒ Late and harsh braking
- ☒ Driving in lower gears
- ☒ Short journeys with a cold engine
- ☒ Rapid acceleration

Question 3.69

Which THREE of the following are most likely to waste fuel?

Mark three answers

- ☒ Reducing your speed
- ☒ Carrying unnecessary weight
- ☒ Using the wrong grade of fuel
- ☒ Under-inflated tyres
- ☒ Using different brands of fuel
- ☒ A fitted, empty roof rack

Question 3.70

In which of these containers may you carry petrol in a motor vehicle?

Mark one answer

☒   ☒

☒   ☒

Answers

- ✗ **Reducing your road speed**
- ✗ **Planning well ahead**

Harsh braking, constant gear changes and acceleration use more fuel. An engine will always use less fuel when travelling at a constant low speed. You need to look well ahead so you are able to anticipate hazards early. Easing off the accelerator and timing your approach could actually improve the miles per gallon of your vehicle.

Answers

- ✗ **Carrying unnecessary weight**
- ✗ **Under-inflated tyres**
- ✗ **A fitted, empty roof rack**

Wasting fuel costs you, the driver, hard earned cash. It also causes unnecessary pollution to the atmosphere. Failing to carry out basic maintenance checks, such as tyre pressures, can affect the handling of your vehicle.

Answer

✗

Petrol may be carried in your vehicle, but it must be carried in a container designed for that purpose. Don't use other types as they might leak or perish. Suitable containers are available in most motor shops and petrol stations.

Question 3.71

You have a loose filler cap on your diesel fuel tank. This will

Mark two answers

- ☒ waste fuel and money
- ☒ make roads slippery for other road users
- ☒ improve your vehicle's fuel consumption
- ☒ increase the level of exhaust emissions

Answers

- ☒ **waste fuel and money**
- ☒ **make roads slippery for other road users**

Diesel fuel is especially slippery if spilled on a wet road. At the end of a dry spell of weather you should be aware that the road surfaces may have a high level of diesel spillage that hasn't been washed away by rain.

Question 3.72

To avoid spillage after refuelling, you should make sure that

Mark one answer

- ☒ your tank is only 3/4 full
- ☒ you have used a locking filler cap
- ☒ you check your fuel gauge is working
- ☒ your filler cap is securely fastened

Answer

- ☒ **your filler cap is securely fastened**

As a learner driver it is sensible to practise filling your car with fuel. Ask your instructor if you can use a petrol station and fill the fuel tank yourself. You need to know where the filler cap is located on the car you are driving in order to park on the correct side of the pump. When filling the car, watch what you are doing to prevent overfilling and fuel spillage. Secure the filler cap as soon as you have replaced the fuel nozzle.

Question 3.73

Extra care should be taken when refuelling, because diesel fuel when spilt is

Mark one answer

- ☒ sticky
- ☒ odourless
- ☒ clear
- ☒ slippery

Answer

- ☒ **slippery**

If you are using diesel or are at a pump which has a diesel facility, be aware that the surface could be slippery. The fuel contamination on the soles of your shoes may cause them to slip when using the foot pedals.

Question 3.74

You must NOT sound your horn

Mark one answer

- [ ] between 10 pm and 6 am in a built-up area
- [ ] at any time in a built-up area
- [ ] between 11.30 pm and 7 am in a built-up area
- [ ] between 11.30 pm and 6 am on any road

Answer

- [x] **between 11.30 pm and 7 am in a built-up area**

Vehicles can be noisy. Every effort must be made to prevent excessive noise, especially in built-up areas at night. Don't

- rev the engine
- sound the horn between 11.30 pm and 7 am.

Question 3.75

When MUST you NOT use your horn in a built-up area?

Mark one answer

- [ ] Between 8 pm and 8 am
- [ ] Between 9 pm and dawn
- [ ] Between dusk and 8 am
- [ ] Between 11.30 pm and 7 am

Answer

- [x] **Between 11.30 pm and 7 am**

Flash your headlights as an alternative. Only sound your horn to prevent an accident.

Question 3.76

Why are mirrors on the outside of vehicles often slightly curved (convex)?

Mark one answer

- [ ] They give a wider field of vision
- [ ] They totally cover blind spots
- [ ] They make it easier to judge the speed of following traffic
- [ ] They make following traffic look bigger

Answer

- [x] **They give a wider field of vision**

Modern vehicles provide the driver with equipment to help increase the field of vision. However, you should always be aware that even these mirrors might not reflect all that is around the vehicle. A check over the shoulder before you move off is required.

Question 3.77

You cannot see clearly behind when reversing. What should you do?

Mark one answer

 Open your window to look behind

Open the door and look behind

Look in the nearside mirror

Ask someone to guide you

Answer

 Ask someone to guide you

If you want to turn your car around, try to find a place where you have good all-round vision. If this isn't possible and you're unable to see clearly, then get someone to guide you.

 Question 3.78

Why can it be helpful to have mirrors fitted on each side of your motorcycle?

Mark one answer

To judge the gap when filtering in traffic

To give protection when riding in poor weather

To make your machine appear larger to other drivers

To give you the best view of the road behind

Answer

To give you the best view of the road behind

When riding on the road you need to know as much about following traffic as you can. A mirror fitted on each side of your motorcycle will help give you the best view of the road behind.

Question 3.79

When MUST you use a dipped headlight during the day?

Mark one answer

On country roads

In poor visibility

Along narrow streets

When parking

Answer

❌ **In poor visibility**

It's important that other road users can see you clearly at all times. It will help other road users to see you if you use a dipped headlight during the day. If there's limited visibility you MUST use them.

Question 3.80

Your side stand is not raised fully when you start to ride. What could this do?

Mark one answer

Alter the machine's centre of gravity

Catch on your feet

Dig into the ground when you are cornering

Cause the machine to steer badly

Answer

❌ **Dig into the ground when you are cornering**

Make sure that your side stand's fully up before you move off. If it isn't up it could dig into the ground as you move away and might lead to an accident.

Question 3.81

What will cause high fuel consumption?

Mark one answer

- ☒ Poor steering control
- ☒ Accelerating around bends
- ☒ Driving in high gears
- ☒ Harsh braking and accelerating

Answer

☒ **Harsh braking and accelerating**

Look after your vehicle or machine. Have it regularly serviced and keep all the lights and windows (on a vehicle) clean. Driving or riding 'sympathetically' will help you to keep fuel consumption down. This practice is kinder to the environment and will also save you money.

Question 3.82

A properly serviced vehicle will give

Mark two answers

- ☒ lower insurance premiums
- ☒ you a refund on your road tax
- ☒ better fuel economy
- ☒ cleaner exhaust emissions

Answers

☒ **better fuel economy**
☒ **cleaner exhaust emissions**

When you purchase your vehicle, check at what intervals you should have it serviced. This can vary depending on model or manufacturer. Use the service manual and keep it up to date. The cleaner the engine, the cleaner it's emissions.

Question 3.83

Driving at 70 mph uses more fuel than driving at 50 mph by up to

Mark one answer

- ☒ 10%
- ☒ 30%
- ☒ 75%
- ☒ 100%

Answer

☒ **30%**

Your vehicle will be cheaper to run if you avoid heavy acceleration. The higher the engine revs, the more fuel you will use.

When driving a car fitted with automatic transmission what would you use 'kick down' for?

Mark one answer

- ❌ Cruise control
- ❌ Quick acceleration
- ❌ Slow braking
- ❌ Fuel economy

Answer

❌ **Quick acceleration**

'Kick down' selects a lower gear, enabling the vehicle to accelerate faster.

When a roof rack is not in use it should be removed. Why is this?

Mark one answer

- ❌ It will affect the suspension
- ❌ It is illegal
- ❌ It will affect your braking
- ❌ It will waste fuel

Answer

❌ **It will waste fuel**

We are all responsible for the environment we live in. If every driver takes individual responsibility for conserving fuel, together we will make a difference.

A roof rack fitted to your car will

Mark one answer

- ❌ reduce fuel consumption
- ❌ improve the road handling
- ❌ make your car go faster
- ❌ increase fuel consumption

Answer

❌ **increase fuel consumption**

Make sure that any cover is securely fitted and does not flap about in the wind when driving. There are roof boxes available which will reduce wind resistance and, in turn, fuel consumption.

Question 3.87

The pictured vehicle is 'environmentally friendly' because it

Mark three answers

- [ ] reduces noise pollution
- [ ] uses diesel fuel
- [ ] uses electricity
- [ ] uses unleaded fuel
- [ ] reduces parking spaces
- [ ] reduces town traffic

Answers

- [x] **reduces noise pollution**
- [x] **uses electricity**
- [x] **reduces town traffic**

The electric motors of trams don't emit dirty fumes which would add to those already emitted by the other town traffic. These types of motor are also much quieter than petrol or diesel engines.

Question 3.88

Supertrams or Light Rapid Transit (LRT) systems are environmentally friendly because

Mark one answer

- [ ] they use diesel power
- [ ] they use quieter roads
- [ ] they use electric power
- [ ] they do not operate during rush hour

Answer

- [x] **they use electric power**

This means that they do not emit toxic fumes which add to city pollution problems. They are also a lot quieter and smoother to ride on.

Question 3.89

'Red routes' in major cities have been introduced to

Mark one answer

- [ ] raise the speed limits
- [ ] help the traffic flow
- [ ] provide better parking
- [ ] allow lorries to load more freely

Answer

- [x] **help the traffic flow**

Traffic jams today are often caused by the volume of traffic. However, selfish parking can block an inside lane or cause traffic to wait for oncoming vehicles, and this will also cause delays. When traffic is moving slowly, each engine is emitting toxic fumes for a longer time.

Question 3.90

To reduce the volume of traffic on the roads you could

Mark three answers

- use public transport more often
- share a car when possible
- walk or cycle on short journeys
- travel by car at all times
- use a car with a smaller engine
- drive in a bus lane

Answers

- ❌ **use public transport more often**
- ❌ **share a car when possible**
- ❌ **walk or cycle on short journeys**

Travelling by public transport is an opportunity to get regular exercise by walking to the train or bus station. Exercise is good for everyone. Leave the car at home.

Question 3.91

In some narrow residential streets you will find a speed limit of

Mark one answer

- 20 mph
- 25 mph
- 35 mph
- 40 mph

Answer

- ❌ **20 mph**

There are numerous hazards to deal with in residential areas. These hazards can be unpredictable, hidden, static or moving. You need to allow yourself the time and space to deal with them. The safest way to do this is to reduce your speed.

Question 3.92

Road humps, chicanes, and narrowings are

Mark one answer

- always at major road works
- used to increase traffic speed
- at toll-bridge approaches only
- traffic calming measures

Answer

- ❌ **traffic calming measures**

Remember that the car is a relatively late addition to our environment. Many areas, especially residential ones, were not built to allow for fast moving traffic. Drivers failing to consider the many dangers has led to measures being taken to slow the traffic down. It may be quicker to walk.

Question 3.93

You enter a road where there are road humps. What should you do?

Mark one answer

- [x] Maintain a reduced speed throughout
- [x] Accelerate quickly between each one
- [x] Always keep to the maximum legal speed
- [x] Drive slowly at school times only

Answer

❌ **Maintain a reduced speed throughout**

The humps are there for a reason – to reduce the speed of the traffic. Don't accelerate harshly between them as you will only have to brake harshly to negotiate the next one. Harsh braking and accelerating uses more fuel.

Question 3.94

A motorcyclist may only carry a pillion passenger when

Mark three answers

- [x] the rider has successfully completed CBT
- [x] the rider holds a full licence for the category of machine
- [x] the motorcycle is fitted with rear foot pegs
- [x] the rider has a full car licence and is over 21
- [x] there is a proper passenger seat fitted
- [x] there is no sidecar fitted to the machine

Answers

❌ **the rider holds a full licence for the category of machine**

❌ **the motorcycle is fitted with rear foot pegs**

❌ **there is a proper passenger seat fitted**

Before carrying a passenger on a motorcycle the rider must hold a full licence for the category being ridden and make sure that

- passenger footrests are fitted
- a proper passenger seat is fitted.

Question 3.95

On your vehicle, where would you find a catalytic converter?

Mark one answer

☒ In the fuel tank

☒ In the air filter

☒ On the cooling system

☒ On the exhaust system

Answer

☒ **On the exhaust system**

Although carbon dioxide is still produced, a catalytic converter reduces the toxic and polluting gases by up to 90%. Unleaded fuel must be used in vehicles fitted with a catalytic converter.

Question 3.96

Leaded petrol must NOT be used in vehicles fitted with

Mark one answer

☒ a fuel injection system

☒ a catalytic converter

☒ an engine of less than 1000 cc

☒ a stainless steel exhaust

Answer

☒ **a catalytic converter**

Leaded petrol can damage the system. Using fuel without lead is better for the environment; it is also cheaper and so will save you money.

Question 3.97

New vehicles are fitted with catalytic converters if they use

Mark one answer

☒ gas power

☒ unleaded petrol

☒ leaded petrol

☒ battery power

Answer

☒ **unleaded petrol**

Motor manufacturers are making efforts to reduce the levels of pollution caused by their vehicles. Catalytic converters can reduce damaging toxic waste by up to 90%. They must not be used with leaded fuel as this can damage them.

DSA THEORY TEST for car drivers and motorcyclists

Question 3.98

For which TWO of these may you use hazard warning lights?

Mark two answers

- ☒ When driving on a motorway, to warn other drivers behind of a hazard ahead
- ☒ When you are double parked on a two-way road
- ☒ When your direction indicators are not working
- ☒ When warning oncoming traffic that you intend to stop
- ☒ When your vehicle has broken down and is causing an obstruction

Answers

- ☒ **When driving on a motorway, to warn other drivers behind of a hazard ahead**
- ☒ **When your vehicle has broken down and is causing an obstruction**

Don't use them as an excuse to park illegally, such as when using a cash machine or postbox. They are an important safety feature and should only be used to warn other road users of a hazard.

Question 3.99

Daytime visibility is poor but not seriously reduced. You should switch on

Mark one answer

- ☒ headlights and fog lights
- ☒ front fog lights
- ☒ dipped headlights
- ☒ rear fog lights

Answer

- ☒ **dipped headlights**

Only use your fog lights when visibility is seriously reduced. Use dipped headlights in poor conditions.

Question 3.100

Why are vehicles fitted with rear fog lights?

Mark one answer

- ☒ To be seen when driving at high speed
- ☒ To use if broken down in a dangerous position
- ☒ To make them more visible in thick fog
- ☒ To warn drivers following closely to drop back

Answer

- ☒ **To make them more visible in thick fog**

It makes it easier to spot a vehicle ahead in difficult conditions. Do not use other vehicle lights as a guide, however, as it will give you a false sense of security.

SECTION 4 SAFETY MARGINS

This section looks at safety margins and how they can be affected by conditions.

The questions will ask you about

- stopping distances
- road surfaces
- skidding
- weather conditions.

Question 4.1

Your vehicle is fitted with anti-lock brakes. To stop quickly in an emergency you should

Mark one answer

- ☒ brake firmly and pump the brake pedal on and off
- ☒ brake rapidly and firmly without releasing the brake pedal
- ☒ brake gently and pump the brake pedal on and off
- ☒ brake rapidly once, and immediately release the brake pedal

Answer

☒ **brake rapidly and firmly without releasing the brake pedal**

Once you have applied the brake keep your foot firmly on the pedal. Releasing the brake and re-applying it will disable the anti-lock capability of the brake system.

Question 4.2

Your car is fitted with anti-lock brakes. You need to stop in an emergency. You should

Mark one answer

- ☒ brake normally and avoid turning the steering wheel
- ☒ press the brake pedal rapidly and firmly until you have stopped
- ☒ keep pushing and releasing the foot brake quickly to prevent skidding
- ☒ apply the handbrake to reduce the stopping distance

Answer

☒ **press the brake pedal rapidly and firmly until you have stopped**

Keep pressure on the brake pedal until you have come to a stop. You need to prevent the car from stalling, so depress the clutch pedal.

Question 4.3

You are driving a vehicle fitted with anti-lock brakes. You need to stop in an emergency. You should apply the footbrake

Mark one answer

- ☒ slowly and gently
- ☒ slowly but firmly
- ☒ rapidly and gently
- ☒ rapidly and firmly

Answer

☒ **rapidly and firmly**

Look well ahead down the road as you drive. You will see clues about the hazards ahead, such as road signs or brake lights. Give yourself time and space to react safely. You may have to stop in an emergency. This may be due to a misjudgement by another driver or a hazard that has given you little time to react, such as a child running out into the road. If your vehicle has anti-lock brakes you should apply the brakes immediately *and keep them applied* until you stop.

Question 4.4

Anti-lock brakes reduce the chances of a skid occurring particularly when

Mark one answer

- [ ] driving down steep hills
- [ ] braking during normal driving
- [ ] braking in an emergency
- [ ] driving on good road surfaces

Answer

- [x] **braking in an emergency**

The anti-lock braking system will operate when the brakes have been applied harshly. It will reduce the chances of your car skidding, but you must be aware that on wet or icy roads it is not a miracle cure for careless driving.

Question 4.5

Your vehicle has anti-lock brakes, but they may not always prevent skidding. This is most likely to happen when driving

Mark two answers

- [ ] in foggy conditions
- [ ] on surface water
- [ ] on loose road surfaces
- [ ] on dry tarmac
- [ ] at night on unlit roads

Answers

- [x] **on surface water**
- [x] **on loose road surfaces**

In very wet weather water can build up between the tyre and the road surface. As a result your vehicle actually rides on a thin film of water and your tyres will not grip the road. Gravel or shingle road surfaces also offer less grip and can present problems when braking.

Question 4.6

Anti-lock brakes prevent wheels from locking. This means the tyres are less likely to

Mark one answer

- [ ] aquaplane
- [ ] skid
- [ ] puncture
- [ ] wear

Answer

- [x] **skid**

Electronic sensors detect when the wheels are about to lock, momentarily releasing the brakes and re-applying them. It then repeats the process in a very short space of time, reducing the risk of skidding.

Question 4.7

Anti-lock brakes are most effective when you

Mark one answer

keep pumping the foot brake to prevent skidding

brake normally, but grip the steering wheel tightly

brake rapidly and firmly until you have slowed down

apply the handbrake to reduce the stopping distance

Answer

 brake rapidly and firmly until you have slowed down

Releasing the brake before you have slowed right down will disable the system. If you have to brake in an emergency ensure that you keep your foot firmly on the brake pedal until the vehicle has stopped.

Question 4.8

Vehicles fitted with anti-lock brakes

Mark one answer

are impossible to skid

can be steered while you are braking

accelerate much faster

are not fitted with a handbrake

Answer

 can be steered while you are braking

Preventing the wheels from locking means that the vehicle's steering and stability can be maintained, leading to safer stopping. However, you must ensure that the engine does not stall, as this could disable the power steering. When stopping in an emergency, and braking harshly, depress the clutch pedal as you brake.

Question 4.9

Anti-lock brakes may not work as effectively if the road surface is

Mark two answers

dry

loose

wet

good

firm

Answers

 loose

 wet

Poor contact with the road surface could cause one or more of the tyres to lose grip on the road. Be especially wary when driving in poor weather conditions when the road surface is uneven or has loose chippings.

Anti-lock brakes are of most use when you are

Mark one answer

- [ ] braking gently
- [ ] driving on worn tyres
- [ ] braking excessively
- [ ] driving normally

Answer

✗ braking excessively

Anti-lock brakes will not be required when braking normally. Looking well down the road and anticipating possible hazards could prevent you having to brake late and harshly. Knowing you have anti-lock brakes should not encourage you to drive less carefully.

Question 4.11

Driving a vehicle fitted with anti-lock brakes allows you to

Mark one answer

- [ ] brake harder because it is impossible to skid
- [ ] drive at higher speeds
- [ ] steer and brake at the same time
- [ ] pay less attention to the road ahead

Answer

✗ steer and brake at the same time

Anti-lock brakes will help you continue to steer when braking, but in poor weather conditions they will be less effective. Depress the clutch pedal to prevent the car stalling. The power steering system uses an engine driven pump and will only operate when the engine is running.

Question 4.12

When would an anti-lock braking system start to work?

Mark one answer

- [ ] After the parking brake has been applied
- [ ] Whenever pressure on the brake pedal is applied
- [ ] Just as the wheels are about to lock
- [ ] When the normal braking system fails to operate

Answer

✗ Just as the wheels are about to lock

Electronic sensors detect when the wheels are about to lock, releases the brakes enough to allow the wheels to revolve and grip, then repeats the process in a very short space of time.

Question 4.13

Anti-lock brakes will take effect when

Mark one answer

- [ ] you do not brake quickly enough
- [ ] excessive brake pressure has been applied
- [ ] you have not seen a hazard ahead
- [ ] speeding on slippery road surfaces

Question 4.14

Anti-lock brakes can greatly assist with

Mark one answer

- [ ] a higher cruising speed
- [ ] steering control when braking
- [ ] control when accelerating
- [ ] motorway driving

Question 4.15

You are on a good, dry road surface and your vehicle has good brakes and tyres. What is the overall stopping distance at 40 mph?

Mark one answer

- [ ] 23 metres (75 feet)
- [ ] 36 metres (118 feet)
- [ ] 53 metres (174 feet)
- [ ] 96 metres (315 feet)

Answer

✗ excessive brake pressure has been applied

If your car is fitted with anti-lock brakes, they will take effect when you use them harshly in an emergency. The system will only activate when it senses the wheels are about to lock.

Answer

✗ steering control when braking

If the wheels of your vehicle lock they will not grip the road. This will have a severe affect on your steering control. In good conditions the anti-lock system will allow you to retain some steering control.

Answer

✗ 36 metres (118 feet)

Factors that affect how long it takes you to stop include

- how fast you're going
- whether you're travelling on the level, uphill or downhill
- the weather and road conditions
- the condition of your tyres, brakes and suspension
- your reaction time.

Question 4.16

You are on a good, dry road surface. Your vehicle has good brakes and tyres. What is the braking distance at 50 mph?

Mark one answer

 38 metres (125 feet)

☒ 14 metres (46 feet)

☒ 24 metres (79 feet)

☒ 55 metres (180 feet)

Answer

✖ 38 metres (125 feet)

The braking distance is how far you travel from the moment you first apply the brakes to the point where you stop. Stopping distance can be divided into

- thinking distance
- braking distance.

The thinking distance is how far you travel from the moment you see the need to brake to the moment you apply the brakes.

Question 4.17

Your overall stopping distance will be longer when riding

Mark one answer

☒ at night

☒ in the fog

☒ with a passenger

☒ up a hill

Answer

✖ with a passenger

When carrying a passenger on a motorcycle the overall weight will be much more than when riding alone. This additional weight will make it harder for you to stop in an emergency.

At 30 mph

Thinking distance	Braking distance	Overall stopping distance
9m (30ft)	14m (45ft)	23m (75ft)

At 50 mph

Thinking distance	Braking distance	Overall stopping distance
15m (50ft)	38m (125ft)	53m (175ft)

At 70 mph

Thinking distance	Braking distance	Overall stopping distance
21m (70ft)	75m (245ft)	96m (315ft)

Question 4.18

Braking hard at speed on a sharp bend can make your vehicle

Mark one answer

- [x] more stable
- [x] unstable
- [x] stall
- [x] corner safely

Answer

[x] **unstable**

Adjust your speed in good time so that you are able to drive around the bend under gentle acceleration.

Question 4.19

You are riding a motorcycle in good road conditions. The most effective way to use the brakes is to

Mark one answer

- [x] apply both brakes with greater pressure on the rear
- [x] apply both brakes with equal pressure
- [x] apply the rear brake first and the front just before you stop
- [x] apply both brakes with greater pressure on the front

Answer

[x] **apply both brakes with greater pressure on the front**

This technique gives the best stopping power in good conditions because

- the combined weight of the machine and rider is thrown forward
- the front tyre is pressed more firmly on the road, giving a better grip.

Question 4.20

What is the shortest stopping distance at 70 mph?

Mark one answer

- [x] 53 metres (174 feet)
- [x] 60 metres (197 feet)
- [x] 73 metres (240 feet)
- [x] 96 metres (315 feet)

Answer

[x] **96 metres (315 feet)**

Note that this is the shortest distance. It will take at least this distance to think, brake and stop.

Question 4.21

You are travelling at 50 mph on a good, dry road. What is your shortest overall stopping distance?

Mark one answer

 36 metres (118 feet)

 53 metres (174 feet)

 75 metres (246 feet)

 96 metres (315 feet)

Answer

✗ **53 metres (174 feet)**

Even in good conditions it will take you further than you think for your car to stop. Don't just learn the figures – understand how far the distance is.

Question 4.22

What is the shortest overall stopping distance on a dry road from 60 mph?

Mark one answer

 53 metres (174 feet)

 58 metres (190 feet)

 73 metres (240 feet)

 96 metres (315 feet)

Answer

✗ **73 metres (240 feet)**

Pace out 73 metres (240 feet) and then look back. It's probably further than you think.

Question 4.23

When driving in fog, which of the following are correct?

Mark three answers

 Use dipped headlights

 Use headlights on full beam

 Allow more time for your journey

 Keep close to the car in front

 Slow down

 Use side lights only

Answers

✗ **Use dipped headlights**

✗ **Allow more time for your journey**

✗ **Slow down**

If your journey is not necessary, don't venture out. You will be taking unnecessary risks. If you have to travel and someone is expecting you at the other end, let them know that you will be taking longer than usual for your journey. This will stop them worrying if you don't turn up on time.

Question 4.24

'Only a fool breaks the Two-Second Rule' refers to

Mark one answer

- [ ] the time recommended when using the choke
- [ ] the separation distance when riding in good conditions
- [ ] restarting a stalled engine in busy traffic
- [ ] the time you should keep your foot down at a junction

Question 4.25

You are on a fast, open road in good conditions. For safety, the distance between you and the vehicle in front should be

Mark one answer

- [ ] a two-second time gap
- [ ] one car length
- [ ] 2 metres (6 feet 6 inches)
- [ ] two car lengths

Question 4.26

The 'Two-Second Rule' helps you to

Mark one answer

- [ ] keep a safe distance from the car in front
- [ ] keep the correct distance from the kerb
- [ ] check your blind spot
- [ ] check your mirrors

Answer

✖ the separation distance when riding in good conditions

It is very important that you always leave a safe gap between yourself and any vehicle you're following. In good conditions you need to leave

- at least one metre for every mile per hour of your speed, or
- a two-second time interval.

Answer

✖ a two-second time gap

One useful method of checking that you've allowed enough room between you and the vehicle in front is the 'Two-Second Rule'. You should allow a two-second time gap as a safe separation distance. Begin by saying 'Only a fool breaks the Two-Second Rule' when the vehicle in front passes a fixed point. You shouldn't reach that point before you finish saying it. If you do, you're travelling too close and should drop back.

Answer

✖ keep a safe distance from the car in front

Some people find it difficult to judge distances in metres or feet. The 'Two-Second Rule' is an easy way to judge your separation distance.

Question 4.27

Your overall stopping distance will be much longer when driving

Mark one answer

- ☒ in the rain
- ☒ in fog
- ☒ at night
- ☒ in strong winds

Answer

 in the rain

Extra care should be taken in wet weather. Wet roads will affect the time it takes you to stop. Your stopping distance could be at least doubled.

Question 4.28

On a wet road what is the safest way to stop?

Mark one answer

- ☒ Change gear without braking
- ☒ Use the back brake only
- ☒ Use the front brake only
- ☒ Use both brakes

Answer

 Use both brakes

Motorcyclists need to take extra care when stopping on wet road surfaces. Plan well ahead so that you're able to brake in good time. You should

- ensure your machine is upright
- brake when travelling in a straight line.

Question 4.29

The road surface is very important to motorcyclists because

Mark one answer

- ☒ there can be many areas where road markings are poor
- ☒ some roads are tarmac and others concrete
- ☒ as traffic increases there is less room for riders
- ☒ only a small part of the tyre touches the road

Answer

 only a small part of the tyre touches the road

A motorcyclist needs to be aware of the affect road conditions have on stability, steering and braking. Only a small part of the tyre is in contact with the road at any time which means that any change in the road surface can affect the grip on the road.

Question 4.30

Road surface is very important to motorcyclists. Which FOUR of these are more likely to reduce the stability of your machine?

Mark four answers

☒ Pot-holes

☒ Drain covers

☒ Concrete

☒ Oil patches

☒ Tarmac

☒ Loose gravel

Answers

☒ **Pot-holes**

☒ **Drain covers**

☒ **Oil patches**

☒ **Loose gravel**

Apart from the weather conditions, the road surface and any changes in it can affect the stability of your motorcycle. Be on the lookout for poor road surfaces.

Question 4.31

What is the main reason why your stopping distance is longer after heavy rain?

Mark one answer

☒ You may not be able to see large puddles

☒ The brakes will be cold because they are wet

☒ Your tyres will have less grip on the road

☒ Water on the windscreen will blur your view of the road ahead

Answer

☒ **Your tyres will have less grip on the road**

When the roads are wet the water will reduce your tyres' grip on the road. When the tyres lose their grip, you lose control. You can cause the tyres to lose their grip by

• excessive acceleration (wheelspin)

• cornering too fast

• braking too hard

• harsh steering (swerving).

Question 4.32

You are riding in town at night. The roads are wet after rain. The reflections from wet surfaces will

Mark one answer

- [ ] affect your stopping distance
- [ ] affect your road holding
- [ ] make it easy to see unlit objects
- [ ] make it hard to see unlit objects

Answer

❌ **make it hard to see unlit objects**

If you can't see clearly, slow down and stop. Make sure that your visor or goggles are clean. Be extra cautious in these conditions.

Question 4.33

What is the most common cause of skidding?

Mark one answer

- [ ] Worn tyres
- [ ] Driver error
- [ ] Other vehicles
- [ ] Pedestrians

Answer

❌ **Driver error**

Skids don't just happen. They're caused by a driver asking too much of the vehicle for the amount of grip the tyres have on the road at the time.

Question 4.34

When braking hard in a straight line, the weight of the vehicle will shift onto the

Mark one answer

- [ ] front wheels
- [ ] rear wheels
- [ ] left wheels
- [ ] right wheels

Answer

❌ **front wheels**

This in turn will throw you and your passengers forward, then back again as the vehicle comes to a stop. This harsh braking could also lead to the wheels locking and skidding on the road surface.

Rear of car skids
to the right

Driver steers
to the right

Question 4.35

You are driving in heavy rain. Your steering suddenly becomes very light. You should

Mark one answer

- ☒ steer towards the side of the road
- ☒ apply gentle acceleration
- ☒ brake firmly to reduce speed
- ☒ ease off the accelerator

Answer

☒ **ease off the accelerator**

Braking harshly in this situation could cause the tyres to lift off the road surface and the wheels to lock, which will result in loss of control. However, if your vehicle's fitted with an anti-lock braking system (ABS) and it starts to slide on the wet road surface, apply and maintain maximum force on the brake pedal.

Question 4.36

You are riding in heavy rain when your rear wheel skids as you accelerate. To get control again you must

Mark one answer

- ☒ change down to a lower gear
- ☒ ease off the throttle
- ☒ brake to reduce speed
- ☒ put your feet down

Answer

☒ **ease off the throttle**

If you feel your back wheel beginning to skid as you pull away, ease off the throttle. This will give your rear tyre the chance to grip the road and stop the skid.

Bike skidding to the left

Direction of steering to correct skid

• **Ease off brake**

You have driven through a flood. What is the first thing you should do?

Mark one answer

 Stop and check the tyres

 Stop and dry the brakes

 Switch on your windscreen wipers

 Test your brakes

Answer

❌ **Test your brakes**

After passing through a flood or ford, test your brakes. Before you do so make sure that you check behind for following traffic. Don't brake sharply. The vehicle behind may not be able to stop quickly. If necessary, signal your intentions.

Question 4.38

You are driving along a country road. You see this sign. AFTER dealing safely with the hazard you should always

Ford

Mark one answer

❌ check your tyre pressures

❌ switch on your hazard warning lights

❌ accelerate briskly

❌ test your brakes

Answer

❌ **test your brakes**

Deep water can affect your brakes, so you should check that they're working properly before you build up speed again. Check your mirrors and consider what's behind you before you do this.

Question 4.39

Braking distances on ice can be

Mark one answer

❌ twice the normal distance

❌ five times the normal distance

❌ seven times the normal distance

❌ ten times the normal distance

Answer

❌ **ten times the normal distance**

Braking and stopping distances will also be affected by icy and snowy weather. You need to take extra care and expect your stopping distance to increase by up to ten times the normal distance.

Question 4.40

Freezing conditions will affect the distance it takes you to come to a stop. You should expect stopping distances to increase by up to

Mark one answer

 two times

 five times

 three times

 ten times

Answer

❌ **ten times**

You must take the road and weather conditions into account when driving. It will take considerably longer to stop in bad weather.

Question 4.41

When driving in icy conditions, the steering becomes light because the tyres

Mark one answer

 have more grip on the road

 are too soft

 are too hard

 have less grip on the road

Answer

❌ **have less grip on the road**

In icy conditions the tyres will lose much of their grip on the road. This could result in the steering becoming light. If you ease off the accelerator you should regain some steering control.

Question 4.42

You are driving on an icy road. How can you avoid wheelspin?

Mark one answer

- ☒ Drive at a slow speed in as high a gear as possible
- ☒ Use the handbrake if the wheels start to slip
- ☒ Brake gently and repeatedly
- ☒ Drive in a low gear at all times

Answer

 Drive at a slow speed in as high a gear as possible

If you're travelling on an icy road extra caution will be required to avoid any loss of control. You can reduce wheelspin by driving

- at a slow speed
- in as high a gear as possible.

Question 4.43

Skidding is mainly caused by

Mark one answer

- ☒ the weather
- ☒ the driver
- ☒ the vehicle
- ☒ the road

Answer

☒ **the driver**

You should always consider the conditions and drive accordingly.

Question 4.44

It is snowing. Before starting your journey you should

Mark one answer

- ☒ think if you need to ride at all
- ☒ try to avoid taking a passenger
- ☒ plan a route avoiding towns
- ☒ take a hot drink before setting out

Answer

☒ **think if you need to ride at all**

Snow is one weather condition when it's better not to ride at all. If you must go out try and keep to main roads which are the most likely to be clear and well gritted.

Question 4.45

How can you avoid wheelspin when driving in freezing conditions?

Mark one answer

- [ ] Stay in first gear all the time
- [ ] Put on your handbrake if the wheels begin to slip
- [ ] Drive in as high a gear as possible
- [ ] Allow the vehicle to coast in neutral

Answer

❌ **Drive in as high a gear as possible**

A low gear will cause the wheels to skid and you'll lose control. A high gear with steady accelerator control will help you to maintain some control.

Question 4.46

You are driving in freezing conditions. What should you do when approaching a sharp bend?

Mark two answers

- [ ] Slow down before you reach the bend
- [ ] Gently apply your handbrake
- [ ] Firmly use your footbrake
- [ ] Coast into the bend
- [ ] Avoid sudden steering movements

Answers

❌ **Slow down before you reach the bend**
❌ **Avoid sudden steering movements**

Avoid steering and braking at the same time. In icy conditions it's very important that you constantly assess what's ahead.

Question 4.47

When riding in extremely cold conditions what can you do to keep warm?

Mark one answer

- [ ] Stay close in behind the vehicles in front
- [ ] Wear suitable clothing
- [ ] Lie flat on the tank
- [ ] Put your hands one at a time on the exhaust pipe

Answer

❌ **Wear suitable clothing**

Motorcyclists are exposed to the elements and can become very cold when riding in wintry conditions. It's important to keep warm or concentration could be affected. The only way to stay warm is to wear suitable clothing. If you do find yourself getting cold then stop at a suitable place to warm up.

Question 4.48

You are turning left on a slippery road. The back of your vehicle slides to the right. You should

Mark one answer

- [ ] brake firmly and not turn the steering wheel
- [ ] steer carefully to the left
- [ ] steer carefully to the right
- [ ] brake firmly and steer to the left

Answer

✗ **steer carefully to the right**

This should stop the sliding and allow you to regain control. Don't

- use the accelerator
- use the brakes
- use the clutch.

Question 4.49

You are braking on a wet road. Your vehicle begins to skid. Your vehicle does not have anti-lock brakes. What is the FIRST thing you should do?

Mark one answer

- [ ] Quickly pull up the handbrake
- [ ] Release the footbrake fully
- [ ] Push harder on the brake pedal
- [ ] Gently use the accelerator

Answer

✗ **Release the footbrake fully**

If the skid has been caused by braking too hard for the conditions, release the brake. This will allow the wheels to turn and so limit the skid.

Skids are much easier to get into than they are to get out of. Prevention is better than cure. Stay alert to the road and weather conditions. Never drive so fast that you can't stop within the distance that you can see to be clear.

Question 4.50

How can you tell when you are driving over black ice?

Mark one answer

- [ ] It is easier to brake
- [ ] The noise from your tyres sounds louder
- [ ] You see black ice on the road
- [ ] Your steering feels light

Answer

✗ **Your steering feels light**

Sometimes you may not be able to see that the road is icy. Black ice makes a road look damp. The signs that you're travelling on black ice can be

- the steering feels light
- the noise from your tyres suddenly dies away.

Question 4.51

Coasting the vehicle

Mark one answer

☒ improves the driver's control

☒ makes steering easier

☒ reduces the driver's control

☒ uses more fuel

Answer

☒ **reduces the driver's control**

'Coasting' is the term used when the clutch is held down and the vehicle is freewheeling. This reduces the driver's control of the vehicle. When you coast, the engine can't drive the wheels to pull you through a corner. Coasting also prevents the engine braking from holding the car back.

Question 4.52

Before starting a journey in freezing weather you should clear ice and snow from your vehicle's

Mark four answers

☒ aerial

☒ windows

☒ bumper

☒ lights

☒ mirrors

☒ number plates

Answers

☒ **windows**

☒ **lights**

☒ **mirrors**

☒ **number plates**

Don't travel in bad weather unless you really have to. Making unnecessary journeys will increase the risk of an accident. It is important that any snow or ice is not covering lights, mirrors, number plates or windows.

Question 4.53

You are driving in falling snow. Your wipers are not clearing the windscreen. You should

Mark one answer

☒ set the windscreen demister to cool

☒ be prepared to clear the windscreen by hand

☒ use the windscreen washers

☒ partly open the front windows

Answer

☒ **be prepared to clear the windscreen by hand**

Before you set off you should ensure that you can see clearly through all the windows. Don't be lazy and rely on the wipers to clear the front and rear, as this will leave dangerous blind spots.

When driving on snow it is best to keep in as high a gear as possible. Why is this?

Mark one answer

- [ ] To help you slow down quickly when you brake
- [ ] So that the wheelspin does not cause your engine to run too fast
- [ ] To leave a lower gear available in case of wheelspin
- [ ] To help to prevent wheelspin

Answer

✘ **To help to prevent wheelspin**

If the ground is covered in snow, move off in as high a gear as possible. Stay in the highest gear you can. This reduces power to the wheels and so lessens the chance of skidding.

Question 4.55

You are trying to move off on snow. You should use

Mark one answer

- [ ] the lowest gear you can
- [ ] the highest gear you can
- [ ] a high engine speed
- [ ] the handbrake and footbrake together

Answer

✘ **the highest gear you can**

If you attempt to move off in a low gear such as first (1) the engine will rev at a higher speed. This could cause the wheels to spin and dig into the snow further.

Question 4.56

When driving in falling snow you should

Mark one answer

- [ ] brake firmly and quickly
- [ ] be ready to steer sharply
- [ ] use sidelights only
- [ ] brake gently in plenty of time

Answer

✘ **brake gently in plenty of time**

Braking on snow can be extremely dangerous. Be gentle with both the accelerator and brake to prevent wheelspin.

Question 4.57

The MAIN benefit of having four-wheel drive is to improve

Mark one answer

- [ ] road holding
- [ ] fuel consumption
- [ ] stopping distances
- [ ] passenger comfort

Answer

❌ **road holding**

This does not replace the skills you need to drive safely. The extra grip which the drive to all four wheels provides helps when travelling on slippery or uneven roads.

Question 4.58

When driving in fog in daylight you should use

Mark one answer

- [ ] sidelights
- [ ] full beam headlights
- [ ] hazard lights
- [ ] dipped headlights

Answer

❌ **dipped headlights**

Don't drive in fog unless you really have to. Use dipped headlights during daylight fog. If the visibility is below 100 metres (328 feet) use fog lights and high-intensity rear lights. Let other road users know that you're there.

Question 4.59

You are at a junction with limited visibility. You should

Mark one answer

- [ ] inch forward, looking to the right
- [ ] inch forward, looking to the left
- [ ] inch forward, looking both ways
- [ ] be ready to move off quickly

Answer

❌ **inch forward, looking both ways**

At some road junctions you might find that you can't see clearly into the road that you're joining. Before you commit yourself you have to inch foward, looking both ways. Only emerge when you can see that it's safe to do so. Don't

- speed out hoping the way will be clear
- look one way only.

Question 4.60

Why should you ride with a dipped headlight on in the daytime?

Mark one answer

 It helps other road users to see you

It means that you can ride faster

Other vehicles will get out of the way

So that it is already on when it gets dark

Answer

❌ **It helps other road users to see you**

Your life could depend on being seen clearly.

Question 4.61

Motorcyclists are only allowed to use high-intensity rear fog lights when

Mark one answer

a pillion passenger is being carried

they ride a large touring machine

visibility is 100 metres (328 feet) or less

they are riding on the road for the first time

Answer

❌ **visibility is 100 metres (328 feet) or less**

If your motorcycle is fitted with high-intensity rear fog lamps you must only use them when visibility is 100 metres (328 feet) or less. This rule applies to all other motor vehicles using these lamps.

Question 4.62

In very hot weather the road surface can get soft. Which TWO of the following will be affected most?

Mark two answers

The suspension

The steering

The braking

The windscreen

Answers

❌ **The steering**
❌ **The braking**

Take care when braking or cornering. Tyres don't grip well on soft tarmac.

Question 4.63

In very hot weather the road surface can get soft. Which TWO of the following will be affected most?

Mark two answers

- ☒ The suspension
- ☒ The grip of the tyres
- ☒ The braking
- ☒ The exhaust

Answers

- ✖ **The grip of the tyres**
- ✖ **The braking**

Only a small part of your motorcycle's tyres are in contact with the road. This is why you must consider and respect the surface you're on.

Question 4.64

You are riding in very hot weather. What are TWO effects that melting tar has on the control of your machine?

Mark two answers

- ☒ It can make the surface slippery
- ☒ It can reduce tyre grip
- ☒ It can reduce stopping distances
- ☒ It can improve braking efficiency

Answers

- ✖ **It can make the surface slippery**
- ✖ **It can reduce tyre grip**

In hot weather never be tempted to ride without protective clothing. If you fall from your machine you'll have no protection from the road surface.

Question 4.65

Where are you most likely to be affected by a sidewind?

Mark one answer

- ☒ On a narrow country lane
- ☒ On an open stretch of road
- ☒ On a busy stretch of road
- ☒ On a long, straight road

Answer

- ✖ **On an open stretch of road**

In windy conditions care must be taken on exposed roads. A strong gust of wind can blow you off course. Watch out for other road users, who may be affected more than you, such as

- cyclists
- motorcyclists
- high-sided lorries
- vehicles towing trailers.

Question 4.66

In windy conditions you need to take extra care when

Mark one answer

- using the brakes
- making a hill start
- turning into a narrow road
- passing pedal cyclists

Answer

X passing pedal cyclists

You should always give cyclists plenty of room when overtaking. When it's windy a sudden gust could blow them off course.

Question 4.67

Your indicators may be difficult to see in bright sunlight. What should you do?

Mark one answer

- Put your indicator on earlier
- Give an arm signal as well as using your indicator
- Touch the brake several times to show the stop lamp(s)
- Turn as quickly as you can

Answer

X Give an arm signal as well as using your indicator

You should always ensure that other road users are aware of your intentions. If you feel your indicator might not be seen, give an arm signal as well.

Question 4.68

What should you do to help you see at night?

Mark one answer

- Allow a gap beneath your visor or goggles
- Keep your visor or goggles clean
- Wear a tinted visor or goggles
- Don't use a visor or goggles at all

Answer

X Keep your visor or goggles clean

If you're riding a motorcycle at night it's important that you can see clearly. Keep your visor or goggles clean and without smears. Don't wear a tinted visor or goggles at night.

Question 4.69

You are riding at night. To be seen more easily you should

Mark two answers

- [ ] ride with your headlight on dipped beam
- [ ] wear reflective clothing
- [ ] keep the motorcycle clean
- [ ] stay well out to the right
- [ ] wear fluorescent clothing

Answers

- [X] **ride with your headlight on dipped beam**
- [X] **wear reflective clothing**

Reflective clothing works by reflecting light from the headlights of the other vehicles. This will make it easier for you to be seen. Fluorescent clothing, although effective during the day, won't show up as well as reflective clothing at night.

Question 4.70

When riding at night you should

Mark two answers

- [ ] ride with your headlight on dipped beam
- [ ] wear reflective clothing
- [ ] wear a tinted visor
- [ ] ride in the centre of the road
- [ ] give arm signals

Answers

- [X] **ride with your headlight on dipped beam**
- [X] **wear reflective clothing**

Fluorescent clothing shows up in daylight, but at night you should wear reflective clothing. This could be a tabard or reflective body strap.

Question 4.71

You MUST use your headlight

Mark three answers

- [ ] when riding in a group
- [ ] at night when street lighting is poor
- [ ] when carrying a passenger
- [ ] on motorways during darkness
- [ ] at times of poor visibility
- [ ] when parked on an unlit road

Answers

- [X] **at night when street lighting is poor**
- [X] **on motorways during darkness**
- [X] **at times of poor visibility**

Your headlight is to help you see in the dark and to help other road users to see you. You must use your headlight at all times when visibility is seriously reduced, or at night

- on all roads where street lighting is more than 185 metres (600 feet) apart
- on all motorways, even when lit.

You are about to go down a steep hill. To control the speed of your vehicle you should

Mark one answer

- ☒ select a high gear and use the brakes carefully
- ☒ select a high gear and use the brakes firmly
- ☒ select a low gear and use the brakes carefully
- ☒ select a low gear and avoid using the brakes

Answer

☒ **select a low gear and use the brakes carefully**

When travelling down a steep hill your vehicle will tend to increase speed. This will also make it more difficult for you to stop. To maintain control and prevent the vehicle running away

- select a lower gear – the engine will then help to control your speed
- use the brakes carefully.

Question 4.73

You are on a long, downhill slope. What should you do to help control the speed of your vehicle?

Mark one answer

- ☒ Select neutral
- ☒ Select a lower gear
- ☒ Grip the handbrake firmly
- ☒ Apply the parking brake gently

Answer

☒ **Select a lower gear**

Selecting a low gear when travelling downhill will help you to control your speed. The engine will assist the brakes and prevent your vehicle gathering speed.

Question 4.74

How can you use the engine of your vehicle as a brake ?

Mark one answer

- ☒ By changing to a lower gear
- ☒ By selecting reverse gear
- ☒ By changing to a higher gear
- ☒ By selecting neutral gear

Answer

☒ **By changing to a lower gear**

You should do this for downhill stretches of road. This will prevent excess use of the brakes, which could lessen their effectiveness.

Question 4.75

You wish to park facing DOWNHILL. Which TWO of the following should you do?

Mark two answers

- [ ] Turn the steering wheel towards the kerb
- [ ] Park close to the bumper of another car
- [ ] Park with two wheels on the kerb
- [ ] Put the handbrake on firmly
- [ ] Turn the steering wheel away from the kerb

Answers

- [X] Turn the steering wheel towards the kerb
- [X] Put the handbrake on firmly

The kerb will help stop any forward movement of the vehicle.

Question 4.76

You are driving in a built-up area. You approach a speed hump. You should

Mark one answer

- [ ] move across to the left-hand side of the road
- [ ] wait for any pedestrians to cross
- [ ] slow your vehicle right down
- [ ] stop and check both pavements

Answer

- [X] slow your vehicle right down

Many towns have speed humps to slow down traffic. They're often where there are pedestrians, so

- slow right down when driving over them
- look out for pedestrians.

They might affect your steering and suspension if you drive too fast.

When approaching a right-hand bend you should keep well to the left. Why is this?

Mark one answer

☒ To improve your view of the road

☒ To overcome the effect of the road's slope

☒ To let faster traffic from behind overtake

☒ To be positioned safely if the vehicle skids

Answer

✘ To improve your view of the road

Don't

- move over to the right to try and straighten the bend. You could endanger yourself by getting too close to oncoming traffic
- cross or straddle unbroken white lines along the centre of the road
- drive so fast that you can't stop within your range of vision.

You are coming up to a right-hand bend. You should

Mark one answer

☒ keep well to the left as it makes the bend faster

☒ keep well to the left for a better view around the bend

☒ keep well to the right to avoid anything in the gutter

☒ keep well to the right to make the bend less sharp

Answer

✘ keep well to the left for a better view around the bend

There could be a hazard just around the bend. Always be aware of this and you'll be better prepared to deal with it if you need to.

Question 4.79

You should not overtake when

Mark three answers

- [ ] intending to turn left shortly afterwards
- [ ] in a one-way street
- [ ] approaching a junction
- [ ] driving up a long hill
- [ ] the view ahead is blocked

Answers

- ☒ **intending to turn left shortly afterwards**
- ☒ **approaching a junction**
- ☒ **the view ahead is blocked**

Before you overtake you should ask yourself if it's really necessary. Getting there safely is more important than taking unnecessary risks.

For
2 miles

This section looks at judgement and hazard perception

The questions will ask you about

- anticipation
- hazard awareness
- attention
- speed and distance
- reaction time
- the effects of alcohol and drugs
- tiredness.

Question 5.1

You see this sign on the rear of a slow-moving lorry that you want to pass. It is travelling in the middle lane of a three lane motorway. You should

Mark one answer

- [ ] cautiously approach the lorry then pass on either side
- [ ] follow the lorry until you can leave the motorway
- [ ] wait on the hard shoulder until the lorry has stopped
- [ ] approach with care and keep to the left of the lorry

Answer

❌ **approach with care and keep to the left of the lorry**

This sign indicates that you should keep to the left of the vehicle. If you wish to overtake then you should do so on the left. Be aware that there might be workmen in the area.

Question 5.2

Where would you expect to see these markers?

Mark two answers

- [ ] On a motorway sign
- [ ] At the entrance to a narrow bridge
- [ ] On a large goods vehicle
- [ ] On a builder's skip placed on the road

Answers

❌ **On a large goods vehicle**
❌ **On a builder's skip placed on the road**

These markers are reflective so that they show up at night. If you see them ahead, then you should be aware that there might be a stationary, slow or long vehicle.

Question 5.3

What does this signal from a police officer, mean to oncoming traffic?

Mark one answer

☒ Go ahead

☒ Stop

☒ Turn left

☒ Turn right

Answer

✗ **Stop**

Police officers might be found at a point where there's heavy traffic or broken down traffic lights. Check your copy of *The Highway Code* for the signals that they use.

Question 5.4

What is the main hazard shown in this picture?

Mark one answer

☒ Vehicles turning right

☒ Vehicles doing U-turns

☒ The cyclist crossing the road

☒ Parked cars around the corner

Answer

✗ **The cyclist crossing the road**

Look at the picture carefully and try to imagine you're there. The cyclist in this picture isn't crossing the road in the correct place. You must be able to deal with the unexpected, especially when you're planning your approach to a hazardous junction. There will be several things to think about on your approach, so look well ahead to give yourself time to deal with them.

Question 5.5

Which road user has caused a hazard?

Mark one answer

- [ ] The parked car (arrowed A)
- [ ] The pedestrian waiting to cross (arrowed B)
- [ ] The moving car (arrowed C)
- [ ] The car turning (arrowed D)

Question 5.6

What should the driver of the car approaching the crossing do?

Mark one answer

- [ ] Continue at the same speed
- [ ] Sound the horn
- [ ] Drive through quickly
- [ ] Slow down and get ready to stop

Answer

✗ The parked car (arrowed A)

The car has parked on the approach to a pedestrian crossing. The road is marked with white zigzag lines. Don't park on these – they're there for a reason. Parking here will

- block the view for pedestrians wishing to cross the road
- restrict the view of the crossing for traffic approaching.

Answer

✗ Slow down and get ready to stop

Look well ahead to see if any hazards are developing. This will give you more time to deal with them in the correct way. The man in the picture is clearly intending to cross the road. You should be travelling at a speed that allows you to check your mirror, slow down and stop in good time. You shouldn't have to brake harshly.

Question 5.7

What should the driver of the red car do?

Mark one answer

☒ Wave the pedestrians who are waiting to cross

☒ Wait for the pedestrian in the road to cross

☒ Quickly drive behind the pedestrian in the road

☒ Tell the pedestrian in the road she should not have crossed

Question 5.8

What THREE things should the driver of the grey car (arrowed) be especially aware of?

Mark three answers

☒ Pedestrians stepping out between cars

☒ Other cars behind the grey car

☒ Doors opening on parked cars

☒ The bumpy road surface

☒ Cars leaving parking spaces

☒ Empty parking spaces

Answer

☒ **Wait for the pedestrian in the road to cross**

Some people might take longer to cross the road. They may be elderly or have a disability. Be patient and don't hurry them by showing your impatience. They might have poor eyesight or not be able to hear traffic approaching.

Don't signal or wave the pedestrian to cross the road. Other road users may not have seen your signal and this could lead the pedestrian into a hazardous situation.

Answers

☒ **Pedestrians stepping out between cars**

☒ **Doors opening on parked cars**

☒ **Cars leaving parking spaces**

Your awareness in hazardous situations is very important. In a busy street like the one in the picture there are many potential dangers. You might not be able to see a pedestrian crossing from between the parked vehicles. A driver or passenger of a parked car might open a door. Drive or ride at a speed that will allow you to stop in good time if a hazard suddenly appears. It could happen at any time.

Question 5.9

What should the driver of the red car (arrowed) do?

Mark one answer

- Sound the horn to tell other drivers where he is
- Squeeze through the gap
- Wave the driver of the white car to go on
- Wait until the car blocking the way has moved

Answer

☒ **Wait until the car blocking the way has moved**

If you're in slow-moving traffic think ahead so that you don't block junctions or stop others' progress. Don't

- force others to give way to you
- sound the horn to gain priority
- flash your lights to gain or give priority
- give any other misleading signal.

Question 5.10

What should the driver of the grey car (arrowed) do?

Mark one answer

- Cross if the way is clear
- Reverse out of the box junction
- Wait in the same place until the lights are green
- Wait until the lights are red then cross

Answer

☒ **Cross if the way is clear**

Yellow markings are marked on the road to prevent busy junctions becoming blocked with traffic. Don't enter the box unless your exit road is clear.

When turning right you can wait in the box if your exit road is clear but you can't proceed due to the oncoming traffic.

Question 5.11

What should the driver of a car coming up to this level crossing do?

Mark one answer

- [ ] Drive through quickly
- [ ] Drive through carefully
- [ ] Stop before the barrier
- [ ] Switch on hazard warning lights

Answer

✗ Stop before the barrier

Approach and cross level crossings with care. If you need to stop, wait patiently. In this picture there's a junction on the left, before the crossing; keep clear of the defined road markings. Don't

- try to beat the barrier by driving through
- drive or ride onto the crossing unless the road is clear on the other side
- drive or ride nose-to-tail over it
- stop on or just over the crossing.

Question 5.12

What are TWO main hazards a driver should be aware of when driving along this street?

Mark two answers

- [ ] Glare from the sun
- [ ] Car doors opening suddenly
- [ ] Lack of road markings
- [ ] The headlights on parked cars being switched on
- [ ] Large goods vehicles
- [ ] Children running out from between vehicles

Answers

✗ Car doors opening suddenly
✗ Children running out from between vehicles

When driving or riding on roads where there are many parked vehicles, you must take extra care. Always be ready for the unexpected and drive or ride accordingly.

Children are small and you might not be able to see them about to emerge from between cars. Drivers may be getting in and out of their vehicles, providing another potential hazard. If the road is narrow, as it is in this picture, you'll also need to look well down the road. This will help you to deal with any oncoming traffic safely.

Question 5.13

What is the main hazard a driver should be aware of when following this cyclist?

Mark one answer

- [ ] The cyclist may move into the left and dismount
- [ ] The cyclist may swerve out into the road
- [ ] The contents of the cyclist's carrier may fall onto the road
- [ ] The cyclist may wish to turn right at the end of the road

Answer

✗ The cyclist may swerve out into the road

When following a cyclist be aware that they also have to deal with the hazards around them. They may wobble or swerve to avoid a pot-hole in the road. They might see a potential hazard and change direction suddenly.

Don't drive or ride very close to them or rev your engine impatiently. This will only add to their perception of a hazard and may rush them into a dangerous decision.

Question 5.14

The driver of which car has caused a hazard?

Mark one answer

- [ ] Car A
- [ ] Car B
- [ ] Car C
- [ ] Car D

Answer

✗ Car A

The driver of car A has forced the approaching vehicle to the right onto the hatch-marked area of the road. It's also blocked the view of the other vehicle trying to emerge.

When dealing with busy junctions consider the other road users around you. Your actions must not put any other driver or rider at risk.

You think the driver of the vehicle in front has forgotten to cancel the right indicator. You should

Mark one answer

- [X] flash your lights to alert the driver
- [X] sound your horn before overtaking
- [X] overtake on the left if there is room
- [X] stay behind and not overtake

Answer

[X] **stay behind and not overtake**

The driver may be unsure of the location of a junction and turn suddenly. Be cautious.

What is the main hazard the driver of the red car (arrowed) should be most aware of?

Mark one answer

- [X] Glare from the sun may affect the driver's vision
- [X] The black car may stop suddenly
- [X] The bus may move out into the road
- [X] Oncoming vehicles will assume the driver is turning right

Answer

[X] **The bus may move out into the road**

You should try to anticipate the actions of the other road users around you. The driver of the red car should have made a mental note that the bus was at the bus stop. If you do this you'll be prepared for the bus pulling out. Look and see how many more passengers are waiting to board. If the last one has just got on, the bus is likely to move off.

Question 5.17

In heavy motorway traffic you are being followed closely by the vehicle behind. How can you lower the risk of an accident?

Mark one answer

- Increase your distance from the vehicle in front
- Tap your foot on the brake pedal
- Switch on your hazard lights
- Move onto the hard shoulder and stop

Answer

 Increase your distance from the vehicle in front

On a busy motorway, traffic might still travel at high speeds although the weight of traffic means the vehicles are close together. Don't follow too close to the vehicle in front. If a driver behind seems to be 'pushing' you, increase your distance from the car in front by easing off the accelerator. This will lessen the risk of an accident involving several vehicles.

Question 5.18

You are driving along this dual carriageway. Why may you need to slow down?

Mark one answer

- There is a broken white line in the centre
- There are solid white lines either side
- There are roadworks ahead of you
- There are no footpaths

Answer

 There are roadworks ahead of you

Look well ahead and read any road signs as you drive. They are there to inform you of what is ahead. In this case you may need to slow right down and change direction. Make sure you are well prepared for the hazard.

Question 5.19

What does the solid white line at the side of the road indicate?

Mark one answer

☒ Traffic lights ahead

☒ Edge of the carriageway

☒ Footpath on the left

☒ Cycle path

Answer

✗ **Edge of the carriageway**

This road marking gives you a warning. This is especially useful in bad weather when visibility is restricted.

Question 5.20

You see this sign ahead. You should expect the road to

Mark one answer

☒ go steeply uphill

☒ go steeply downhill

☒ bend sharply to the left

☒ bend sharply to the right

Answer

✗ **bend sharply to the left**

Adjust your speed in good time so that you are able to select the correct gear for the bend. Driving too fast into the bend will lead to lack of control.

Question 5.21

You are approaching this cyclist. You should

Answer

 slow down and allow the cyclist to turn

Keep well back and allow the cyclist room to take up the correct position for the turn. Don't drive up close behind or try to squeeze past through a narrow gap.

Mark one answer

- overtake before the cyclist gets to the junction
- flash your headlights at the cyclist
- slow down and allow the cyclist to turn
- overtake the cyclist on the left-hand side

Question 5.22

You have just been overtaken by this motorcyclist who is cutting in sharply. You should

Answer

✖ **keep a safe gap**

If you need to, take your foot off the accelerator and drop back to allow a safe separation distance. Try not to react by braking sharply as you could lose control. Any vehicles behind you will have to react in the same way, and it could lead to an accident.

Mark one answer

- sound the horn
- brake firmly
- keep a safe gap
- remember to flash your lights

Question 5.23

Why must you take extra care when turning right at this junction?

Mark one answer

- ☒ Road surface is poor
- ☒ Footpaths are narrow
- ☒ Road markings are faint
- ☒ There is reduced visibility

Answer

☒ **There is reduced visibility**

You may have to pull forward slowly until you can see down the road. Be aware that the traffic approaching the junction can't see you either. If you don't know that it's clear, don't go.

Question 5.24

What is the main hazard in this picture?

Mark one answer

- ☒ The pedestrian
- ☒ The parked cars
- ☒ The junction on the left
- ☒ The driveway on the left

Answer

☒ **The pedestrian**

As you drive make a mental note of pedestrians on the pavement. They could suddenly decide to cross the road or step off the kerb.

Question 5.25

You are driving towards this parked lorry. What is the first hazard you should be aware of?

Mark one answer

- ☒ The lorry moving off
- ☒ The narrowing road
- ☒ The pedestrian crossing
- ☒ The vehicles ahead

Question 5.26

This yellow sign on a vehicle indicates this is

Mark one answer

- ☒ a vehicle broken down
- ☒ a school bus
- ☒ an ice cream van
- ☒ a private ambulance

Answer

☒ **The pedestrian crossing**

Pedestrian crossings are usually provided in shopping areas like the one in the picture. As you approach consider that you may have to slow down and stop to allow pedestrians to cross.

Answer

☒ **a school bus**

Buses which carry children to and from school stop at places other than scheduled bus stops. Be aware that they might pull over to allow children to get on or off. This will normally be in rush hours when traffic is heavy.

You are driving towards this level crossing. What would be the first warning of an approaching train?

Mark one answer

- [ ] Both half barriers down
- [ ] A steady amber light
- [ ] One half barrier down
- [ ] Twin flashing red lights

Answer

❌ **A steady amber light**

This will be followed by a twin flashing red light which gives you a further warning. There is also an audible alarm to alert you. You must obey the lights. Stop.

You are driving along this motorway. It is raining. When following this lorry you should

Mark two answers

- [ ] allow at least a two-second gap
- [ ] move left and drive on the hard shoulder
- [ ] allow at least a four-second gap
- [ ] be aware of spray reducing your vision
- [ ] move right and stay in the right hand lane

Answers

❌ **allow at least a four-second gap**
❌ **be aware of spray reducing your vision**

The two-second time gap will increase to four seconds when the roads are wet. If you stay well back you will increase your

- vision around the vehicle
- visibility through the windscreen
- degree of safety.

Question 5.29

You are behind this cyclist. When the traffic lights change, what should you do?

Mark one answer

- [ ] Try to move off before the cyclist
- [ ] Allow the cyclist time and room
- [ ] Turn right but give the cyclist room
- [ ] Tap your horn and drive through first

Answer

✗ Allow the cyclist time and room

Hold back and allow the cyclist to move off. In some towns, junctions have special areas across the front of the traffic lane where cyclists can wait for the lights to change.

Question 5.30

You are driving towards this left hand bend. What dangers should you be aware of?

Mark one answer

- [ ] A vehicle overtaking you
- [ ] No white lines in the centre of the road
- [ ] No sign to warn you of the bend
- [ ] Pedestrians walking towards you

Answer

✗ Pedestrians walking towards you

Pedestrians walking on a road with no pavement will walk against the direction of the traffic. You can't see around this bend; there may be hidden dangers. Always consider this so you give yourself time to react to them.

Question 5.31

When approaching this bridge you should give way to

Mark one answer

- ⊠ bicycles
- ⊠ buses
- ⊠ motorcycles
- ⊠ cars

Answer

 buses

A double-deck bus will have to take up a position in the centre of the road so that it can clear the bridge. There is normally a sign to indicate this. Look well down the road, through the bridge and consider that you may have to stop and give way to any bus approaching.

Question 5.32

What type of vehicle could you expect to meet in the middle of the road?

Mark one answer

- ⊠ Lorry
- ⊠ Bicycle
- ⊠ Car
- ⊠ Motorcycle

Answer

 Lorry

A large vehicle might have to take up all the road to allow the top of the vehicle to clear the bridge. The arch of the bridge is at its highest point in the centre.

DSA THEORY TEST for car drivers and motorcyclists

Question 5.33

As the driver of this vehicle, why should you slow down?

Mark two answers

- ☒ Because of the bend
- ☒ Because its hard to see to the right
- ☒ Because of approaching trains
- ☒ Because of animals crossing
- ☒ Because of the level crossing

Answers

- ✖ **Because of the bend**
- ✖ **Because of the level crossing**

There are two hazards clearly signed in this picture. You should be preparing for the bend by slowing down and selecting the correct gear. You might also have to stop for the level crossing, so be alert and be prepared.

Question 5.34

While driving, you see this sign ahead. You should

Mark one answer

- ☒ stop at the sign
- ☒ slow, but continue around the bend
- ☒ slow to a crawl and continue
- ☒ stop and look for open farm gates

Answer

- ✖ **slow, but continue around the bend**

Drive around the bend at a steady speed in the correct gear. Be aware that you might have to stop for approaching trains.

Why should the junction on the left be kept clear?

Mark one answer

☒ To allow vehicles to enter and emerge

☒ To allow the bus to reverse

☒ To allow vehicles to make a 'U' turn

☒ To allow vehicles to park

Answer

☒ **To allow vehicles to enter and emerge**

If you are waiting in traffic, look well down the queue. Judge stopping so that you are able to leave a gap allowing traffic to flow in and out of the junction.

What is the first hazard shown in this picture?

Mark one answer

☒ Standing traffic

☒ Oncoming traffic

☒ Junction on the left

☒ Pedestrians

Answer

☒ **Junction on the left**

There may be traffic waiting to emerge, or traffic approaching waiting to turn right into the junction. If there is a queue ahead, leave a gap so that traffic can proceed.

Question 5.37

You are driving in the left lane but want to turn right at the traffic lights. You should

Mark one answer

- [ ] check your mirrors, signal and move to the right
- [ ] weave into the middle and then to the right lane
- [ ] drive up to the lights then turn right
- [ ] stay in your lane and find another way back

Answer

✗ stay in your lane and find another way back

Don't disrupt the flow of traffic by cutting across the lanes. Look out for direction signs as you drive and get into the correct lane in good time.

Question 5.38

When the traffic lights change to green the white car should

Mark one answer

- [ ] wait for the cyclist to pull away
- [ ] move off quickly and turn in front of the cyclist
- [ ] move close up to the cyclist to beat the lights
- [ ] sound the horn to warn the cyclist

Answer

✗ wait for the cyclist to pull away

Before you move away, check all around; cyclists often filter along the nearside of waiting traffic. Allow the cyclist to move off safely.

Question 5.39

You intend to turn left at the traffic lights. Just before turning you should

Mark one answer

- [ ] check your right mirror
- [ ] move close up to the white car
- [ ] straddle the lanes
- [ ] check for bicycles on your left

Answer

✖ check for bicycles on your left

This is especially important if you have been stationary and are about to move off. Cyclists do often try to filter past vehicles in this way. You should always check your nearside.

Question 5.40

You should reduce your speed when driving along this road because

Mark one answer

- [ ] there is a staggered junction ahead
- [ ] there is a low bridge ahead
- [ ] there is a change in the road surface
- [ ] the road ahead narrows

Answer

✖ there is a staggered junction ahead

Traffic could be turning off to the left or right ahead of you. They will be slowing right down or stopping to allow oncoming traffic to clear. Be prepared for this situation as you might have to slow down or stop behind them.

An approaching motorcyclist is easier to see when

Mark three answers

- ☒ the rider is wearing bright clothing
- ☒ the rider has a white helmet
- ☒ the headlight is on
- ☒ the motorcycle is moving slowly
- ☒ the motorcycle is moving quickly
- ☒ the rider has a passenger

Answers

- ☒ **the rider is wearing bright clothing**
- ☒ **the rider has a white helmet**
- ☒ **the headlight is on**

These precautions are sensible measures which can increase the chances of other road users seeing the motorcyclist. As a driver you should not assume that all other vehicles are the width of a car. Motorcyclists can filter between traffic and approach junctions from behind queuing or parked cars. Watch out for them.

You are driving at 60 mph. As you approach this hazard you should

Mark one answer

- ☒ maintain your speed
- ☒ reduce your speed
- ☒ take the next right turn
- ☒ take the next left turn

Answer

- ☒ **reduce your speed**

There could be stationary traffic ahead, waiting to turn right. Other traffic could be emerging and will take time to gather speed.

The traffic ahead of you in the left lane is slowing. You should

Mark two answers

- [X] be wary of cars on your right cutting in

- [X] accelerate past the vehicles in the left lane

- [X] pull up on the left hand verge

- [X] move across and continue in the right hand lane

- [X] slow down keeping a safe separation distance

What might you expect to happen in this situation?

Mark one answer

- [X] Traffic will move into the right-hand lane

- [X] Traffic speed will increase

- [X] Traffic will move into the left-hand lane

- [X] Traffic will not need to change position

Answers

- [X] **be wary of cars on your right cutting in**

- [X] **slow down keeping a safe separation distance**

Allow the traffic to merge into the nearside lane. Leave enough room so that your separation distance is not shortened drastically if a vehicle pulls into the left-hand lane ahead of you.

Answer

- [X] **Traffic will move into the left-hand lane**

Be courteous and allow the traffic to merge into the left-hand lane. Try not to cut the vehicle off so that the driver has to steer sharply at the end of the lane.

Question 5.45

You are driving on a road with several lanes. You see these signs above the lanes. What do they mean?

Mark one answer

- [ ] The two right lanes are open
- [ ] The two left lanes are open
- [ ] Traffic in the left lanes should stop
- [ ] Traffic in the right lanes should stop

Answer

 The two left lanes are open

If you see a red cross above your lane it means that there is an obstruction ahead. You will have to move into the lane which is showing the green light. If all the lanes are showing a red cross, then you must stop.

Question 5.46

At this blind junction you must stop

Mark one answer

- [ ] behind the line, then edge forward to see clearly
- [ ] beyond the line at a point where you can see clearly
- [ ] only if there is traffic on the main road
- [ ] only if you are turning to the right

Answer

 behind the line, then edge forward to see clearly

The 'stop' sign has been put here because it is a dangerous junction. You must stop. It will not be possible to assess the situation on the move, however slowly.

Question 5.47

When must you stop at this junction?

Mark one answer

- [ ] During rush hour only
- [ ] Only when the area is busy
- [ ] When turning right only
- [ ] At all times

Answer

✗ At all times

Attempting to emerge from this junction without stopping is highly dangerous. Even the most experienced driver would not be able to assess the situation without stopping.

Question 5.48

As a provisional licence holder, you must not drive a motor car

Mark two answers

- [ ] at more than 50 mph
- [ ] on your own
- [ ] on the motorway
- [ ] under the age of 18 years of age at night
- [ ] with passengers in the rear seats

Answers

✗ on your own
✗ on the motorway

When you have passed your practical test you will be able to drive on a motorway. It is recommended that you have instruction on motorway driving before you venture out on your own. Ask your instructor about this.

Question 5.49

To drive you MUST be able to read a number plate from what distance?

Mark one answer

- [ ] 10 metres (32 feet)
- [ ] 15 metres (50 feet)
- [ ] 20.5 metres (67 feet)
- [ ] 25.5 (84 feet)

Answer

✗ 20.5 metres (67 feet)

When you take your practical test your examiner will ask you to read a number plate from a distance of 20.5 metres (67 feet). This is a legal requirement to ensure that you see situations around you on the road.

DSA THEORY TEST for car drivers and motorcyclists

Question 5.50

A driver can only read a number plate at the required distance with glasses on. The glasses should be worn

Mark one answer

- [x] all the time when driving
- [x] only when driving long distances
- [x] only when reversing
- [x] only in poor visibility

Answer

❌ **all the time when driving**

You might find you need glasses or contact lenses to read number plates. This is fine, but you must then wear them when you drive or ride.

Question 5.51

You are about to drive home. You cannot find the glasses you need to wear when driving. You should

Mark one answer

- [x] drive home slowly, keeping to quiet roads
- [x] borrow a friend's glasses and drive home
- [x] drive home at night, so that the lights will help you
- [x] find a way of getting home without driving

Answer

❌ **find a way of getting home without driving**

Don't be tempted to drive if you've lost or forgotten your glasses. It's obvious that you must be able to see clearly when driving.

Question 5.52

You MUST wear glasses or contact lenses when driving on public roads if

Mark one answer

- [x] you are the holder of an orange badge
- [x] you cannot read a vehicle number plate from a distance of 36 metres (120 feet) without them
- [x] there is an eyesight problem in your family
- [x] you cannot read a vehicle number plate from a distance of 20.5 metres (67 feet) without them

Answer

❌ **you cannot read a vehicle number plate from a distance of 20.5 metres (67 feet) without them**

When you take your practical test your examiner will test your eyesight. You may wear glasses or contact lenses to do this, but you must then wear them every time you drive.

Question 5.53

As a driver you find that your eyesight has become very poor. Your optician says he cannot help you. The law says that you should tell

Mark one answer

- [ ] the licensing authority
- [ ] your own doctor
- [ ] the local police station
- [ ] another optician

Answer

✗ the licensing authority

This will have a serious affect on your judgement and concentration. The Driver and Vehicle Licensing Agency can be contacted by telephoning 01792 772 151

Question 5.54

You find that you need glasses to read vehicle number plates. When MUST you wear them?

Mark one answer

- [ ] Only in bad weather conditions
- [ ] At all times when driving
- [ ] Only when you think it necessary
- [ ] Only in bad light or at night time

Answer

✗ At all times when driving

Have your eyesight tested before you start your practical training. Then, throughout your driving life, have periodical checks to ensure that your eyesight hasn't deteriorated.

Question 5.55

After passing your driving test, you suffer from ill health. This affects your driving. You MUST

Mark one answer

- [ ] inform your local police station
- [ ] get on as best you can
- [ ] not inform anyone as you hold a full licence
- [ ] inform the licensing authority

Answer

✗ inform the licensing authority

The licensing authority won't automatically take away your licence without investigation. Contact the Driver and Vehicle Licensing Agency for advice.

Question 5.56

Which THREE result from drinking alcohol and driving?

Mark three answers

- ☒ Less control
- ☒ A false sense of confidence
- ☒ Faster reactions
- ☒ Poor judgement of speed
- ☒ Greater awareness of danger

Answers

- ☒ **Less control**
- ☒ **A false sense of confidence**
- ☒ **Poor judgement of speed**

You must understand the dangers of mixing alcohol with driving or riding. One drink is too many if you're going to drive or ride. Alcohol will reduce your ability to drive or ride safely.

Question 5.57

Which THREE of these are likely effects of drinking alcohol on driving?

Mark three answers

- ☒ Reduced co-ordination
- ☒ Increased confidence
- ☒ Poor judgement
- ☒ Increased concentration
- ☒ Faster reactions
- ☒ Colour blindness

Answers

- ☒ **Reduced co-ordination**
- ☒ **Increased confidence**
- ☒ **Poor judgement**

Alcohol can increase confidence to a point where a driver or rider's behaviour might become 'out of character'. Someone who normally behaves sensibly suddenly takes risks and enjoys it. Never let yourself or your friends get into this situation.

Question 5.58

Drinking any amount of alcohol is likely to

Mark three answers

- ☒ slow down your reactions to hazards
- ☒ increase the speed of your reactions
- ☒ worsen your judgement of speed
- ☒ improve your awareness of danger
- ☒ give a false sense of confidence

Answers

- ☒ **slow down your reactions to hazards**
- ☒ **worsen your judgement of speed**
- ☒ **give a false sense of confidence**

Never drink if you are going to drive. It's always the safest option not to drink at all. Don't be tempted, it's not worth it.

Question 5.59

You are invited to a pub lunch. You know that you will have to drive in the evening. What is your best course of action?

Mark one answer

- ☒ Avoid mixing your alcoholic drinks
- ☒ Not drink any alcohol at all
- ☒ Have some milk before drinking alcohol
- ☒ Eat a hot meal with your alcoholic drinks

Answer

☒ **Not drink any alcohol at all**

Alcohol will stay in the body for this length of time. Drinking during the day will affect your performance at work or study. Avoid drinking at all, even if you have not planned to drive in the evening.

Question 5.60

What else can seriously affect your concentration when driving, other than alcoholic drinks?

Mark three answers

- ☒ Drugs
- ☒ Tiredness
- ☒ Tinted windows
- ☒ Contact lenses
- ☒ Loud music

Answers

☒ **Drugs**
☒ **Tiredness**
☒ **Loud music**

The least distraction can allow your concentration to drift. Think about your driving, and that only, to stay in full control of your vehicle.

Question 5.61

How does alcohol affect your driving?

Mark one answer

- ☒ It speeds up your reactions
- ☒ It increases your awareness
- ☒ It improves your co-ordination
- ☒ It reduces your concentration

Answer

☒ **It reduces your concentration**

Concentration and good judgement at all times are needed to be a good, safe driver.

Question 5.62

After drinking alcohol heavily you should not drive the following day. Why is this?

Mark two answers

- [ ] You may still be over the legal limit
- [ ] Your concentration will not be badly affected
- [ ] You will be well under the legal limit
- [ ] Your concentration may still be badly affected

Answers

- ❌ **You may still be over the legal limit**
- ❌ **Your concentration may still be badly affected**

Think about this before you go to get into your car for work. You might still be over the limit, which means that your judgement and decision making will still be impaired.

Question 5.63

You have been convicted of driving whilst unfit through drink or drugs. You will find this is likely to cause the cost of one of the following to rise considerably. Which one?

Mark one answer

- [ ] Road fund licence
- [ ] Insurance premiums
- [ ] Vehicle test certificate
- [ ] Driving licence

Answer

- ❌ **Insurance premiums**

You have proved yourself to be a risk to yourself and others on the road. For this reason insurance companies may charge you a high premium.

Question 5.64

What advice should you give to a driver who has had a few alcoholic drinks at a party?

Mark one answer

- [ ] Have a strong cup of coffee and then drive home
- [ ] Drive home carefully and slowly
- [ ] Go home by public transport
- [ ] Wait a short while and then drive home

Answer

- ❌ **Go home by public transport**

Drinking black coffee or waiting a few hours won't make any difference. Alcohol takes time to leave the body. You might even be unfit to drive or ride the following morning.

Question 5.65

You go to a social event and need to drive a short time after. What precaution should you take?

Mark one answer

- [ ] Avoid drinking alcohol on an empty stomach
- [ ] Drink plenty of coffee after drinking alcohol
- [ ] Avoid drinking alcohol completely
- [ ] Drink plenty of milk before drinking alcohol

Answer

✗ Avoid drinking alcohol completely

This is always going to be the safest option. One drink could be too many.

Question 5.66

It is eight hours since you last had an alcoholic drink. Which of the following applies?

Mark two answers

- [ ] You will certainly be under the legal limit
- [ ] You will have no alcohol in your system
- [ ] You may still be unfit to drive
- [ ] You may still be over the legal limit

Answers

✗ You may still be unfit to drive
✗ You may still be over the legal limit

Alcohol can take several hours to leave the body. You may feel alright to drive, but it's effect will last for several hours.

Question 5.67

Your doctor has given you a course of medicine. Why should you ask if it is OK to drive?

Mark one answer

- [ ] Drugs make you a better driver by quickening your reactions
- [ ] You will have to let your insurance company know about the medicine
- [ ] Some types of medicine can cause your reactions to slow down
- [ ] The medicine you take may affect your hearing

Answer

✗ Some types of medicine can cause your reactions to slow down

Always check the label of any medication container. The contents might affect your driving. If you aren't sure, ask your doctor or pharmacist.

Question 5.68

You have been taking medicine for a few days which made you feel drowsy. Today you feel better but still need to take the medicine. You should only drive

Mark one answer

- [ ] if your journey is necessary
- [ ] at night on quiet roads
- [ ] if someone goes with you
- [ ] after checking with your doctor

Answer

✗ after checking with your doctor

Take care, it's not worth taking risks. Always check to be really sure. The medicine may have an affect on you later in the day.

Question 5.69

You are about to return home from holiday when you become ill. A doctor prescribes drugs which are likely to affect your driving. You should

Mark one answer

- [ ] drive only if someone is with you
- [ ] avoid driving on motorways
- [ ] not drive yourself
- [ ] never drive at more than 30 mph

Answer

✗ not drive yourself

Find another way to get home. This may be very inconvenient, but it isn't worth the risk to other road users, your passengers or yourself.

Question 5.70

During periods of illness your ability to drive may be impaired. You MUST

Mark two answers

- [ ] see your doctor each time before you drive
- [ ] only take smaller doses of any medicines
- [ ] be medically fit to drive
- [ ] not drive after taking certain medicines
- [ ] take all your medicines with you when you drive

Answers

✗ be medically fit to drive
✗ not drive after taking certain medicines

Medication can affect your concentration and your judgement when dealing with hazards. This, of course, is highly dangerous; be responsible.

Question 5.71

You are not sure if your cough medicine will affect your driving. What TWO things could you do?

Mark two answers

- [X] Ask your doctor
- [X] Check the medicine label
- [X] Drive if you feel alright
- [X] Ask a friend or relative for advice

Answers

X Ask your doctor

X Check the medicine label

If you're taking medicine or drugs prescribed by your doctor, check to ensure that they won't make you drowsy. If you forget to ask at the time of your visit to the surgery, check with your pharmacist.

Question 5.72

You take some cough medicine given to you by a friend. What should you do before driving?

Mark one answer

- [X] Ask your friend if taking the medicine affected their driving
- [X] Drink some strong coffee one hour before driving
- [X] Check the label to see if the medicine will affect your driving
- [X] Drive a short distance to see if the medicine is affecting your driving

Answer

X Check the label to see if the medicine will affect your driving

Never drive or ride having taken drugs you don't know about. They might affect your judgement and perception, and therefore endanger lives.

Question 5.73

You have taken medication that may make you feel drowsy. Your friends tell you it is safe to drive. What should you do?

Mark one answer

- [X] Take their advice and drive
- [X] Ignore your friends' advice and do not drive
- [X] Only drive if they come with you
- [X] Drive for short distances only

Answer

X Ignore your friends' advice and do not drive

Friends may have their own reasons for wanting you to drive. Don't take the risk; it's never worth it.

Question 5.74

You feel drowsy when driving. You should

Mark two answers

- [ ] stop and rest as soon as possible
- [ ] turn the heater up to keep you warm and comfortable
- [ ] make sure you have a good supply of fresh air
- [ ] continue with your journey but drive more slowly
- [ ] close the car windows to help you concentrate

Answers

- [X] **stop and rest as soon as possible**
- [X] **make sure you have a good supply of fresh air**

You will be putting other road users at risk if you continue to drive. Pull over and stop in a safe place. If you are driving a long distance, think about finding some accommodation in order to get some sleep before continuing your journey.

Question 5.75

You are driving along a motorway and become tired. You should

Mark two answers

- [ ] stop at the next service area and rest
- [ ] leave the motorway at the next exit and rest
- [ ] increase your speed and turn up the radio volume
- [ ] close all your windows and set heating to warm
- [ ] pull up on the hard shoulder and change drivers

Answers

- [X] **stop at the next service area and rest**
- [X] **leave the motorway at the next exit and rest**

If you have planned your journey properly, to include rest stops, you will arrive at your destination in good time.

Question 5.76

You are taking drugs that are likely to affect your driving. What should you do?

Mark one answer

- [ ] Seek medical advice before driving
- [ ] Limit your driving to essential journeys
- [ ] Only drive if accompanied by a full licence-holder
- [ ] Drive only for short distances

Answer

- [X] **Seek medical advice before driving**

Check with your doctor or pharmacist if you think that the drugs you're taking are likely to make you feel drowsy.

Question 5.77

You are about to drive home. You feel very tired and have a severe headache. You should

Mark one answer

- [ ] wait until you are fit and well before driving
- [ ] drive home, but take a tablet for headaches
- [ ] drive home if you can stay awake for the journey
- [ ] wait for a short time, then drive home slowly

Answer

☒ **wait until you are fit and well before driving**

All your concentration should be on your driving. Any pain you feel will distract you. Change your plans and be safe.

Question 5.78

If you are feeling tired it is best to stop as soon as you can. Until then you should

Mark one answer

- [ ] increase your speed to find a stopping place quickly
- [ ] ensure a supply of fresh air
- [ ] gently tap the steering wheel
- [ ] keep changing speed to improve concentration

Answer

☒ **ensure a supply of fresh air**

If you're travelling on a long journey, plan your route before you leave. This will help you to

- be decisive at intersections and junctions
- plan your rest stops
- know approximately how long the journey will take.

Make sure that the vehicle you're travelling in is well ventilated. A warm, stuffy atmosphere can make you drowsy, which will impair your judgement and perception.

Question 5.79

Your reactions will be much slower when driving

Mark one answer

- [ ] if tired
- [ ] in fog
- [ ] too quickly
- [ ] in rain

Answer

☒ **if tired**

Try to prevent becoming tired by

- taking plenty of rest stops
- allowing fresh air into the vehicle.

Question 5.80

You are driving on a motorway. You feel tired. You should

Mark one answer

- carry on but drive slowly
- leave the motorway at the next exit
- complete your journey as quickly as possible
- stop on the hard shoulder

Answer

❌ **leave the motorway at the next exit**

If you do feel tired and there's no service station for many miles, leave the motorway at the next exit. Find a road off the motorway where you can pull up and stop safely.

Question 5.81

If your motorway journey seems boring and you feel drowsy whilst driving you should

Mark one answer

- open a window and drive to the next service area
- stop on the hard shoulder for a sleep
- speed up to arrive at your destination sooner
- slow down and let other drivers overtake

Answer

❌ **open a window and drive to the next service area**

Never stop on the hard shoulder to rest. If there is not a service station for several miles, leave the motorway at the next exit.

Question 5.82

You are planning a long journey. It should take about six hours. Do you need to plan rest stops?

Mark one answer

- Yes, you should plan to stop after about four hours driving
- Yes, regular stops help concentration
- No, you will be less tired if you get there as soon as possible
- No, only fuel stops will be needed

Answer

❌ **Yes, regular stops help concentration**

Plan your journey so that you can take rest stops. A minimum break of at least 15 minutes after every two hours of driving is recommended. You will need to stop for something to eat within this six hours in order to keep up your energy level. If this is allowed to drop you will become tired and lose concentration.

Question 5.83

Driving long distances can be tiring. You can prevent this by

Mark three answers

☒ stopping every so often for a walk

☒ opening a window for some fresh air

☒ ensuring plenty of refreshment breaks

☒ completing the journey without stopping

☒ eating a large meal before driving

Answers

☒ **stopping every so often for a walk**

☒ **opening a window for some fresh air**

☒ **ensuring plenty of refreshment breaks**

A stuffy, warm vehicle will cause you to feel tired. Playing loud music could prevent you hearing the approach of an emergency vehicle.

Question 5.84

To help concentration on long journeys you should stop frequently and

Mark one answer

☒ have a rest

☒ fill up with fuel

☒ eat a meal

☒ take a shower

Answer

☒ **have a rest**

Feeling tired will affect your ability to concentrate fully. This could have dangerous results leading to injury or even death.

Question 5.85

Which TWO things would help to keep you alert during a long journey?

Mark two answers

☒ Finishing your journey as fast as you can

☒ Keeping off the motorways and using country roads

☒ Making sure that you get plenty of fresh air

☒ Making regular stops for refreshments

Answers

☒ **Making sure that you get plenty of fresh air**

☒ **Making regular stops for refreshments**

Make sure that the vehicle you're driving is well ventilated. A warm, stuffy atmosphere will make you feel drowsy. Open a window or turn down the heating.

Question 5.86

Which THREE are likely to make you lose concentration while driving?

Mark three answers

- ☒ Looking at road maps
- ☒ Listening to loud music
- ☒ Using your windscreen washers
- ☒ Looking in your wing mirror
- ☒ Using a mobile phone

Answers

- ☒ **Looking at road maps**
- ☒ **Listening to loud music**
- ☒ **Using a mobile phone**

Looking at road maps while driving is very dangerous. If you aren't sure of your route, stop in a safe place and check the map. You must not allow anything to take your attention away from the road.

If you need to use a mobile phone, stop in a safe place before doing so. If you use a mobile phone frequently, have a 'hands free' phone fitted in your vehicle.

Question 5.87

You get cold and wet when riding. Which TWO are likely to happen?

Mark two answers

- ☒ You may lose concentration
- ☒ You may slide off the seat
- ☒ Your visor may freeze up
- ☒ Your reaction times may be slower
- ☒ Your helmet may loosen

Answers

- ☒ **You may lose concentration**
- ☒ **Your reaction times may be slower**

If you're riding a motorcycle you should ensure that you're wearing suitable clothing. If you become cold and uncomfortable this could cause you to lose concentration.

Question 5.88

A correct seating position will enable you to

Mark three answers

- ☒ rest your head against the head restraint
- ☒ comfortably reach the pedals
- ☒ have good visibility through the windows
- ☒ talk to all your passengers
- ☒ have a suitable grip on the steering wheel
- ☒ rest your hand on the gear lever

Answers

- ☒ **comfortably reach the pedals**
- ☒ **have good visibility through the windows**
- ☒ **have a suitable grip on the steering wheel**

You need to be in control of your vehicle at all times. You should be able to reach all the controls comfortably, without stretching. Also, check the position of the mirrors and adjust them if you need to.

A driver pulls out of a side road in front of you. You have to brake hard. You should

Mark one answer

☒ ignore the error and stay calm

☒ flash your lights to show your annoyance

☒ sound your horn to show your annoyance

☒ overtake as soon as possible

Answer·

☒ **ignore the error and stay calm**

If you're driving or riding where there are a number of side roads, be alert. Drivers approaching or emerging from a side road might not be able to see you. Be especially careful if there are a lot of parked vehicles. If a vehicle does emerge and you have to stop quickly

• try to be tolerant

• learn from the experience.

A car driver pulls out causing you to brake. You should

Mark one answer

☒ keep calm and not retaliate

☒ overtake and sound your horn

☒ drive close behind and sound your horn

☒ flag the driver down and explain the mistake

Answer

☒ **keep calm and not retaliate**

You have to understand that others on the road might disobey the rules or make an error of judgement at times. Try to accept this calmly and learn from other people's mistakes.

Another driver does something that upsets you. You should

Mark one answer

☒ try not to react

☒ let them know how you feel

☒ flash your headlights several times

☒ sound your horn

Answer

☒ **try not to react**

There are occasions when other drivers or riders make a misjudgement or a mistake. If this happens try not to let it worry you. Don't react by showing anger. Sounding the horn, flashing the headlights or shouting at the other driver won't help the situation. Good anticipation will help to prevent these incidents becoming accidents.

Question 5.92

Another driver's behaviour has upset you. It may help if you

Mark one answer

- [ ] stop and take a break
- [ ] shout abusive language
- [ ] gesture to them with your hand
- [ ] follow their car, flashing the headlights

Answer

✖ **stop and take a break**

Tiredness may make you more irritable than you would be normally. You might react differently to situations because of it. If you feel yourself becoming tense, take a break.

Question 5.93

An elderly person's driving ability could be affected because they may be unable to

Mark one answer

- [ ] obtain car insurance
- [ ] understand road signs
- [ ] react very quickly
- [ ] give signals correctly

Answer

✖ **react very quickly**

Poor judgement of speed and distances may cause them to be more hesitant. Be tolerant of other drivers on the road and allow them time and room.

Question 5.94

You take the wrong route and find you are on a one-way street. You should

Mark one answer

- [ ] reverse out of the road
- [ ] turn round in a side road
- [ ] continue to the end of the road
- [ ] reverse into a driveway

Answer

✖ **continue to the end of the road**

Never reverse or turn your vehicle around in a one-way street. This is highly dangerous. Carry on and find another route, checking the direction signs as you drive.

If you need to check a map, stop in a safe place.

SECTION 6 | VULNERABLE ROAD USERS

This section looks at the risks when dealing with vulnerable road users

The questions will ask you about

- pedestrians
- children
- elderly drivers
- disabled people
- cyclists
- motorcycles
- animals
- new drivers.

Question 6.1

You should not ride too closely behind a lorry because

Mark one answer

- ☒ you will breathe in the lorry's exhaust fumes
- ☒ wind from the lorry will slow you down
- ☒ drivers behind you may not be able to see you
- ☒ it will reduce your view ahead

Answer

❌ **it will reduce your view ahead**

If you're following a large vehicle your view beyond it will be restricted. Drop back. This will help you to see more of the road ahead.

Question 6.2

You are riding in fast-flowing traffic. The vehicle behind is following too closely. You should

Mark one answer

- ☒ slow down gradually to increase the gap in front of you
- ☒ slow down as quickly as possible by braking
- ☒ accelerate to get away from the vehicle behind you
- ☒ apply the brakes briefly to warn the driver behind

Answer

❌ **slow down gradually to increase the gap in front of you**

Vehicles travelling too close together are dangerous. Increase the safety margin by dropping back.

Question 6.3

You are riding along a main road with many side roads. Why should you be particularly careful?

Mark one answer

- ☒ Gusts of wind from the side roads may push you off course
- ☒ Drivers coming out from side roads may not see you
- ☒ The road will be more slippery where cars have been turning
- ☒ Drivers will be travelling slowly when they approach a junction

Answer

❌ **Drivers coming out from side roads may not see you**

If you're riding along a main road where there are many side roads, be alert. Drivers approaching or emerging from side roads may not be able to see you. Be especially careful if there are a lot of parked vehicles.

Always drive at a speed that will enable you to slow down and stop in good time. If you look well ahead and anticipate the actions of other road users, you'll avoid having to brake suddenly or harshly.

Question 6.4

You are driving on a country road. What should you expect to see coming towards you on YOUR side of the road?

Mark one answer

 Motorcycles

 Bicycles

 Pedestrians

 Horse riders

Answer

 Pedestrians

On a quiet country road always be aware that there may be a hazard just around the next bend, such as a slow-moving vehicle or pedestrians. There might not be a pavement and people may be walking on your side of the road.

Question 6.5

Which sign means that there may be people walking along the road?

Mark one answer

Answer

Always check the road signs as you drive. They'll keep you informed of hazards ahead and help you to anticipate any problems.

There are different types of signs showing pedestrians. Learn the meaning of each one. This will help you to be aware of the hazard ahead.

Question 6.6

What does this sign mean?

Mark one answer

 Pedestrian crossing

 Pedestrians in the road ahead

 No pedestrians

 Route for pedestrians

Answer

 No pedestrians

Always be aware that, although the sign restricts pedestrians, there may be some about.

Question 6.7

You are turning left into a side road. Pedestrians are crossing the road near the junction. You must

Mark one answer

- ☒ wave them on
- ☒ sound your horn
- ☒ switch on your hazard lights
- ☒ wait for them to cross

Answer

❌ **wait for them to cross**

Before you turn into a junction, check that it's clear. Check the pavement in each direction. If there are pedestrians crossing, let them cross in their own time.

Question 6.8

You are turning left at a junction. Pedestrians have started to cross the road. You should

Mark one answer

- ☒ go on, giving them plenty of room
- ☒ stop and wave at them to cross
- ☒ blow your horn and proceed
- ☒ give way to them

Answer

❌ **give way to them**

If you're turning into a side road you should give way to pedestrians already crossing. They have priority. Don't

- wave them across the road
- sound your horn
- flash your lights
- give any other misleading signal – other road users may misinterpret your signal and you might lead the pedestrian into a dangerous situation.

If a pedestrian is slow or indecisive, be patient and wait. Don't hurry them across by revving the engine.

You are turning left from a main road into a side road. People are already crossing the road into which you are turning. You should

Mark one answer

☒ continue, as it is your right of way

☒ signal to them to continue crossing

☒ wait and allow them to cross

☒ sound your horn to warn them of your presence

Answer

☒ **wait and allow them to cross**

Always check the road you're turning into. Approaching at the correct speed will allow you enough time to observe and react.

You are at a road junction, turning into a minor road. There are pedestrians crossing the minor road. You should

Mark one answer

☒ stop and wave the pedestrians across

☒ sound your horn to let the pedestrians know that you are there

☒ give way to the pedestrians who are already crossing

☒ carry on; the pedestrians should give way to you

Answer

☒ **give way to the pedestrians who are already crossing**

Always look into the road you're turning into. If there are pedestrians crossing, be considerate, but don't wave or signal to them to cross. Signal your intention to turn as you approach.

Question 6.11

You are turning left into a side road. What hazards should you be especially aware of?

Mark one answer

☒ One way street

☒ Pedestrians

☒ Traffic congestion

☒ Parked vehicles

Answer

☒ **Pedestrians**

Make sure that you have reduced your speed and are in the correct gear for the turn. Look into the road before you turn and always give way to any pedestrians who are crossing.

Question 6.12

You want to reverse into a side road. You are not sure that the area behind your car is clear. What should you do?

Mark one answer

☒ Look through the rear window only

☒ Get out and check

☒ Check the mirrors only

☒ Carry on, assuming it is clear

Answer

☒ **Get out and check**

It's always safer to be sure. You may not be able to see a small child close behind your car. The shape and size of your vehicle can restrict visibility.

Question 6.13

You are about to reverse into a side road. A pedestrian wishes to cross behind you. You should

Mark one answer

☒ wave to the pedestrian to stop

☒ give way to the pedestrian

☒ wave to the pedestrian to cross

☒ reverse before the pedestrian starts to cross

Answer

☒ **give way to the pedestrian**

If you need to reverse into a side road, try to find a place that's free from traffic and pedestrians.

Look all around before and during the manoeuvre. Always stop and give way to any pedestrians who wish to cross behind you.

Question 6.14

Who is especially in danger of not being seen as you reverse your car?

Mark one answer

- [ ] Motorcyclists
- [ ] Car drivers
- [ ] Cyclists
- [ ] Children

Question 6.15

You are reversing around a corner when you notice a pedestrian walking behind you. What should you do?

Mark one answer

- [ ] Slow down and wave the pedestrian across
- [ ] Continue reversing and steer round the pedestrian
- [ ] Stop and give way
- [ ] Continue reversing and sound your horn

Question 6.16

You intend to turn right into a side road. Just before turning you should check for motorcyclists who might be

Mark one answer

- [ ] overtaking on your left
- [ ] following you closely
- [ ] emerging from the side road
- [ ] overtaking on your right

Answer

 Children

As you look through the rear of your vehicle you will not be able to see a small child. Be aware of this before you reverse. If there are children about, get out and check that it is clear.

Answer

❌ **Stop and give way**

Wait until the pedestrian has passed, then look around again before you start to reverse. Don't forget that you may not be able to see a small child directly behind your vehicle. Be aware of the possibility of hidden dangers.

Answer

 overtaking on your right

Never attempt to change direction to the right without checking your right-hand mirror. A motorcyclist might not have seen your signal, which may be hidden by the car behind you. This action should become a matter of routine.

Question 6.17

You want to turn right from a junction but your view is restricted by parked vehicles. What should you do?

Mark one answer

⊠ Move out quickly, but be prepared to stop

⊠ Sound your horn and pull out if there is no reply

⊠ Stop, then move slowly forward until you have a clear view

⊠ Stop, get out and look along the main road to check

Answer

❌ **Stop, then move slowly forward until you have a clear view**

If you want to turn right from a junction and your view's restricted, STOP. Ease forward until you can see – there might be something approaching.

IF YOU DON'T KNOW, DON'T GO.

Question 6.18

You are at the front of a queue of traffic waiting to turn right into a side road. Why is it important to check your right mirror just before turning?

Mark one answer

⊠ To look for pedestrians about to cross

⊠ To check for overtaking vehicles

⊠ To make sure the side road is clear

⊠ To check for emerging traffic

Answer

❌ **To check for overtaking vehicles**

There could be a motorcyclist riding along the outside of the queue. Always check your mirror, situations behind you can change in the time you have been waiting to turn.

Question 6.19

In which THREE places would parking your vehicle cause danger or obstruction to other road users?

Mark three answers

⊠ In front of a property entrance

⊠ At or near a bus stop

⊠ On your driveway

⊠ In a marked parking space

⊠ On the approach to a level crossing

Answers

❌ **In front of a property entrance**
❌ **At or near a bus stop**
❌ **On the approach to a level crossing**

Don't park your vehicle where parking restrictions apply. Think carefully before you slow down and stop. Look at road markings and signs to ensure that you aren't parking illegally.

Question 6.20

In which three places would parking cause an obstruction to others ?

Mark three answers

- ☒ Near the brow of a hill
- ☒ In a lay-by
- ☒ Where the kerb is raised
- ☒ Where the kerb has been lowered for wheelchairs
- ☒ At or near a bus stop

Answers

- ☒ **Near the brow of a hill**
- ☒ **Where the kerb has been lowered for wheelchairs**
- ☒ **At or near a bus stop**

Think about the affect your parking will have on other road users. Don't forget that not all vehicles are the size of a car. Large vehicles will need more room to pass and might need more time to do so. Leaving the traffic unsighted, as before the brow of a hill, causes unnecessary danger. Think before you park your car.

Question 6.21

What must a driver do at a pelican crossing when the amber light is flashing?

Mark one answer

- ☒ Signal the pedestrian to cross
- ☒ Always wait for the green light before proceeding
- ☒ Give way to any pedestrians on the crossing
- ☒ Wait for the red-and-amber light before proceeding

Answer

- ☒ **Give way to any pedestrians on the crossing**

The flashing amber light allows pedestrians already on the crossing to get to the other side before a green light shows to the traffic. Let them do this at their own pace.

Question 6.22

You have stopped at a pelican crossing. A disabled person is crossing slowly in front of you. The lights have now changed to green. You should

Mark two answers

- ☒ allow the person to cross
- ☒ drive in front of the person
- ☒ drive behind the person
- ☒ sound your horn
- ☒ be patient
- ☒ edge forward slowly

Answers

- ☒ **allow the person to cross**
- ☒ **be patient**

At a pelican crossing the green light means you may proceed as long as the crossing is clear. If someone hasn't finished crossing, be patient and wait for them to do so.

Question 6.23

As you approach a pelican crossing the lights change to green. Elderly people are halfway across. You should

Mark one answer

- [ ] wave them to cross as quickly as they can
- [ ] rev your engine to make them hurry
- [ ] flash your lights in case they have not heard you
- [ ] wait because they will take longer to cross

Answer

- [X] **wait because they will take longer to cross**

Even if the lights turn to green, wait for them to clear the crossing. Allow them to cross the road in their own time.

Question 6.24

A toucan crossing is different from other crossings because

Mark one answer

- [ ] moped riders can use it
- [ ] it is controlled by a traffic warden
- [ ] it is controlled by two flashing lights
- [ ] cyclists can use it

Answer

- [X] **cyclists can use it**

Pedestrians and cyclists are shown the green light together. The signals are push button operated, and there is no flashing amber phase.

Question 6.25

At toucan crossings

Mark two answers

- [ ] there is no flashing amber light
- [ ] cyclists are not permitted
- [ ] there is a continuously flashing amber beacon
- [ ] pedestrians and cyclists may cross
- [ ] you only stop if someone is waiting to cross

Answers

- [X] **there is no flashing amber light**
- [X] **pedestrians and cyclists may cross**

There are some crossings where cycle routes lead the cyclists to cross at the same place as pedestrians. Always look out for cyclists, as they're likely to be approaching faster than pedestrians.

Look at this picture. What is the danger you should be most aware of?

Mark one answer

- ☒ The ice cream van may move off
- ☒ The driver of the ice cream van may get out
- ☒ The car on the left may move off
- ☒ The child may run out into the road

Answer

☒ **The child may run out into the road**

Extra care must be taken when there are children about. Look out for them at all times but especially

- in residential areas
- near parks
- near schools.

Where there are crossing places used by children be extra cautious. Don't

- overtake
- drive at high speed.

If you see an ice cream van ask yourself: 'where are the children?' They might run across the road to it. Their small size may prevent you from seeing them emerging from behind parked vehicles.

You are driving past parked cars. You notice a wheel of a bicycle sticking out between them. What should you do?

Mark one answer

- ☒ Accelerate past quickly and sound your horn
- ☒ Slow down and wave the cyclist across
- ☒ Brake sharply and flash your headlights
- ☒ Slow down and be prepared to stop for a cyclist

Answer

☒ **Slow down and be prepared to stop for a cyclist**

Scan the road as you drive. Try to anticipate hazards by being aware of the places where they are likely to occur. You'll then be able to react in good time, if necessary.

Question 6.28

You are driving past a line of parked cars. You notice a ball bouncing out into the road ahead. What should you do?

Mark one answer

- [ ] Continue driving at the same speed and sound your horn
- [ ] Continue driving at the same speed and flash your headlights
- [ ] Slow down and be prepared to stop for children
- [ ] Stop and wave the children across to fetch their ball

Answer

✖ **Slow down and be prepared to stop for children**

Beware of children playing in the street and running out into the road. If a ball bounces out from the pavement slow down and stop. Don't encourage anyone to retrieve it. Other road users may not see your signal and you might lead a child into a dangerous situation.

Question 6.29

What does this sign tell you?

Mark one answer

- [ ] No cycling
- [ ] Cycle route ahead
- [ ] Route for cycles only
- [ ] End of cycle route

Answer

✖ **Cycle route ahead**

With people's concern today for the environment, cycle routes are being created in our towns and cities. These can be defined by road markings and signs. Don't straddle or drive in them. Respect the presence of cyclists on the road, and give them plenty of room if you need to pass.

How will a school crossing patrol signal you to stop?

Mark one answer

- ☒ By pointing to children on the opposite pavement
- ☒ By displaying a red light
- ☒ By displaying a stop sign
- ☒ By giving you an arm signal

Answer

☒ **By displaying a stop sign**

If someone steps out into the road with a school crossing sign you must stop. Don't

- wave anyone across the road
- get impatient or rev your engine.

You are approaching a school crossing patrol. When this sign is held up you must

Mark one answer

- ☒ stop and allow any children to cross
- ☒ stop and beckon the children to cross
- ☒ stop only if the children are on a pedestrian crossing
- ☒ stop only when the children are actually crossing the road

Answer

☒ **stop and allow any children to cross**

If you see a school sign anticipate that there might be a school crossing patrol. Always drive carefully where there might be children.

Question 6.32

Where would you see this sign?

Mark one answer

☒ In the window of a car taking children to school

☒ At the side of the road

☒ At playground areas

☒ On the rear of a school bus or coach

Answer

☒ On the rear of a school bus or coach

Vehicles that are used to carry children to and from school will be travelling at busy times of the day. If you're following a vehicle with this sign, be prepared for it to make frequent stops. It might pick up or set down passengers in places other than normal bus stops.

Question 6.33

Where would you see this sign?

Mark one answer

☒ On the approach to a school crossing

☒ At a playground entrance

☒ On a school bus

☒ At a 'pedestrians only' area

Answer

☒ On a school bus

Watch out for children crossing the road from the other side of the bus.

Question 6.34

You are parking your vehicle in the street. The car parked in front of you is displaying an orange badge. You should

Mark one answer

- [ ] park close to it to save road space
- [ ] allow room for a wheelchair
- [ ] wait until the orange-badge holder returns
- [ ] park with two wheels on the pavement

Answer

❌ **allow room for a wheelchair**

Think about the room that's needed to open the rear of the vehicle and lift a chair in. Room might be needed to manoeuvre a chair between the two cars.

Question 6.35

You are following a car driven by an elderly driver. You should

Mark one answer

- [ ] expect the driver to drive badly
- [ ] flash your lights and overtake
- [ ] be aware that the driver's reactions may not be as fast as yours
- [ ] stay close behind and drive carefully

Answer

❌ **be aware that the driver's reactions may not be as fast as yours**

You must show consideration to other road users. Their reactions may be slower and they might need more time to deal with a situation. Be tolerant and don't lose patience or show your annoyance.

Question 6.36

Which sign tells you that pedestrians may be walking in the road as there is no pavement?

Mark one answer

Answer

If you have to pass pedestrians who are walking at the side of the road, you must give them plenty of room. The draught caused by your vehicle could unsteady them, or they could turn around when they hear your car engine and step sideways into the road.

Question 6.37

Which sign means there may be elderly pedestrians likely to cross the road?

Mark one answer

Answer

You will often find this sign where there is a nursing home or retirement accommodation. Be patient if elderly people are crossing the road. They will need more time. Be aware that they might be deaf, or that their vision might be limited.

Question 6.38

What does this sign mean?

Mark one answer

 No route for pedestrians and cyclists

 A route for pedestrians only

 A route for cyclists only

 A route for pedestrians and cyclists

Answer

 A route for pedestrians and cyclists

This shared route is for pedestrians and cyclists only. Be aware that when it ends the cyclists will be rejoining the main road.

Question 6.39

You see a pedestrian carrying a white stick. This shows that the person is

Mark one answer

☒ disabled

☒ deaf

☒ elderly

☒ blind

Answer

☒ **blind**

If you see a pedestrian carrying a white stick it will mean that the person is partially sighted or blind. Make allowances for their hesitation at crossings or junctions.

You see a pedestrian with a white stick and red band. This means that the person is

Mark one answer

- [ ] physically disabled
- [ ] deaf only
- [ ] blind only
- [ ] deaf and blind

Answer

✖ **deaf and blind**

If the person is deaf as well as blind the stick will have a red band. You can't tell if a pedestrian is deaf. Don't assume everyone can hear you approaching.

Question 6.41

You are driving towards a zebra crossing. Waiting to cross is a person in a wheelchair. You should

Mark one answer

- [ ] continue on your way
- [ ] wave to the person to cross
- [ ] wave to the person to wait
- [ ] be prepared to stop

Answer

✖ **be prepared to stop**

As with an able-bodied pedestrian, you should prepare to slow down and stop. Don't wave the pedestrian across as they, due to their seated position, might not be able to see traffic beyond in a right hand lane. There might be a motorcyclist on your offside.

Question 6.42

What action would you take when elderly people are crossing the road?

Mark one answer

- [ ] Wave them across so they know that you have seen them
- [ ] Be patient and allow them to cross in their own time
- [ ] Rev the engine to let them know that you are waiting
- [ ] Tap the horn in case they are hard of hearing

Answer

✖ **Be patient and allow them to cross in their own time**

Don't hurry elderly people across the road by driving up close to them or revving the engine. Be aware that they might take longer to cross. They might also be hard of hearing and not able to hear your approach.

Question 6.43

You see two elderly pedestrians about to cross the road ahead. You should

Mark one answer

- expect them to wait for you to pass
- speed up to get past them quickly
- stop and wave them across the road
- be careful, they may misjudge your speed

Answer

 be careful, they may misjudge your speed

Their concentration, judgement, hearing and/or vision could be impaired. Be aware that if they proceed to cross they will take more time to do so.

Question 6.44

You are following a motorcyclist on an uneven road. You should

Mark one answer

- allow less room to ensure that you can be seen in their mirrors
- overtake immediately
- allow extra room in case they swerve to avoid pot-holes
- allow the same room as normal because motorcyclists are not affected by road surfaces

Answer

 allow extra room in case they swerve to avoid pot-holes

Pot-holes in the road can unsteady a motorcyclist. For this reason the rider might swerve to avoid an uneven road surface. Watch out at places where this is likely to occur.

Question 6.45

What does this sign mean?

Mark one answer

- Contra-flow pedal cycle lane
- With-flow pedal cycle lane
- Pedal cycles and buses only
- No pedal cycles or buses

Answer

 With-flow pedal cycle lane

This will be marked on the road, sometimes with a different colour surface. Leave it clear for cyclists, and don't pass too closely when you overtake.

Question 6.46

You should NEVER attempt to overtake a cyclist

Mark one answer

- [ ] just before you turn left
- [ ] just before you turn right
- [ ] on a one-way street
- [ ] on a dual carriageway

Answer

❌ **just before you turn left**

If you want to turn left and there's a cyclist in front of you, hold back. Wait until the cyclist has passed the junction and then turn left behind them.

Question 6.47

You are driving behind a cyclist. You wish to turn left just ahead. You should

Mark one answer

- [ ] overtake the cyclist before the junction
- [ ] pull alongside the cyclist and stay level until after the junction
- [ ] hold back until the cyclist has passed the junction
- [ ] go around the cyclist on the junction

Answer

❌ **hold back until the cyclist has passed the junction**

When driving or riding make allowances for cyclists. Allow them plenty of room. If you're following a cyclist, be aware that they also have to deal with hazards around them. They might swerve or change direction suddenly to avoid an uneven road surface.

Question 6.48

You are coming up to a roundabout. A cyclist is signalling to turn right. What should you do?

Mark one answer

- [ ] Overtake on the right
- [ ] Give a horn warning
- [ ] Signal the cyclist to move across
- [ ] Give the cyclist plenty of room

Answer

❌ **Give the cyclist plenty of room**

If you're following a cyclist who's signalling to turn right at a roundabout, leave plenty of room. Give them space and time to get into the correct lane.

Question 6.49

You are driving behind two cyclists. They approach a roundabout in the left-hand lane. In which direction should you expect the cyclists to go?

Mark one answer

- Left
- Right
- Any direction
- Straight ahead

Question 6.50

You are approaching this roundabout and see the cyclist signal right. Why is the cyclist keeping to the left?

Mark one answer

- It is a quicker route for the cyclist
- The cyclist is going to turn left instead
- The cyclist thinks *The Highway Code* does not apply to bicycles
- The cyclist is slower and more vulnerable

Answer

✖ **Any direction**

If you're following a cyclist into a roundabout be aware of them as they might not be taking the exit you anticipate. Cyclists approaching in the left-hand lane may be turning right but may not have been able to get into the correct lane due to heavy traffic. Give them room.

Answer

✖ **The cyclist is slower and more vulnerable**

Cycling in today's heavy traffic can be hazardous. Some cyclists may not feel happy about crossing the path of traffic to take up a position in an outside lane. Be aware of this and understand that, although in the left-hand lane, the cyclist might be turning right.

Question 6.51

When you are overtaking a cyclist you should leave as much room as you would give to a car. What is the main reason for this?

Mark one answer

- [ ] The cyclist might change lanes
- [ ] The cyclist might get off the bike
- [ ] The cyclist might swerve
- [ ] The cyclist might have to make a right turn

Answer

- [X] **The cyclist might swerve**

If you intend to overtake a cyclist look at the road ahead. Check if the cyclist needs to change direction for a parked vehicle or an uneven road surface. When you have a safe place to overtake leave as much room as you would for a car. Don't cut in sharply or pass too closely.

Question 6.52

Which TWO should you allow extra room when overtaking?

Mark two answers

- [ ] Motorcycles
- [ ] Tractors
- [ ] Bicycles
- [ ] Road-sweeping vehicles

Answers

- [X] **Motorcycles**
- [X] **Bicycles**

Don't pass riders too closely as this may cause them to lose balance. Leave them extra room, and don't cut in.

Question 6.53

Why should you allow extra room when overtaking a motorcyclist on a windy day?

Mark one answer

- [ ] The rider may turn off suddenly to get out of the wind
- [ ] The rider may be blown across in front of you
- [ ] The rider may stop suddenly
- [ ] The rider may be travelling faster than normal

Answer

- [X] **The rider may be blown across in front of you**

A motorcyclist's position on the road can be affected by high winds. If you're driving or riding on a windy day, be aware that the conditions might force a motorcyclist to swerve or wobble. Take this into consideration if you're following or wish to overtake.

Question 6.54

Which type of vehicle is most affected by strong winds?

Mark one answer

- ☒ Tractor
- ☒ Motorcycle
- ☒ Car
- ☒ Tanker

Answer

☒ **Motorcycle**

Pass a motorcyclist leaving plenty of room. Allow space in case the wind blows the motorcyclist across the lane.

Question 6.55

Why should you look particularly for motorcyclists and cyclists at junctions?

Mark one answer

- ☒ They may want to turn into the side road
- ☒ They may slow down to let you turn
- ☒ They are harder to see
- ☒ They might not see you turn

Answer

☒ **They are harder to see**

These road users could be hazards that are hidden from your view. Parked cars could cause you to lose sight of them. Consider that cyclists may need more time to make a turn.

Question 6.56

You are waiting to come out of a side road. Why should you watch carefully for motorcycles?

Mark one answer

- ☒ Motorcycles are usually faster than cars
- ☒ Police patrols often use motorcycles
- ☒ Motorcycles are small and hard to see
- ☒ Motorcycles have right of way

Answer

☒ **Motorcycles are small and hard to see**

If you're waiting to emerge from a side road watch out for motorcyclists. They're smaller and more difficult to see. Be especially careful if there are parked vehicles restricting your view. There might be a motorcyclist approaching.

IF YOU DON'T KNOW, DON'T GO.

Question 6.57

Where should you take particular care to look out for motorcyclists and cyclists?

Mark one answer

- On dual carriageways
- At junctions
- At zebra crossings
- On one-way streets

Answer

 At junctions

Motorcyclists and cyclists may be more difficult to see on the road. This is especially the case at junctions. You may not be able to see a motorcyclist approaching a junction if your view's blocked by other traffic. Be aware of the possibility. A motorcycle may be travelling as fast as a car, or faster. Make sure that you judge speeds correctly before you emerge.

Question 6.58

In daylight, an approaching motorcyclist is using a dipped headlight. Why?

Mark one answer

- So that the rider can be seen more easily
- To stop the battery overcharging
- To improve the rider's vision
- The rider is inviting you to proceed

Answer

 So that the rider can be seen more easily

A motorcycle can be lost out of sight behind another vehicle. The use of the headlight helps to make it more conspicuous and therefore more easily seen.

Question 6.59

Where in particular should you look out for motorcyclists?

Mark one answer

- In a filling station
- At a road junction
- Near a service area
- When entering a car park

Answer

 At a road junction

Always look ahead and try to make use of the information you see. This will enable you to anticipate possible hazards, and give you more time to deal with them as they occur.

Motorcycle riders are vulnerable because they

Mark one answer

- [ ] are easy for other road users to see
- [ ] are difficult for other road users to see
- [ ] are likely to have breakdowns
- [ ] cannot give arm signals

Answer

- ☒ **are difficult for other road users to see**

Motorcyclists don't always wear bright clothing. Look out for them, especially at junctions.

Motorcyclists should wear bright clothing mainly because

Mark one answer

- [ ] they must do so by law
- [ ] it helps keep them cool in summer
- [ ] the colours are popular
- [ ] drivers often do not see them

Answer

- ☒ **drivers often do not see them**

Although they're advised to wear clothing that's bright or reflective, motorcyclists often wear black. This means that they're difficult to see. Look out for them.

Motorcyclists ride in daylight with their headlights switched on because

Mark one answer

- [ ] it is a legal requirement
- [ ] there is a speed trap ahead
- [ ] they need to be seen
- [ ] there are speed humps ahead

Answer

- ☒ **they need to be seen**

Motorcyclists using their headlights in this way aren't indicating any priority. They want you to see them. Riding with the headlight on warns of their approach.

Question 6.63

There is a slow-moving motorcyclist ahead of you. You are unsure what the rider is going to do. You should

Mark one answer

 pass on the left

pass on the right

stay behind

move closer

Answer

 stay behind

Be patient. The motorcyclist might be turning right or changing direction.

Question 6.64

You are driving behind a moped. You want to turn left just ahead. You should

Mark one answer

overtake the moped before the junction

pull alongside the moped and stay level until just before the junction

sound your horn as a warning and pull in front of the moped

stay behind until the moped has passed the junction

Answer

 stay behind until the moped has passed the junction

Passing the moped and turning into the junction could mean that you cut across the front of the rider. This might force them to slow down, stop or even lose control.

Question 6.65

Motorcyclists will often look round over their right shoulder just before turning right. This is because

Mark one answer

they need to listen for following traffic

motorcycles do not have mirrors

looking around helps them balance as they turn

they need to check for traffic in their blind area

Answer

they need to check for traffic in their blind area

If you're behind a motorcyclist who takes a quick glance over their shoulder, expect them to be changing direction. They should do this before turning. By observing this you'll get an early signal of their intention.

Question 6.66

At road junctions which of the following are most vulnerable?

Mark three answers

- Cyclists
- Motorcyclists
- Pedestrians
- Car drivers
- Lorry drivers

Answers

- ✖ **Cyclists**
- ✖ **Motorcyclists**
- ✖ **Pedestrians**

Good effective observation, coupled with appropriate action, can save lives.

Question 6.67

When emerging from a side road into a queue of traffic which vehicles can be especially difficult to see?

Mark one answer

- Motorcycles
- Tractors
- Milk floats
- Cars

Answer

- ✖ **Motorcycles**

When emerging into queuing traffic, take extra care, and look for cyclists and motorcyclists, who may be approaching faster than you expect.

Question 6.68

You want to turn right from a main road into a side road. Just before turning you should

Mark one answer

- cancel your right-turn signal
- select first gear
- check for traffic overtaking on your right
- stop and set the handbrake

Answer

- ✖ **check for traffic overtaking on your right**

Motorcyclists often overtake queues of vehicles. Always make that last check in the mirror to avoid turning across their path.

Question 6.69

Motorcyclists are particularly vulnerable

Mark one answer

☒ when moving off

☒ on dual carriageways

☒ when approaching junctions

☒ on motorways

Answer

☒ **when approaching junctions**

Another road user failing to see a motorcyclist at a junction is a major cause of collision accidents. Wherever streams of traffic join or cross there's the potential for this type of accident to occur.

Question 6.70

Which of the following are hazards motorcyclists present in queues of traffic?

Mark three answers

☒ Cutting in just in front of you

☒ Riding in single file

☒ Passing very close to your car

☒ Riding with their headlamp on dipped beam

☒ Filtering between the lanes

Answers

☒ **Cutting in just in front of you**

☒ **Passing very close to your car**

☒ **Filtering between the lanes**

Where there's more than one lane of queuing traffic motorcyclists use the opportunity to make progress by riding between the lanes. Be aware that they may be passing on either side. Check your mirrors before you move off.

Question 6.71

You are driving on a main road. You intend to turn right into a side road. Just before turning you should

Mark one answer

☒ adjust your interior mirror

☒ flash your headlamps

☒ steer over to the left

☒ check for traffic overtaking on your offside

Answer

☒ **check for traffic overtaking on your offside**

A last check in the offside mirror will allow you sight of any cyclist or motorcyclist passing on your offside.

Question 6.72

When driving, ahead of you there is a vehicle with a flashing amber beacon. This means it is

Mark one answer

- slow moving
- broken down
- a doctor's car
- a school crossing patrol

Answer

✗ **slow moving**

As you approach the vehicle assess the situation. Due to it's slow progress you will need to judge whether it is safe to overtake.

Question 6.73

You are driving in slow-moving queues of traffic. Just before changing lane you should

Mark one answer

- sound the horn
- look for motorcyclists filtering through the traffic
- give a 'slowing down' arm signal
- change down to first gear

Answer

✗ **look for motorcyclists filtering through the traffic**

In this situation motorcyclists could be passing you on either side. Always check before you change lanes or change direction.

Question 6.74

An injured motorcyclist is lying unconscious in the road. You should

Mark one answer

- remove the safety helmet
- seek medical assistance
- move the person off the road
- remove the leather jacket

Answer

✗ **seek medical assistance**

When someone is injured, the sooner proper medical attention is given the better. Either send someone to phone for help or go yourself. Only move an injured person if further danger is threatened.

You are riding on a country lane. You see cattle on the road. You should

Mark three answers

- [ ] slow down
- [ ] stop if necessary
- [ ] give plenty of room
- [ ] rev your engine
- [ ] sound your horn
- [ ] ride up close behind them

Answers

- **✗ slow down**
- **✗ stop if necessary**
- **✗ give plenty of room**

Try not to startle the animals. They can be easily frightened by noise or by traffic passing too closely.

You are driving in town. There is a bus at the bus stop on the other side of the road. Why should you be careful?

Mark one answer

- [ ] The bus may have broken down
- [ ] Pedestrians may come from behind the bus
- [ ] The bus may move off suddenly
- [ ] The bus may remain stationary

Answer

- **✗ Pedestrians may come from behind the bus**

If you see a bus ahead, watch out for pedestrians. They may not be able to see you if they're crossing behind the bus.

Question 6.77

You are about to overtake horse riders. Which of the following could scare the horses?

Mark two answers

- [ ] Sounding your horn
- [ ] Giving arm signals
- [ ] Riding slowly
- [ ] Revving your engine

Answers

✗ Sounding your horn
✗ Revving your engine

When passing horses allow plenty of space and slow down. Animals can become frightened by sudden or loud noises, so don't sound your horn or rev the engine.

Question 6.78

How should you overtake horse riders?

Mark one answer

- [ ] Drive up close and overtake as soon as possible
- [ ] Speed is not important but allow plenty of room
- [ ] Use your horn just once to warn them
- [ ] Drive slowly and leave plenty of room

Answer

✗ Drive slowly and leave plenty of room

If you're driving or riding on a country road then take extra care. Be ready for

- farm animals
- horses
- pedestrians
- farm vehicles.

Always be prepared to slow down or stop.

You notice horse riders in front. What should you do FIRST?

Mark one answer

- [ ] Pull out to the middle of the road
- [ ] Be prepared to slow down
- [ ] Accelerate around them
- [ ] Signal right

Answer

 Be prepared to slow down

When you're driving or riding you must always look well ahead and be ready to deal with hazards as they occur.

Question 6.80

You are driving on a narrow country road. Where would you find it most difficult to see horses and riders ahead of you?

Mark one answer

- [ ] On left-hand bends
- [ ] When travelling downhill
- [ ] When travelling uphill
- [ ] On right-hand bends

Answer

 On left-hand bends

You're more likely to come across horses on country roads. These roads can be narrow so extra care must be taken when approaching left-hand bends as your view of the road ahead will be restricted.

Question 6.81

A horse rider is in the left-hand lane approaching a roundabout. The driver behind should expect the rider to

Mark one answer

- [ ] go in any direction
- [ ] turn right
- [ ] turn left
- [ ] go ahead

Answer

 go in any direction

Horses and their riders will move more slowly than other road users. They might not have time to cut across busy traffic to take up positions in the offside lane. For this reason a horse and rider may approach a roundabout in the left-hand lane, even though they're turning right.

Question 6.82

You are approaching a roundabout. There are horses just ahead of you. You should

Mark two answers

- [ ] be prepared to stop
- [ ] treat them like any other vehicle
- [ ] give them plenty of room
- [ ] accelerate past as quickly as possible
- [ ] sound your horn as a warning

Answers

- ☒ **be prepared to stop**
- ☒ **give them plenty of room**

Horse riders often keep to the outside of the roundabout even if they are turning right. Give them room in case they have to cross lanes of traffic.

Question 6.83

You see some horse riders as you approach a roundabout. They are signalling right but keeping well to the left. You should

Mark one answer

- [ ] proceed as normal
- [ ] keep close to them
- [ ] cut in front of them
- [ ] stay well back

Answer

- ☒ **stay well back**

Allow the riders to enter and exit the roundabout in their own time. Don't drive up close behind or alongside them, this could disturb the horses.

Question 6.84

Which THREE should you do when passing sheep on a road?

Mark three answers

☒ Allow plenty of room

☒ Drive very slowly

☒ Pass quickly but quietly

☒ Be ready to stop

☒ Briefly sound your horn

Answers

☒ **Allow plenty of room**

☒ **Drive very slowly**

☒ **Be ready to stop**

If you see animals in the road ahead, slow down and be ready to stop. Animals are easily frightened by

• noise

• vehicles passing too close to them.

Stop if signalled to do so by the person in charge. Switch off your engine if the animals are taking a long time to clear the road.

Question 6.85

What is the most common factor in causing road accidents?

Mark one answer

☒ Weather conditions

☒ Driver error

☒ Road conditions

☒ Mechanical failure

Answer

☒ **Driver error**

Bad weather and different conditions will increase the risks, so you must drive accordingly. Be aware of the distance it will take you to stop .

• in good conditions

• during wet or icy weather

• when you're tired

• when you aren't concentrating or are distracted. (Your thinking distance will increase.)

Question 6.86

You have a collision whilst your car is moving. What is the first thing you must do?

Mark one answer

☒ Stop only if there are injured people

☒ Call the emergency services

☒ Stop at the scene of the accident

☒ Call your insurance company

Answer

☒ **Stop at the scene of the accident**

It is the law. Apart from taking responsibility for any mistake you have made, the incident will have shaken you. You will need time to take stock before you drive on.

Question 6.87

Riders are more likely to have a serious accident if they

Mark one answer

- [ ] wear glasses or contact lenses
- [ ] have recently passed their test
- [ ] are carrying pillion passengers
- [ ] have not taken a theory test

Answer

✗ have recently passed their test

It takes time to experience different situations on the road. Develop safe habits and a responsible attitude from the start. This will help you to become a better rider.

Question 6.88

How would you react to other drivers who appear to be inexperienced?

Mark one answer

- [ ] Sound your horn to warn them of your presence
- [ ] Be patient and prepared for them to react more slowly
- [ ] Flash your headlights to indicate that it is safe for them to proceed
- [ ] Overtake them as soon as possible

Answer

✗ Be patient and prepared for them to react more slowly

Learners might not have confidence when they first start to drive. Allow them plenty of room and don't react adversely to their hesitation. We all learn from experience, but new drivers will have had less practice in dealing with all the situations that might occur.

Question 6.89

As a new driver, how can you decrease your risk of accidents on the motorway?

Mark one answer

- [ ] By keeping up with the car in front
- [ ] By never driving over 45 mph
- [ ] By driving only in the nearside lane
- [ ] By taking further training

Answer

✗ By taking further training

You're more likely to have an accident in the first year after taking your test. Lack of experience means that you might not react to hazards as quickly as a more experienced driver or rider. Further training will help you to become safer on the roads. If you're a motorcyclist ask your Compulsory Basic Training (CBT) instructor about this.

Question 6.90

Which age group is most likely to be involved in a road accident?

Mark one answer

- [x] 36 to 45-year-olds
- [x] 55-year-olds and over
- [x] 46 to 55-year-olds
- [x] 17 to 25-year-olds

Answer

✗ 17 to 25-year-olds

Statistics show that if you're between the ages of 17 and 25 you're more likely to be involved in a road accident. There are several reasons contributing to this, but in most cases accidents are due to driver or rider error.

Question 6.91

You are following a learner driver who stalls at a junction. You should

Mark one answer

- [x] be patient as you expect them to make mistakes
- [x] drive up close behind and flash your headlights
- [x] start to rev your engine if they take too long to restart
- [x] immediately steer around them and drive on

Answer

✗ be patient as you expect them to make mistakes

Learning is a process of practice and experience. Try to understand this and tolerate others who are at the beginning of this process.

Question 6.92

A learner driver has begun to emerge into your path from a side road on the left. You should

Mark one answer

- [x] be ready to slow down and stop
- [x] let them emerge then ride close behind
- [x] turn into the side road
- [x] brake hard, then wave them out

Answer

✗ be ready to slow down and stop

If you see another vehicle begin to emerge into your path you should ride defensively. Always be ready to slow down or stop if necessary.

Question 6.93

The vehicle ahead is being driven by a learner. You should

Mark one answer

- [ ] keep calm and be patient
- [ ] ride up close behind
- [ ] put your headlight on full beam
- [ ] sound your horn and overtake

Answer

 keep calm and be patient

Learners might take longer to react to traffic situations. Don't unnerve them by riding up close behind.

Question 6.94

A friend wants to teach you to drive a car. They must

Mark one answer

- [ ] be over 21 and have held a full licence for at least two years
- [ ] be over 18 and hold an advanced driver's certificate
- [ ] be over 18 and have fully comprehensive insurance
- [ ] be over 21 and have held a full licence for at least three years

Answer

 be over 21 and have held a full licence for at least three years

Teaching someone to drive is a responsible task. You're advised to contact a qualified Approved Driving Instructor (ADI) about learning to drive. This will ensure that you're taught the correct procedures from the start.

Question 6.95

Your vehicle hits a pedestrian at 40 mph. The pedestrian will

Mark one answer

- certainly be killed
- certainly survive
- probably be killed
- probably survive

Answer

❌ **probably be killed**

If you're a car driver ask your Approved Driving Instructor (ADI) about the Pass Plus scheme. This is a course designed to give you further instruction, which includes driving

- in town
- out of town
- in all weathers
- at night
- on dual carriageways
- on motorways.

Taking further training with a professional will help you to gain experience and positive driving skills. Whether driving or riding, you must always be aware that there may be others on the road who are particularly vulnerable. Always be on the lookout for danger and adjust your speed accordingly.

Although Northern Ireland doesn't have a Pass Plus scheme, your instructor will be willing to give you details of further instruction.

Question 6.96

At night you see a pedestrian wearing reflective clothing and carrying a bright red light. What does this mean?

Mark one answer

- You are approaching roadworks
- You are approaching an organised walk
- You are approaching a slow-moving vehicle
- You are approaching an accident black spot

Answer

❌ **You are approaching an organised walk**

The people involved in the march should be keeping to the left, but this can't be assumed. Pass slowly, ensuring that you have the time to do so safely. Be aware that the pedestrians have their backs to you and might not know that you're there.

Question 6.97

You are dazzled at night by a vehicle behind you. You should

Mark one answer

- [ ] set your mirror to anti-dazzle
- [ ] set your mirror to dazzle the other driver
- [ ] brake sharply to a stop
- [ ] switch your rear lights on and off

Answer

 set your mirror to anti-dazzle

Most modern vehicles have this facility. The interior mirror of your vehicle can be set to the anti-dazzle position. This prevents distraction from the lights of traffic behind you. You will still be able to see the lights but the dazzle will be greatly reduced.

This section looks at the risks when dealing with different types of vehicle.

The questions will ask you about

- motorcycles
- lorries
- buses.

Question 7.1

The road is wet. Why might a motorcyclist steer round drain covers on a bend?

Mark one answer

- [ ] To avoid puncturing the tyres on the edge of the drain covers
- [ ] To prevent the motorcycle sliding on the metal drain covers
- [ ] To help judge the bend using the drain covers as marker points
- [ ] To avoid splashing pedestrians on the pavement

Question 7.2

It is very windy. You are behind a motorcyclist who is overtaking a high-sided vehicle. What should you do?

Mark one answer

- [ ] Overtake the motorcyclist immediately
- [ ] Keep well back
- [ ] Stay level with the motorcyclist
- [ ] Keep close to the motorcyclist

Answer

✗ To prevent the motorcycle sliding on the metal drain covers

The actions other drivers take may be due to the size or characteristics of their vehicle. If you understand this it will help you to anticipate their actions. Motorcyclists will be checking the road ahead for uneven or slippery surfaces, especially in wet weather. They may need to move across their lane to avoid road surface hazards.

Answer

✗ Keep well back

Motorcyclists are affected more by windy weather than other vehicles. Keep well back as they could be blown off course.

CROSSWIND

CROSSWIND

A drop in pressure can pull the rider towards the large vehicle.

Question 7.3

It is very windy. You are about to overtake a motorcyclist. You should

Mark one answer

 overtake slowly

 allow extra room

 sound your horn

 keep close as you pass

Question 7.4

You are about to overtake a slow-moving motorcyclist. Which one of these signs would make you take special care?

Mark one answer

Question 7.5

You are waiting to emerge left from a minor road. A large vehicle is approaching from the right. You have time to turn, but you should wait. Why?

Mark one answer

 The large vehicle can easily hide an overtaking vehicle

 The large vehicle can turn suddenly

 The large vehicle is difficult to steer in a straight line

 The large vehicle can easily hide vehicles from the left

Answer

 allow extra room

Side winds can blow a motorcyclist across the lane. Passing too close could also cause a draught, unsteadying the rider.

Answer

In windy weather watch out for motorcyclists, as they can be blown sideways and veer into your path. Pass them leaving plenty of room and check your mirror as you pass and pull back in.

Answer

 The large vehicle can easily hide an overtaking vehicle

Don't only consider the hazards you can see. The possible hidden hazards are the most dangerous as they are often unexpected. By considering the possible dangers when emerging, you can lessen the risk.

Question 7.6

You are following a large articulated vehicle. It is going to turn left into a narrow road. What action should you take?

Mark one answer

☒ Move out and overtake on the offside

☒ Pass on the left as the vehicle moves out

☒ Be prepared to stop behind

☒ Overtake quickly before the lorry moves out

Answer

✗ **Be prepared to stop behind**

Lorries are larger and longer than other vehicles. This will affect their position when approaching junctions – especially when turning left. They need more room so that they don't cut in and mount the kerb when turning.

Question 7.7

You are following a long vehicle. It approaches a crossroads and signals left, but moves out to the right. You should

Mark one answer

☒ get closer in order to pass it quickly

☒ stay well back and give it room

☒ assume the signal is wrong and it is really turning right

☒ overtake as it starts to slow down

Answer

✗ **stay well back and give it room**

Approaching a left turn a lorry may swing out to the right. This is to allow the rear wheels to clear the kerb as it turns. If you see a gap on the nearside don't try to filter through.

Question 7.8

You are riding behind a long vehicle. There is a mini-roundabout ahead. The vehicle is signalling left, but positioned to the right. You should

Mark one answer

- [ ] sound your horn
- [ ] overtake on the left
- [ ] keep well back
- [ ] flash your headlights

Answer

✗ keep well back

The long vehicle needs more room to make the left turn. Don't overtake on the left. Staying well back will also give you a better view around the vehicle.

Question 7.9

You are following a long vehicle approaching a crossroads. The driver signals right but moves close to the left-hand kerb. What should you do?

Mark one answer

- [ ] Warn the driver of the wrong signal
- [ ] Wait behind the long vehicle
- [ ] Report the driver to the police
- [ ] Overtake on the right-hand side

Answer

✗ Wait behind the long vehicle

When a long vehicle is going to turn right it may need to keep close to the left-hand kerb. This is to prevent the rear end of the trailer cutting the corner. You need to be aware of how long vehicles behave in such situations. Don't overtake the lorry because it could turn as you're alongside. Stay behind and give plenty of room.

Question 7.10

You are approaching a mini-roundabout. The long vehicle in front is signalling left but positioned over to the right. You should

Mark one answer

- [ ] sound your horn
- [ ] overtake on the left
- [ ] follow the same course as the lorry
- [ ] keep well back

Answer

✖ **keep well back**

At mini-roundabouts there isn't much room for a long vehicle to manoeuvre. It will have to swing out wide so that it can complete the turn safely. Keep well back and allow plenty of room. Don't drive or ride along its nearside.

Question 7.11

You are following a large vehicle. Side and end markers are being displayed. This means the load

Mark one answer

- [ ] is higher than normal
- [ ] may be flammable
- [ ] is in two parts
- [ ] overhangs at the rear

Answer

✖ **overhangs at the rear**

Always keep a safe distance from the vehicle in front. In this case you should judge your separation distance from the extreme rear of the load the vehicle is carrying.

Question 7.12

You are towing a caravan. Which is the safest type of rear view mirror to use?

Mark one answer

- [ ] Interior wide-angle-view mirror
- [ ] Extended-arm side mirrors
- [ ] Ordinary door mirrors
- [ ] Ordinary interior mirror

Answer

✗ Extended-arm side mirrors

Towing a large trailer or caravan can greatly reduce your view of the road. The correct equipment will help you to get a better view behind and around the unit.

Question 7.13

You keep well back while waiting to overtake a large vehicle. Another car fills the gap. You should

Mark one answer

- [ ] sound your horn
- [ ] drop back further
- [ ] flash your headlights
- [ ] start to overtake

Answer

✗ drop back further

It's very frustrating when your separation distance is shortened by another car. React positively and consider your own and your passengers' safety.

Question 7.14

Before overtaking a large vehicle you should keep well back. Why is this?

Mark one answer

- [ ] To give acceleration space to overtake quickly on blind bends
- [ ] To get the best view of the road ahead
- [ ] To leave a gap in case the vehicle stops and rolls back
- [ ] To offer other drivers a safe gap if they want to overtake you

Answer

✗ To get the best view of the road ahead

When following a large vehicle keep well back. If you're too close

- you won't be able to see the road ahead
- the driver of the long vehicle might not be able to see you in the mirrors.

Question 7.15

You wish to overtake a long, slow moving vehicle on a busy road. You should

Mark one answer

☒ follow it closely and keep moving out to see the road ahead

☒ flash your headlights for the oncoming traffic to give way

☒ stay behind until the driver waves you past

☒ keep well back until you can see that it is clear

Answer

✖ **keep well back until you can see that it is clear**

If you wish to overtake a long vehicle, stay well back so that you can see the road ahead. Don't

- get up close to the vehicle – this will restrict your view of the road ahead

- get impatient – overtaking on a busy road calls for sound judgement

- take a gamble – only overtake when you can see that you can safely complete the manoeuvre.

Question 7.16

You are driving downhill. There is a car parked on the other side of the road. Large, slow lorries are coming towards you. You should

Mark one answer

☒ keep going because you have the right of way

☒ slow down and give way

☒ speed up and get past quickly

☒ pull over on the right behind the parked car

Answer

✖ **slow down and give way**

Large vehicles need several gear changes to build up speed and this takes time, especially on an uphill gradient. You should keep this in mind and give way so that they can maintain momentum up the hill.

Question 7.17

When about to overtake a long vehicle you should

Mark one answer

- [ ] sound the horn to warn the driver that you are there
- [ ] stay well back from the lorry to obtain a better view
- [ ] drive close to the lorry in order to pass more quickly
- [ ] flash your lights and wait for the driver to signal when it is safe

Answer

✗ stay well back from the lorry to obtain a better view

If you're thinking about overtaking ask yourself if it's really necessary. An unladen large vehicle can accelerate surprisingly quickly.

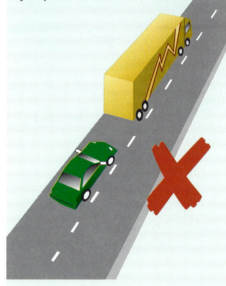

Question 7.18

Why is passing a lorry more risky than passing a car?

Mark one answer

- [ ] Lorries are longer than cars
- [ ] Lorries may suddenly pull up
- [ ] The brakes of lorries are not as good
- [ ] Lorries climb hills more slowly

Answer

✗ Lorries are longer than cars

Hazards to watch for include

- oncoming traffic
- junctions
- bends or dips, which could restrict your view
- any signs or road markings prohibiting overtaking.

Never begin to overtake unless you can see that it's safe to complete the manoeuvre.

Question 7.19

As a driver, why should you be more careful where trams operate?

Mark two answers

☒ Because they do not have a horn

☒ Because they do not stop for cars

☒ Because they are silent

☒ Because they cannot steer to avoid you

☒ Because they do not have lights

Answers

☒ **Because they are silent**

☒ **Because they cannot steer to avoid you**

You should take extra care when you first encounter trams. You will have to get used to dealing with a different traffic system. As well as being silent, they can travel very quickly.

Question 7.20

You are driving along a road and you see this signal. It means

Mark one answer

☒ cars must stop

☒ trams must stop

☒ both trams and cars must stop

☒ both trams and cars can continue

Answer

☒ **trams must stop**

Trams are popular in some cities, not least because they don't create fumes, so they're cleaner. You may not live in an area that has trams, but you should still learn the signs. You never know when you might drive through a town that has them.

Question 7.21

You are travelling behind a bus that pulls up at a bus stop. What should you do?

Mark two answers

☒ Accelerate past the bus sounding your horn

☒ Watch carefully for pedestrians

☒ Be ready to give way to the bus

☒ Pull in closely behind the bus

Answers

☒ **Watch carefully for pedestrians**

☒ **Be ready to give way to the bus**

There might be pedestrians crossing from in front of the bus. Look out for them if you intend to pass. Consider staying back and waiting. How many people are waiting to get on the bus? Check the queue if you can. The bus might be moving off straight away.

Question 7.22

You are driving in town. Ahead of you a bus is at a bus stop. Which two of the following should you do?

Mark two answers

☒ Be prepared to give way if the bus suddenly moves off

☒ Continue at the same speed but sound your horn as a warning

☒ Watch carefully for the sudden appearance of pedestrians

☒ Pass the bus as quickly as you possibly can

Question 7.23

When you approach a bus signalling to move off from a bus stop you should

Mark one answer

☒ get past before it moves

☒ allow it to pull away, if it is safe to do so

☒ flash your headlights as you approach

☒ signal left and wave the bus on

Answers

☒ **Be prepared to give way if the bus suddenly moves off**

☒ **Watch carefully for the sudden appearance of pedestrians**

As you approach, look out for any signal the driver might make. If you pass the vehicle, watch out for pedestrians attempting to cross the road from the other side of the bus. They will be hidden from view until the last moment.

Answer

☒ **allow it to pull away, if it is safe to do so**

Give way to buses whenever you can do so safely, especially when they signal to pull away from bus stops. Look out for people who've got off the bus and may try to cross the road. Don't

• try to accelerate past before it moves away

• flash your lights – other road users may be misled by this signal.

Question 7.24

Which of these vehicles is LEAST likely to be affected by crosswinds?

Mark one answer

- [×] Cyclists
- [×] Motorcyclists
- [×] High-sided vehicles
- [×] Cars

Answer

[×] **Cars**

Crosswinds can take you by surprise

- after overtaking a large vehicle
- when passing gaps between hedges or buildings
- on exposed sections of road.

Question 7.25

What does 'tailgating' mean?

Mark one answer

- [×] When a vehicle delivering goods has its tailgate down
- [×] When a vehicle is travelling with its back doors open
- [×] When a driver is following another vehicle too closely
- [×] When stationary vehicles are too close in a queue

Answer

[×] **When a driver is following another vehicle too closely**

This can often be seen on motorways, when traffic is travelling at high speeds. Tailgating is a highly dangerous practice and could lead to a serious accident.

Question 7.26

You are following a large lorry on a wet road. Spray makes it difficult to see. You should

Mark one answer

- [ ] drop back until you can see better
- [ ] put your headlights on full beam
- [ ] keep close to the lorry, away from the spray
- [ ] speed up and overtake quickly

Question 7.27

You are driving on a wet motorway with surface spray. You should use

Mark one answer

- [ ] your hazard flashers
- [ ] your dipped headlights
- [ ] your rear fog lights
- [ ] your sidelights

Answer

❌ **drop back until you can see better**

In the wet, large vehicles may throw up a lot of spray. This will make it difficult to see ahead. Dropping back further will

- move you out of the spray and so allow you to see further
- increase your separation distance.

It takes longer to stop in the wet and you need to allow more room. Don't

- get up close behind
- overtake, unless you can see the way ahead is clear.

Answer

❌ **your dipped headlights**

When surface spray reduces visibility, switch on your dipped headlights. This will help other road users to see you.

Question 7.28

You are driving in heavy traffic on a wet road. Spray makes it difficult to be seen. You should use your

Mark two answers

- [ ] full beam headlights
- [ ] rear fog lights if visibility is less than 100 metres (328 feet)
- [ ] rear fog lights if visibility is more than 100 metres (328 feet)
- [ ] dipped headlights
- [ ] side lights only

Answers

- ✖ **rear fog lights if visibility is less than 100 metres (328 feet)**
- ✖ **dipped headlights**

You must ensure that you can be seen by others on the road. Use your lights during the day if the visibility is bad. If you use your rear fog lights, don't forget to turn them off when the visibility improves.

Question 7.29

Some two way roads are divided into three lanes. Why are these particularly dangerous?

Mark one answer

- [ ] Traffic in both directions can use the middle lane to overtake
- [ ] Traffic can travel faster in poor weather conditions
- [ ] Traffic can overtake on the left
- [ ] Traffic uses the middle lane for emergencies only

Answer

- ✖ **Traffic in both directions can use the middle lane to overtake**

If you intend to overtake you must consider that approaching traffic could be intending the same manoeuvre. When you have judged the situation and decided it is safe, indicate your intentions early. This will show the approaching traffic that you intend to pull out.

This section looks at the handling of your vehicle in different conditions

The questions will ask you about

- weather conditions
- road conditions
- the time of day
- speed
- traffic calming.

Question 8.1

To gain basic skills in how to ride a motorcycle you should

Mark one answer

- [ ] practise off-road with an approved training body
- [ ] ride on the road on the first dry day
- [ ] practise off-road in a public park or in a quiet cul-de-sac
- [ ] ride on the road as soon as possible

Answer

✗ practise off-road with an approved training body

All new motorcyclists must complete a course of basic training with an approved training body before going on the road. This training is given on a site which has been authorised by the Driving Standards Agency as suitable for off-road training.

Question 8.2

When you are seated on a stationary motorcycle, your position should allow you to

Mark one answer

- [ ] just touch the ground with your toes
- [ ] place both feet on the ground
- [ ] operate the centre stand
- [ ] reach the switches by stretching

Answer

✗ place both feet on the ground

When sitting astride a stationary motorcycle you should be able to place both feet on the ground for maximum control and stability.

Question 8.3

As a safety measure before starting your engine, you should

Mark two answers

- [ ] push the motorcycle forward to check the rear wheel turns freely
- [ ] engage first gear and apply the rear brake
- [ ] engage first gear and apply the front brake
- [ ] glance at the neutral light on your instrument panel

Answers

✗ push the motorcycle forward to check the rear wheel turns freely

✗ glance at the neutral light on your instrument panel

Before starting the engine you should ensure the motorcycle is in neutral. This can be done by

- moving the motorcycle to see that the rear wheel turns freely
- checking that the neutral lamp is lit when the ignition is turned on.

Question 8.4

You should not ride with your clutch lever pulled in for longer than necessary because it

Mark one answer

- [ ] increases wear on the gearbox
- [ ] increases petrol consumption
- [ ] reduces your control of the motorcycle
- [ ] reduces the grip of the tyres

Answer

- [X] **reduces your control of the motorcycle**

Coasting

- gives you less steering control
- reduces the traction on the road surface
- causes the machine to pick up speed.

If you're travelling downhill your machine will gather speed quickly. The engine won't be able to assist the braking.

Question 8.5

What are TWO main reasons why coasting downhill is wrong?

Mark two answers

- [ ] Fuel consumption will be higher
- [ ] The vehicle will pick up speed
- [ ] It puts more wear and tear on the tyres
- [ ] You have less braking and steering control
- [ ] It damages the engine

Answers

- [X] **The vehicle will pick up speed**
- [X] **You have less braking and steering control**

It's especially important that you don't coast your vehicle

- at junctions
- approaching hazards
- on bends
- downhill.

Question 8.6

You should avoid 'coasting' your vehicle because it could

Mark one answer

- [ ] damage the suspension
- [ ] increase tyre wear
- [ ] flatten the battery
- [ ] reduce steering control

Answer

- [X] **reduce steering control**

Coasting your vehicle or machine will

- cause it to pick up speed
- give you less steering and braking control
- make selecting the correct gear difficult.

Question 8.7

Why is coasting wrong?

Mark one answer

- ☒ It will cause the car to skid
- ☒ It will make the engine stall
- ☒ The engine will run faster
- ☒ There is no engine braking

Answer

☒ **There is no engine braking**

Try to look ahead and read the road. Plan your approach to junctions and select the correct gear in good time. This will give you the control you need to deal with any hazards that occur. You'll coast a little every time you change gear. This can't be avoided, but it should be kept to a minimum.

Question 8.8

Hills can affect the performance of your vehicle. Which TWO apply when driving up steep hills?

Mark two answers

- ☒ Higher gears will pull better
- ☒ You will slow down sooner
- ☒ Overtaking will be easier
- ☒ The engine will work harder
- ☒ The steering will feel heavier

Answers

☒ **You will slow down sooner**
☒ **The engine will work harder**

The engine will need more power to pull the vehicle up the hill. When approaching a steep hill you should select a lower gear to maintain your speed. You should do this without hesitation, so that you don't lose too much speed.

Question 8.9

You are approaching a bend at speed. You should begin to brake

Mark one answer

- ☒ on the bend
- ☒ after the bend
- ☒ after changing gears
- ☒ before the bend

Answer

☒ **before the bend**

Full control of the vehicle is essential at all times. Adjust your speed before the bend. Change gear if necessary and drive round it under gentle acceleration.

Question 8.10

You should brake

Mark one answer

- ☒ by using the rear brake first and then the front
- ☒ when the machine is being turned or ridden through a bend
- ☒ by pulling in the clutch before using the front brake
- ☒ when the machine is upright and moving in a straight line

Answer

☒ **when the machine is upright and moving in a straight line**

A motorcycle is most stable when it's upright and moving in a straight line. This is the best time to brake and normally both brakes should be used, with the front brake being applied just before the rear.

Question 8.11

You are following a vehicle at a safe distance on a wet road. Another driver overtakes you and pulls into the gap you have left. What should you do?

Mark one answer

- ☒ Flash your headlights as a warning
- ☒ Try to overtake safely as soon as you can
- ☒ Drop back to regain a safe distance
- ☒ Stay close to the other vehicle until it moves on

Answer

☒ **Drop back to regain a safe distance**

The weather will affect the way your vehicle or machine behaves. It will increase the time it takes for you to stop and can affect your control.

Drive at a speed that will allow you to stop safely and in good time. If another vehicle pulls into the gap you've left, ease back until you've regained your stopping distance. Don't flash your lights or drive up close to it.

Question 8.12

You are driving in the left-hand lane of a dual carriageway. Another vehicle overtakes and pulls in front of you leaving you without enough separation distance. You should

Mark one answer

- ☒ move to the right-hand lane
- ☒ continue as you are
- ☒ drop back
- ☒ sound your horn

Answer

☒ **drop back**

Dual carriageways have at least two lanes in each direction. There will be a central reserve where there may be a safety barrier. If you're overtaken by another vehicle and it cuts in too closely, don't react by flashing your lights or giving any other signal. Gradually increase your distance from the vehicle so that you have a safe gap if you need to stop.

Question 8.13

In which THREE of these situations may you overtake another vehicle on the left?

Mark three answers

☒ When you are in a one-way street

☒ When approaching a motorway slip road where you will be turning off

☒ When the vehicle in front is signalling to turn right

☒ When a slower vehicle is travelling in the right-hand lane of a dual carriageway

☒ In slow-moving traffic queues when traffic in the right-hand lane is moving more slowly

Answers

❌ **When you are in a one-way street**

❌ **When the vehicle in front is signalling to turn right**

❌ **In slow-moving traffic queues when traffic in the right-hand lane is moving more slowly**

At certain times of the day traffic might be heavy. If traffic is moving in queues and vehicles in the right-hand lane are moving more slowly, you may overtake on the left. Don't keep changing lanes to try and beat the queue.

Question 8.14

You are driving on the motorway in windy conditions. When passing high-sided vehicles you should

Mark one answer

☒ increase your speed

☒ be wary of a sudden gust

☒ drive alongside very closely

☒ expect normal conditions

Answer

❌ **be wary of a sudden gust**

The draught caused by other vehicles could be strong enough to push you out of your lane. Keep both hands on the steering wheel to maintain full control.

Question 8.15

When coming to a normal stop on a motorcycle, you should

Mark one answer

☒ only apply the front brake

☒ rely just on the rear brake

☒ apply both brakes smoothly

☒ apply either of the brakes gently

Answer

❌ **apply both brakes smoothly**

In normal riding you should always use both brakes. Harsh or poorly-controlled use of the brakes can cause loss of control and skidding.

Question 8.16

Which THREE of the following will affect your stopping distance?

Mark three answers

- ☒ How fast you are going
- ☒ The tyres on your vehicle
- ☒ The time of day
- ☒ The weather
- ☒ The street lighting

Answers

- ☒ **How fast you are going**
- ☒ **The tyres on your vehicle**
- ☒ **The weather**

You should be aware that there are several factors that can affect the distance it takes to stop your vehicle. Your stopping distance in wet weather will increase. You should double the separation distance from the car in front. Your tyres will have less grip on the road and, therefore, you'll need more time to stop. Always drive in accordance with the conditions.

Question 8.17

You are travelling in very heavy rain. Your overall stopping distance is likely to be

Mark one answer

- ☒ doubled
- ☒ halved
- ☒ up to ten times greater
- ☒ no different

Answer

- ☒ **doubled**

Apart from the lack of visibility, the road will be extremely wet. This will lessen the grip the tyres have on the road and increase the distance it takes to stop. Double your separation distance.

Question 8.18

You are riding in heavy rain. What clears the water between your tyres and the road surface to prevent aquaplaning?

Mark one answer

- ☒ Tread depth
- ☒ Your speed
- ☒ Your mudguards
- ☒ Harsh braking

Answer

- ☒ **Tread depth**

When riding in the wet you rely on the tyres' tread to clear the water and let the tyres grip the road. As tread wears it cannot clear the water as quickly, so increasing the risk of aquaplaning.

Question 8.19

Motorcyclists are more at risk from other road users because they

Mark one answer

- [ ] are less experienced than other drivers
- [ ] are more likely to break down than other motorists
- [ ] are always faster than other drivers
- [ ] are more difficult to see than other drivers

Answer

✗ are more difficult to see than other drivers

A motorcycle is one of the smallest motor vehicles on our roads. Being small they are not always easy to see. This makes them more at risk from other road users, who may not see them, particularly at junctions.

Question 8.20

You are approaching this junction. As the motorcyclist you should

Mark two answers

- [ ] prepare to slow down
- [ ] sound your horn
- [ ] keep near the left kerb
- [ ] speed up to clear the junction
- [ ] stop, as the car has right of way

Answers

✗ prepare to slow down
✗ sound your horn

Look out for road signs indicating side roads, even if you aren't turning off. A driver emerging might not be able to see you due to parked cars or heavy traffic. Always be prepared, and stop if it's necessary. Remember, no one has priority at unmarked crossroads.

Question 8.21

What can you do to improve your safety on the road as a motorcyclist?

Mark one answer

 Anticipate the actions of others

Stay just above the speed limits

Keep positioned close to the kerbs

Remain well below speed limits

Answer

✗ Anticipate the actions of others

Always ride defensively. This means looking and planning ahead as well as anticipating the actions of other road users.

Question 8.22

Which FOUR types of road surface increase the risk of skidding for motorcyclists?

Mark four answers

White lines

Dry tarmac

Tar banding

Yellow grid lines

Loose chippings

Answers

✗ White lines
✗ Tar banding
✗ Yellow grid lines
✗ Loose chippings

If you're riding a motorcycle you must look at the road surface ahead. The stability of your machine will depend on it. Also, look out for

• pot-holes
• drain covers (especially in the wet)
• oily surfaces
• road markings
• tram tracks
• wet mud and leaves.

Question 8.23

You have to brake sharply and your machine starts to skid. You should

Mark one answer

continue braking and select a low gear

apply the brakes harder for better grip

select neutral and use the front brake only

release the brakes and re-apply

Answer

✗ release the brakes and re-apply

If you skid as a result of too much braking you need to

• release the brakes to stop the skid
• re-apply them progressively to stop.

Question 8.24

Which THREE of these can cause skidding?

Mark three answers

- [ ] Braking too gently
- [ ] Leaning too far over when cornering
- [ ] Staying upright when cornering
- [ ] Braking too hard
- [ ] Changing direction suddenly

Answers

- [x] **Leaning too far over when cornering**
- [x] **Braking too hard**
- [x] **Changing direction suddenly**

In order to keep control of your vehicle and prevent skidding you must plan well ahead to avoid harsh, late braking. Take the road and weather conditions into consideration and ride accordingly.

Question 8.25

To correct a rear-wheel skid you should

Mark one answer

- [ ] not steer at all
- [ ] steer away from it
- [ ] steer into it
- [ ] apply your handbrake

Answer

- [x] **steer into it**

Prevention is better than cure, so it's important that you take every precaution to prevent a skid. If you do feel your vehicle beginning to skid, try to steer to recover control. Don't brake suddenly – this will only make the situation worse.

Question 8.26

It is very cold and the road looks wet. You cannot hear any road noise. You should

Mark two answers

- [ ] continue riding at the same speed
- [ ] ride slower in as high a gear as possible
- [ ] ride in as low a gear as possible
- [ ] keep revving your engine
- [ ] slow down as there may be black ice

Answers

- [x] **ride slower in as high a gear as possible**
- [x] **slow down as there may be black ice**

If the road surface looks wet but your tyres make no noise, suspect black ice. This is caused by rain freezing on roads as it falls, and it's very dangerous because it's almost invisible. The first indication you might have of it is when the steering becomes very light. You need to keep your speed down and ride according to the weather conditions.

Question 8.27

You are approaching a road with a surface of loose chippings. What should you do?

Mark one answer

- ☒ Ride normally
- ☒ Speed up
- ☒ Slow down
- ☒ Stop suddenly

Answer

☒ **Slow down**

You should

- ride at an appropriate speed
- apply both front and rear brakes evenly
- brake when travelling in a straight line with your machine upright.

Don't make sudden changes of direction unless you are trying to avoid an accident. The handling of your machine will be greatly affected by the road surface that you're riding on. Look at the road ahead and be alert if it looks uneven or has loose chippings. Slow down in good time – braking harshly may cause you to skid.

Question 8.28

When snow is falling heavily you should

Mark one answer

- ☒ drive as long as your headlights are used
- ☒ not drive unless you have a mobile phone
- ☒ drive only when your journey is short
- ☒ not drive unless it is essential

Answer

☒ **not drive unless it is essential**

Consider if the increased risk is worth it. If the weather conditions are bad and your journey isn't essential, then stay at home.

Question 8.29

You are driving on an icy road. What distance should you drive from the car in front?

Mark one answer

- ☒ Eight times the normal distance
- ☒ Six times the normal distance
- ☒ Ten times the normal distance
- ☒ Four times the normal distance

Answer

☒ **Ten times the normal distance**

Think about how far this is. It's a long way; probably further than you imagine.

Question 8.30

You are driving in very wet weather. Your vehicle begins to slide. This effect is called

Mark one answer

 hosing

 weaving

 aquaplaning

fading

Answer

 aquaplaning

Water can build up between your tyres and the road until the tyres lose contact with the road. Your vehicle will then 'float' on the film of water, causing the steering to feel light and you to lose proper control.

Question 8.31

Why should you test your brakes after this hazard?

Mark one answer

 Because you will be driving on a slippery road

 Because your brakes will be soaking wet

 Because you will have driven down a long hill

Because you will have just crossed a long bridge

Answer

Because your brakes will be soaking wet

A ford is a crossing over a stream that's shallow enough to drive through. If you've driven through a ford or a deep puddle the water can affect your brakes. Be sure you check that they're working before returning to normal speed.

Question 8.32

You have to make a journey in fog. What are the TWO most important things you should do before you set out?

Mark two answers

- [✗] Top up the radiator with antifreeze
- [✗] Make sure that you have a warning triangle in the vehicle
- [✗] Check that your lights are working
- [✗] Check the battery
- [✗] Make sure that the windows are clean

Answers

- [✗] **Check that your lights are working**
- [✗] **Make sure that the windows are clean**

Don't drive in fog unless you really have to. Drive in accordance with the conditions.

Question 8.33

When riding a motorcycle you should wear full protective clothing

Mark one answer

- [✗] at all times
- [✗] only on faster, open roads
- [✗] just on long journeys
- [✗] only during bad weather

Answer

- [✗] **at all times**

Protective clothing is designed to protect you from

- the cold and wet
- some kinds of injury.

If you allow yourself to become cold and wet when riding, you'll lose concentration.

Question 8.34

You have to make a journey in fog. What are the TWO most important things you should do before you set out?

Mark two answers

- [✗] Fill up with fuel
- [✗] Make sure that you have a warm drink with you
- [✗] Check that your lights are working
- [✗] Check the battery
- [✗] Make sure that your visor is clean

Answers

- [✗] **Check that your lights are working**
- [✗] **Make sure that your visor is clean**

If you're riding a motorcycle, keep your visor as clean as possible to give you a clear view of the road. It's a good idea to carry a clean, damp cloth in a polythene bag for this purpose. When the weather is foggy or misty ensure that your lights are clean and can be seen clearly by other road users.

DSA THEORY TEST for car drivers and motorcyclists

Question 8.35

You have to make a journey in foggy conditions. You should

Mark one answer

- ☒ follow closely other vehicles' tail lights
- ☒ never use demisters and windscreen wipers
- ☒ leave plenty of time for your journey
- ☒ keep two seconds behind other vehicles

Answer

❌ **leave plenty of time for your journey**

If you're planning to make a journey in foggy conditions, listen to the weather reports on the radio or television. Don't drive if visibility is very low or your journey isn't necessary. If you do travel, leave plenty of time for your journey. If there's someone expecting you at the other end of your journey, let them know that you'll be taking longer than normal to arrive. Take your time and don't hurry.

Question 8.36

Front fog lights may be used ONLY if

Mark one answer

- ☒ visibility is seriously reduced
- ☒ they are fitted above the bumper
- ☒ they are not as bright as the headlights
- ☒ an audible warning device is used

Answer

❌ **visibility is seriously reduced**

Your fog lights should have a warning light which illuminates when they are being used. You should be familiar with the layout of your dashboard so that you are aware if they have been switched on in error, or you have forgotten to switch them off.

Question 8.37

Front fog lights may be used ONLY

Mark one answer

- ☒ if they are not as bright as the headlights
- ☒ when visibility is seriously reduced
- ☒ between dusk and dawn
- ☒ during 'lighting up' times only

Answer

❌ **when visibility is seriously reduced**

Driving around with front fog lights on when visibility is good is inexcusable. It is unnecessary and the glare can dazzle other road users, particularly when the roads are wet.

Question 8.38

Front fog lights may be used ONLY if

Mark one answer

- [ ] your headlights are not working
- [ ] they are operated with rear fog lights
- [ ] they were fitted by the vehicle manufacturer
- [ ] visibility is seriously reduced

Answer

 visibility is seriously reduced

It is illegal to use fog lights unless visibility is seriously reduced. Check that they have been switched off when conditions improve.

Question 8.39

Front fog lights may be used ONLY if

Mark one answer

- [ ] they prevent headlight glare on a wet road
- [ ] you wish to overtake in bad weather
- [ ] visibility is seriously reduced
- [ ] fitted by the manufacturer

Answer

 visibility is seriously reduced

Do not use them at any other time; it is illegal.

Question 8.40

You may drive with front fog lights switched-on

Mark one answer

- [ ] when visibility is less than 100 metres (328 feet)
- [ ] at any time to be noticed
- [ ] instead of headlights on high speed roads
- [ ] when dazzled by the lights of oncoming vehicles

Answer

 when visibility is less than 100 metres (328 feet)

Consider if the distance you are able to see is more than 100 metre (328 feet). Turn off your fog lights as the weather improves.

Question 8.41

Front fog lights should be used ONLY when

Mark one answer

- [ ] travelling in very light rain
- [ ] visibility is seriously reduced
- [ ] daylight is fading
- [ ] driving after midnight

Answer

✗ **visibility is seriously reduced**

It will help others see you, but remember, they must only be used if visibility is reduced to less than 100 metres (328 feet).

Question 8.42

Front fog lights should be used

Mark one answer

- [ ] when visibility is reduced to 100 metres (328 feet)
- [ ] as a warning to oncoming traffic
- [ ] when driving during the hours of darkness
- [ ] in any conditions and at any time

Answer

✗ **when visibility is reduced to 100 metres (328 feet)**

As visibility reduces to less than 100 metres (328 feet) switch on your fog lights if you have them fitted. It is essential, not only that you can see ahead, but that other drivers are able to see you.

Question 8.43

Using front fog lights in clear daylight will

Mark one answer

- [ ] flatten the battery
- [ ] dazzle other drivers
- [ ] improve your visibility
- [ ] increase your awareness

Answer

✗ **dazzle other drivers**

Fog lights can be brighter than normal dipped headlights. If the weather has improved, turn them off so as not to dazzle other road users.

Question 8.44

You may use front fog lights with headlights ONLY when visibility is reduced to less than

Mark one answer

- 100 metres (328 feet)
- 200 metres (656 feet)
- 300 metres (984 feet)
- 400 metres (1312 feet)

Answer

 100 metres (328 feet)

It is an offence to use them if the visibility is better than 100 metres (328 feet). Deal with patchy fog sensibly to avoid dazzling other road users in the clear patches.

Question 8.45

You are following other vehicles in fog with your lights on. How else can you reduce the chances of being involved in an accident?

Mark one answer

- Keep close to the vehicle in front
- Use your main beam instead of dipped headlights
- Keep together with the faster vehicles
- Reduce your speed and increase the gap

Answer

 Reduce your speed and increase the gap

Always ensure that you have your lights on and that you can be seen by all other road users. Use dipped headlights. If visibility is below 100 metres (328 feet) use fog lights and high-intensity rear lights. Drive at a sensible speed and don't follow the car in front too closely. You'll need to adjust your stopping distance as the road is likely to be wet and slippery.

Question 8.46

Why should you always reduce your speed when driving in fog?

Mark one answer

- Because the brakes do not work as well
- Because you could be dazzled by other people's fog lights
- Because the engine's colder
- Because it is more difficult to see events ahead

Answer

✗ Because it is more difficult to see events ahead

Driving in fog is hazardous. Only travel if it's really necessary. To drive or ride safely you must always look well ahead. In fog this won't be possible and you'll have less time to react to any hazards. You must reduce your speed.

Question 8.47

You are driving in fog. Why should you keep well back from the vehicle in front?

Mark one answer

- [ ] In case it changes direction suddenly
- [ ] In case its fog lights dazzle you
- [ ] In case it stops suddenly
- [ ] In case its brake lights dazzle you

Answer

✗ In case it stops suddenly

If you're following another road user in fog stay well back. The driver in front won't be able to see hazards until they're close and might brake suddenly. You'll need a good separation distance as the road surface is likely to be wet and slippery.

Question 8.48

You should switch your rear fog lights on when visibility drops below

Mark one answer

- [ ] your overall stopping distance
- [ ] ten car lengths
- [ ] 200 metres (656 feet)
- [ ] 100 metres (328 feet)

Answer

✗ 100 metres (328 feet)

They will help other road users to see you. Don't forget to turn off fog lights once visibility improves; they might be mistaken for brake lights.

Question 8.49

You should only use rear fog lights when you cannot see further than about

Mark one answer

- [ ] 100 metres (328 feet)
- [ ] 200 metres (656 feet)
- [ ] 250 metres (820 feet)
- [ ] 150 metres (492 feet)

Answer

✗ 100 metres (328 feet)

They will help other road users to see you. Don't forget to switch them off when visibility improves. Driving with them on at other times, such as in heavy rain, can dazzle the car behind.

Question 8.50

You should use rear fog lights when

Mark one answer

- [ ] vehicles are following too closely
- [ ] visibility is reduced to 100 metres (328 feet)
- [ ] very bright sunshine is dazzling motorists
- [ ] driving in busy fast moving traffic

Answer

- [X] **visibility is reduced to 100 metres (328 feet)**

You must ensure that other traffic can see you. This should prevent traffic behind following too closely.

Question 8.51

Using rear fog lights in clear daylight will

Mark one answer

- [ ] be useful when towing a trailer
- [ ] give extra protection
- [ ] dazzle other drivers
- [ ] make following drivers keep back

Answer

- [X] **dazzle other drivers**

Rear fog lights shine brighter than normal rear lights so that they show up in poor visibility. When the weather is clear they could dazzle the driver behind, so switch them off.

Question 8.52

You are driving on a clear dry night with your rear fog lights switched on. This may

Mark two answers

- [ ] reduce glare from the road surface
- [ ] make other drivers think you are braking
- [ ] give a better view of the road ahead
- [ ] dazzle following drivers
- [ ] help your indicators to be seen more clearly

Answers

- [X] **make other drivers think you are braking**
- [X] **dazzle following drivers**

A warning light will show on the dashboard to indicate when your rear fog lights are on. You should know the meaning of all the lights on your dashboard and check them before you move off and as you drive.

NI

Question 8.53
Why is it dangerous to leave rear fog lights on when they are not needed?

Mark two answers

- [ ] Brake lights are less clear
- [ ] Following drivers can be dazzled
- [ ] Electrical systems could be overloaded
- [ ] Direction indicators may not work properly
- [ ] The battery could fail

Answers

- ☒ **Brake lights are less clear**
- ☒ **Following drivers can be dazzled**

The drivers behind you may be confused by your fog lights. On a wet road surface the glare caused by bright lights makes it difficult for following drivers to know if you are braking, or if you have forgotten to turn off your rear fog lights. This can be a real problem at speed on motorways.

Question 8.54
Whilst driving, the fog clears and you can see more clearly. You must remember to

Mark one answer

- [ ] switch off the fog lights
- [ ] reduce your speed
- [ ] switch off the demister
- [ ] close any open windows

Answer

- ☒ **switch off the fog lights**

Bright rear fog lights might be mistaken for brake lights and could be misleading for the traffic behind.

Question 8.55
You are driving in thick fog using fog lights. When visibility improves you MUST

Mark one answer

- [ ] maintain your speed
- [ ] keep them on
- [ ] increase your speed
- [ ] switch them off

Answer

- ☒ **switch them off**

If visibility improves you should switch off your fog lights. Don't forget to turn off your rear fog lights as well. These could be mistaken for brake lights by traffic behind you.

Question 8.56

You have just driven out of fog. Visibility is now good. You MUST

Mark one answer

- [x] switch off all your fog lights
- [x] keep your rear fog lights on
- [x] keep your front fog lights on
- [x] leave fog lights on in case fog returns

Answer

[x] **switch off all your fog lights**

Be prepared for the fact that the fog may be patchy. You must turn off your fog lights if visibility is more than 100 metres (328 feet)

NI

Question 8.57

You forget to switch off your rear fog lights when the fog has cleared. This may

Mark three answers

- [x] dazzle other road users
- [x] reduce battery life
- [x] cause brake lights to be less clear
- [x] be breaking the law
- [x] seriously affect engine power

Answers

[x] **dazzle other road users**
[x] **cause brake lights to be less clear**
[x] **be breaking the law**

You could be prosecuted for driving with fog lights on in good visibility. Don't forget to switch them off as the weather improves. The high intensity of the rear fog lights can look like brakes lights, and on a high speed road this may cause following traffic to brake unnecessarily.

NI

Question 8.58

You have been driving in thick fog which has now cleared. You must switch OFF your rear fog lights because

Mark one answer

- [x] they use a lot of power from the battery
- [x] they make your brake lights less clear
- [x] they will cause dazzle in your rear view mirrors
- [x] they may not be properly adjusted

Answer

[x] **they make your brake lights less clear**

It is essential that the traffic behind is given a clear warning when you brake. As the rear fog lights could be mistaken for brake lights, following drivers will not be able to detect whether you are applying the brakes. Switch off your fog lights as the visibility improves.

Question 8.59

Front and rear fog lights MUST be

Mark one answer

- [ ] connected to an audible warning signal
- [ ] used outside built up areas only
- [ ] switched off in night-time fog
- [ ] switched off if visibility is not seriously reduced

Answer

 switched off if visibility is not seriously reduced

They can be misleading for other road users and can dazzle in clear weather.

Question 8.60

You are driving with your front fog lights switched on. Earlier fog has now cleared. What should you do?

Mark one answer

- [ ] Leave them on if other drivers have their lights on
- [ ] Switch them off as long as visibility remains good
- [ ] Flash them to warn oncoming traffic that it is foggy
- [ ] Drive with them on instead of your headlights

Answer

 Switch them off as long as visibility remains good

Switch off your fog lights if the weather improves, but be prepared to use them again if visibility reduces to less than 100 metres (328 feet).

Question 8.61

While you are driving in fog, it becomes necessary to use front fog lights. You should

Mark one answer

- [ ] only turn them on in heavy traffic conditions
- [ ] remember not to use them on motorways
- [ ] only use them at night
- [ ] remember to switch them off as visibility improves

Answer

✗ **remember to switch them off as visibility improves**

It is an offence to have your fog lights on in conditions other than seriously reduced visibility, i.e., less than 100 metres (328 feet).

Question 8.62

You have to park on the road in fog. You should

Mark one answer

- [ ] leave sidelights on
- [ ] leave dipped headlights and fog lights on
- [ ] leave dipped headlights on
- [ ] leave main beam headlights on

Answer

✗ **leave sidelights on**

If you have to park your vehicle in foggy conditions it's important that it can be seen by other road users. Try to find a place to park off the road. If this isn't possible, leave it facing in the same direction as the traffic flow. Make sure that your lights are clean and that you leave your sidelights on.

Question 8.63

On a foggy day you unavoidably have to park your car on the road. You should

Mark one answer

- [ ] leave your headlights on
- [ ] leave your fog lights on
- [ ] leave your sidelights on
- [ ] leave your hazard lights on

Answer

✗ **leave your sidelights on**

Ensure that your vehicle can be seen by other traffic. If possible, park your car off the road in a car park or driveway to avoid the extra risk to other road users.

The best place to park your motorcycle is

Mark one answer

- ☒ on soft tarmac
- ☒ on bumpy ground
- ☒ on grass
- ☒ on firm, level ground

Answer

☒ on firm, level ground

Parking your machine on soft ground might cause the stand to sink and the bike to fall over. The ground should be firm and level to ensure that the bike is stable. If possible, park your machine off the road.

You are driving on a motorway in fog. The left-hand edge of the motorway can be identified by reflective studs. What colour are they?

Mark one answer

- ☒ Green
- ☒ Amber
- ☒ Red
- ☒ White

Answer

☒ Red

Be especially careful if you're driving on a motorway in fog. You must be able to stop well within the distance that you can see to be clear. Keep in the left-hand lane. Reflective studs are used on motorways to help you in poor visibility. The studs are coloured so that you'll know which lane you're in and where slip roads join or leave the motorway.

When riding in windy conditions, you should

Mark one answer

- ☒ stay close to large vehicles
- ☒ keep your speed up
- ☒ keep your speed down
- ☒ stay close to the gutter

Answer

☒ keep your speed down

Strong winds can blow motorcycles off course and even across the road. In windy conditions you need to

- slow down
- avoid riding on exposed roads
- watch for gaps in buildings and hedges, where you may be affected by a sudden gust of wind.

Question 8.67

In normal riding your position on the road should be

Mark one answer

- [ ] about a foot from the kerb
- [ ] about central in your lane
- [ ] on the right of your lane
- [ ] near the centre of the road

Answer

✗ about central in your lane

If you're riding a motorcycle it's very important to ride where other road users can see you. In normal weather you should ride in the centre of your lane. This will

- help you to be seen in the mirror of the vehicle in front
- avoid uneven road surfaces in the gutter
- allow others to overtake on the right if they wish.

Question 8.68

Should lights be used when travelling at night on a well lit motorway?

Mark one answer

- [ ] Yes, but only sidelights are needed
- [ ] Yes, dipped headlights are needed
- [ ] No, unless the weather is bad
- [ ] No, lights are not needed

Answer

✗ Yes, dipped headlights are needed

Due to the higher speeds on a motorway you must ensure that your vehicle can be seen much earlier. Some motorways are only lit in parts, throwing you into a pool of darkness when you drive onto an unlit stretch.

Question 8.69

You are driving on a well-lit motorway at night. You must

Mark one answer

- [ ] use only your sidelights
- [ ] always use your headlights
- [ ] always use rear fog lights
- [ ] use headlights only in bad weather

Answer

✗ always use your headlights

If you're driving on a motorway at night you must always use your headlights, even if the road is well lit. The vehicles in front must be able to see you in their mirrors.

Question 8.70

You are driving on a motorway at night. You MUST have your headlights switched on unless

Mark one answer

- ☒ there are vehicles close in front of you
- ☒ you are travelling below 50 mph
- ☒ the motorway is lit
- ☒ your vehicle is broken down on the hard shoulder

Answer

☒ **your vehicle is broken down on the hard shoulder**

Always use your headlights at night on a motorway unless you're stopped on the hard shoulder. If you break down and have to stop on the hard shoulder, switch off your headlights. Leave the sidelights on so that other road users can see your vehicle or machine.

Question 8.71

You are travelling on a motorway at night with other vehicles just ahead of you. Which lights should you have on?

Mark one answer

- ☒ Front fog lights
- ☒ Main beam headlights
- ☒ Sidelights only
- ☒ Dipped headlights

Answer

☒ **Dipped headlights**

If you're driving or riding behind other traffic at night on the motorway

- leave a two-second time gap
- dip your headlights.

Full beam will dazzle the driver ahead. Your light beam should fall short of the vehicle in front.

Question 8.72

Which TWO of the following are correct? When overtaking at night you should

Mark two answers

- ☒ wait until a bend so that you can see the oncoming headlights
- ☒ sound your horn twice before moving out
- ☒ be careful because you can see less
- ☒ beware of bends in the road ahead
- ☒ put headlights on full beam

Answers

☒ **be careful because you can see less**
☒ **beware of bends in the road ahead**

Only overtake the vehicle in front if it's really necessary. At night the risks are increased due to the poor visibility. Don't overtake if there's a possibility of

- road junctions
- bends ahead
- the brow of a bridge or hill, except on a dual carriageway
- pedestrian crossings
- double white lines ahead
- vehicles changing direction
- any other potential hazard.

Question 8.73

You are overtaking a car at night. You must be sure that

Mark one answer

- [x] you flash your headlamps before overtaking
- [x] your rear fog lights are switched on
- [x] you have switched your lights to full beam before overtaking
- [x] you do not dazzle other road users

Answer

[x] **you do not dazzle other road users**

If you wish to overtake at night, ensure that your lights don't reflect in the mirror of the car in front. Wait until you've overtaken before switching to full beam.

Question 8.74

When riding at night you should

Mark two answers

- [x] wear fluorescent clothing
- [x] ride closer to the vehicle in front
- [x] keep your goggles or visor clean
- [x] ride just left of centre
- [x] use your headlights

Answers

[x] **keep your goggles or visor clean**

[x] **use your headlights**

Always make sure that you can see clearly and that other road users can see you. Make sure that your visor or goggles don't have any scratches which might distort your view or cause dazzle. Wearing bright clothing is a good idea, but remember, only reflective clothing will adequately show up at night.

Question 8.75

You are travelling at night. You are dazzled by headlights coming towards you. You should

Mark one answer

- [x] pull down your sun visor
- [x] slow down or stop
- [x] switch on your main beam headlights
- [x] put your hand over your eyes

Answer

[x] **slow down or stop**

If you're driving at night there will be extra hazards to deal with. The lights of oncoming vehicles can often distract. If you're dazzled by them don't

- close your eyes
- flash your headlights. This will only distract the other driver too.

DSA THEORY TEST for car drivers and motorcyclists

Question 8.76

You are dazzled by oncoming headlights when driving at night. What should you do?

Mark one answer

- ☒ Slow down or stop
- ☒ Brake hard
- ☒ Drive faster past the oncoming car
- ☒ Flash your lights

Answer

☒ **Slow down or stop**

Let your eyes re-adjust. Speed and distance are more difficult to judge at night. You won't be able to see as far as in daylight, so less information will be available. Don't take risks, especially if you're considering overtaking the vehicle in front.

Question 8.77

You are parking on a two-way road at night. The speed limit is 40 mph. You should park on the

Mark one answer

- ☒ left with sidelights on
- ☒ left with no lights on
- ☒ right with sidelights on
- ☒ right with dipped headlights on

Answer

☒ **left with sidelights on**

On a two-way road you may only park at night without lights on

- if the road has a speed limit of 30 mph or less
- you're at least 10 metres (32 feet) away from a junction
- if you're facing in the direction of the traffic flow.

Question 8.78

You are on a narrow road at night. A slower-moving vehicle ahead has been signalling right for some time. What should you do?

Mark one answer

- ☒ Overtake on the left
- ☒ Flash your headlights before overtaking
- ☒ Signal right and sound your horn
- ☒ Wait for the signal to be cancelled before overtaking

Answer

☒ **Wait for the signal to be cancelled before overtaking**

If the vehicle in front has been indicating right for some time, but has made no attempt to turn, wait for the signal to be cancelled. The other driver may have misjudged the distance to the road junction or there might be a hidden hazard.

A rumble device is designed to

Mark two answers

- [ ] give directions
- [ ] prevent cattle escaping
- [ ] alert drivers to low tyre pressure
- [ ] alert drivers to a hazard
- [ ] encourage drivers to reduce speed

Answers

- ✗ **alert drivers to a hazard**
- ✗ **encourage drivers to reduce speed**

A rumble device is usually raised markings or strips on the road's surface. These strips are in places where traffic has constantly ignored warning or restriction signs. They're there for a good reason. Slow down and be ready to deal with a hazard.

Which TWO are correct? The passing places on a single-track road are

Mark two answers

- [ ] for taking a rest from driving
- [ ] to pull into if an oncoming vehicle wants to proceed
- [ ] for stopping and checking your route
- [ ] to turn the car around in, if you are lost
- [ ] to pull into if the car behind wants to overtake

Answers

- ✗ **to pull into if an oncoming vehicle wants to proceed**
- ✗ **to pull into if the car behind wants to overtake**

If you're driving on a single-track road be prepared to pull over and let other road users pass. There are passing places to enable you to do this. These shouldn't be used for parking or turning your car around.

You see a vehicle coming towards you on a single-track road. You should

Mark one answer

- [ ] reverse back to the main road
- [ ] do an emergency stop
- [ ] stop at a passing place
- [ ] put on your hazard warning lights

Answer

- ✗ **stop at a passing place**

You must take extra care when driving on single-track roads. You may not be able to see around bends due to high hedges or fences. Drive with caution and expect to meet oncoming vehicles around the next bend. If you do, pull over and stop in or opposite a passing place.

DSA THEORY TEST for car drivers and motorcyclists

Question 8.82

Your motorcycle is parked on a two-way road. You should get on from the

Mark one answer

- [ ] right and apply the rear brake
- [ ] left and leave the brakes alone
- [ ] left and apply the front brake
- [ ] right and leave the brakes alone

Answer

✗ left and apply the front brake

When you get onto a motorcycle you should

- get on from the left side to avoid putting yourself in danger from passing traffic
- apply the front brake to prevent the machine rolling either forwards or backwards.

Question 8.83

When may you wait in a box junction?

Mark one answer

- [ ] When you are stationary in a queue of traffic
- [ ] When approaching a pelican crossing
- [ ] When approaching a zebra crossing
- [ ] When oncoming traffic prevents you turning right

Answer

✗ When oncoming traffic prevents you turning right

The purpose of this road marking is to keep the junction clear by preventing traffic from stopping in the path of crossing traffic. If there is already a vehicle waiting to turn right you're free to enter behind it and wait to turn right.

Question 8.84

Which of the following may apply when dealing with this hazard?

Mark four answers

- [×] It could be more difficult in winter
- [×] Use a low gear and drive slowly
- [×] Use a high gear to prevent wheelspin
- [×] Test your brakes afterwards
- [×] Always switch on fog lamps
- [×] There may be a depth gauge

Answers

- [×] **It could be more difficult in winter**
- [×] **Use a low gear and drive slowly**
- [×] **Test your brakes afterwards**
- [×] **There may be a depth gauge**

During the winter the stream is likely to flood. It is also possible that, in extreme weather, it could ice over. Assess the situation carefully before you drive through. If you drive a vehicle with limited ground clearance you will have to be extra cautious.

Question 8.85

Which of these plates normally appear with this road sign?

Mark one answer

- [×] Humps for ¹₂ mile
- [×] Hump Bridge
- [×] Low Bridge
- [×] Soft Verge

Answer

- [×] 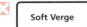 Humps for ¹₂ mile

These are in place to slow down the traffic. You should be aware that they are in places where there are often pedestrians, such as

- shopping areas
- near schools
- residential areas.

Watch out for people close to the kerb or crossing the road.

Question 8.86

How should a scooter be left when parking for some time in a town centre?

Mark three answers

- [ ] On firm and level ground
- [ ] By using the side stand leaning over the kerb
- [ ] On the centre stand if fitted
- [ ] Secure and with the fuel tap off
- [ ] On any very wide pavement

Answers

- ❌ On firm and level ground
- ❌ On the centre stand if fitted
- ❌ Secure and with the fuel tap off

When parking always try to park

- on firm level ground
- with the fuel tap turned off.

You should always secure your vehicle using any steering lock or immobiliser fitted by the manufacturer. An additional visible lock that helps to deter thieves is recommended.

SECTION 9 · MOTORWAY RULES

This section looks at motorway rules.

The questions will ask you about

- speed limits
- lane discipline
- stopping
- lighting
- parking.

Question 9.1

Which of the following CAN travel on a motorway?

Mark one answer

- ☒ Cyclists
- ☒ Vans
- ☒ Farm tractors
- ☒ Learner drivers

Answer

☒ **Vans**

Motorways are designed to help traffic travel quickly. Traffic can only travel safely at high speed if the road is clear. Any slow-moving road user would be a danger to themselves and other traffic. For this reason there are restrictions on which vehicles can use the motorway.

Question 9.2

As a provisional licence-holder you should not drive a car

Mark one answer

- ☒ over 50 mph
- ☒ at night
- ☒ on the motorway
- ☒ with passengers in rear seats

Answer

☒ **on the motorway**

When you've passed your practical test ask your instructor to take you for a lesson on the motorway. You'll need to get used to the speed of traffic and learn how to deal with multiple lanes.

Question 9.3

Which FOUR of these must not use motorways?

Mark four answers

- ☒ Learner car drivers
- ☒ Motorcycles over 50 cc
- ☒ Double-decker buses
- ☒ Farm tractors
- ☒ Horse riders
- ☒ Cyclists

Answers

- ☒ **Learner car drivers**
- ☒ **Farm tractors**
- ☒ **Horse riders**
- ☒ **Cyclists**

In addition, motorways MUST NOT be used by

- pedestrians
- motorcycles under 50 cc
- certain slow-moving vehicles, without permission
- invalid carriages weighing no more than 254 kg (560 lbs).

Question 9.4

Which FOUR of these must NOT use motorways?

Mark four answers

- ☒ Learner car drivers
- ☒ Motorcycles over 50 cc
- ☒ Double-deck buses
- ☒ Farm tractors
- ☒ Learner motorcyclists
- ☒ Cyclists

Answers

- ✖ **Learner car drivers**
- ✖ **Farm tractors**
- ✖ **Learner motorcyclists**
- ✖ **Cyclists**

When you've passed your practical test it's a good idea to have some lessons on motorways. Statistically, motorways are safer than other roads, but they have rules that you need to know before you venture out for the first time. Check with your instructor about this.

Question 9.5

A motorcycle is not allowed on a motorway if it has an engine size smaller than

Mark one answer

- ☒ 50 cc
- ☒ 125 cc
- ☒ 150 cc
- ☒ 250 cc

Answer

- ✖ **50 cc**

The restricted speed of a small machine will cause a hazard to other motorway users. If you're riding a machine with a small engine, choose another route.

Question 9.6

To ride on a motorway your motorcycle must be

Mark one answer

- ☒ 50 cc or more
- ☒ 100 cc or more
- ☒ 125 cc or more
- ☒ 250 cc or more

Answer

- ✖ **50 cc or more**

Traffic on motorways travels at high speeds. Vehicles need to be capable of keeping up with the flow of traffic. For this reason low-powered vehicles are prohibited.

Question 9.7

Why is it particularly important to carry out a check on your vehicle before making a long motorway journey?

Mark one answer

☒ You will have to do more harsh braking on motorways

☒ Motorway service stations do not deal with breakdowns

☒ The road surface will wear down the tyres faster

☒ Continuous high speeds may increase the risk of your vehicle breaking down

Answer

✘ **Continuous high speeds may increase the risk of your vehicle breaking down**

Before you start your journey make sure that your vehicle can cope with the demands of high-speed driving. Before starting a motorway journey check your vehicle's

• oil

• water

• tyres.

Plan your rest stops if you're travelling a long way.

Question 9.8

Immediately after joining a motorway you should normally

Mark one answer

☒ try to overtake

☒ readjust your mirrors

☒ position your vehicle in the centre lane

☒ keep in the left lane

Answer

✘ **keep in the left lane**

Give yourself time to get used to the higher speeds of motorway traffic.

Question 9.9

You are joining a motorway. Why is it important to make full use of the slip road?

Mark one answer

☒ Because there is space available to reverse if you need to

☒ To allow you direct access to the overtaking lanes

☒ To build up a speed similar to traffic on the motorway

☒ Because you can continue on the hard shoulder

Answer

✘ **To build up a speed similar to traffic on the motorway**

Try to join the motorway without affecting the progress of the traffic already travelling on it. At busy times this could also mean slowing down to merge into slow-moving traffic

Question 9.10

You are joining a motorway from a slip road on the left. You should

Mark one answer

- [X] adjust your speed to the speed of the traffic on the motorway
- [X] accelerate as quickly as you can and ride straight out
- [X] ride onto the hard shoulder until a gap appears
- [X] expect drivers on the motorway to give way to you

Question 9.11

When joining a motorway you must always

Mark one answer

- [X] use the hard shoulder
- [X] stop at the end of the acceleration lane
- [X] come to a stop before joining the motorway
- [X] give way to traffic already on the motorway

Answer

✗ adjust your speed to the speed of the traffic on the motorway

Give way to the traffic already on the motorway and join where there's a suitable gap in the traffic. Try to avoid stopping at the end of the slip road. This might not be avoidable, however, if the motorway is exceptionally busy and there isn't a clear gap in the traffic.

Answer

✗ give way to traffic already on the motorway

The traffic may be travelling at high speed so you should adjust your speed and emerge when it's safe to do so.

Question 9.12

You have just joined a motorway. Which lane would you normally stay in to get used to the higher speeds?

Mark one answer

- ☒ Hard shoulder
- ☒ Right-hand lane
- ☒ Centre lane
- ☒ Left-hand lane

Answer

 Left-hand lane

Give yourself time to judge and adjust to the faster speed of the traffic already on the motorway.

Question 9.13

You are riding on a motorway. Unless signs show otherwise you must NOT exceed

Mark one answer

- ☒ 50 mph
- ☒ 60 mph
- ☒ 70 mph
- ☒ 80 mph

Answer

✗ **70 mph**

Ride in accordance with the conditions. Bad weather, heavy traffic or roadworks will limit your speed.

Question 9.14

What is the national speed limit for cars and motorcycles in the centre lane of a three-lane motorway?

Mark one answer

- ☒ 40 mph
- ☒ 50 mph
- ☒ 60 mph
- ☒ 70 mph

Answer

✗ **70 mph**

Unless otherwise indicated, the speed limit for the motorway applies to all the lanes. Be on the lookout for any indication of speed limit changes due to roadworks or traffic flow control.

Question 9.15

What is the national speed limit on motorways for cars and motorcycles?

Mark one answer

- [ ] 30 mph
- [ ] 50 mph
- [ ] 60 mph
- [ ] 70 mph

Answer

 70 mph

Driving or riding at the national speed limit doesn't allow you to hog the outside lane. Always keep to the nearside whenever possible. When leaving the motorway, always adjust your speed in good time to deal with

- bends or curves on the slip road
- traffic queuing at roundabouts.

Question 9.16

You are towing a trailer on a motorway. What is your maximum speed limit?

Mark one answer

- [ ] 40 mph
- [ ] 50 mph
- [ ] 60 mph
- [ ] 70 mph

Answer

 60 mph

Don't forget that you're towing a trailer. If you're towing a small, light trailer it won't reduce your vehicle's performance by very much. Strong winds or buffeting from large vehicles might cause it to snake from side to side. Be aware of your speed and don't exceed the lower limit imposed.

Question 9.17

You are driving a car on a motorway. Unless signs show otherwise you must NOT exceed

Mark one answer

- [ ] 50 mph
- [ ] 60 mph
- [ ] 70 mph
- [ ] 80 mph

Answer

✖ **70 mph**

The national speed limit for a car or motorcycle on the motorway is 70 mph. Lower speed limits may be in force so look out for the signs. There might be a variable speed limit in operation to control a very busy motorway. The speed limit may change depending on the volume of traffic. There may be roadworks requiring a low speed

Question 9.18

On a three-lane motorway which lane should you use for normal driving?

Mark one answer

- [ ] Left
- [ ] Right
- [ ] Centre
- [ ] Either the right or centre

Answer

 Left

On a three-lane motorway you should travel in the left-hand lane unless you're overtaking. This applies regardless of the speed you're travelling at.

Question 9.19

A basic rule when driving on motorways is

Mark one answer

- [ ] use the lane that has least traffic
- [ ] keep to the left lane unless overtaking
- [ ] overtake on the side that is clearest
- [ ] try to keep above 50 mph to prevent congestion

Answer

 keep to the left lane unless overtaking

When you've overtaken, move back into the left-hand lane as soon as it's safe to do so. Don't cut across in front of the vehicle that you're overtaking.

Question 9.20

On a three-lane motorway why should you normally ride in the left lane?

Mark one answer

- ☒ The left lane is only for lorries and motorcycles
- ☒ The left lane should only be used by smaller vehicles
- ☒ The lanes on the right are for overtaking
- ☒ Motorcycles are not allowed in the far right lane

Answer

☒ The lanes on the right are for overtaking

Change lanes only if necessary. When you do change lanes observe, signal and manoeuvre in good time. Always remember your 'lifesaver' check. This is a final, quick rearward glance before you manoeuvre.

Question 9.21

You are driving on a three-lane motorway at 70 mph. There is no traffic ahead. Which lane should you use?

Mark one answer

- ☒ Any lane
- ☒ Middle lane
- ☒ Right lane
- ☒ Left lane

Answer

☒ Left lane

Use the left-hand lane if it's free, regardless of the speed you're travelling at.

Question 9.22

The left-hand lane on a three-lane motorway is for use by

Mark one answer

- ☒ any vehicle
- ☒ large vehicles only
- ☒ emergency vehicles only
- ☒ slow vehicles only

Answer

☒ any vehicle

On a motorway all traffic should use the left-hand lane unless overtaking. If you need to overtake use the centre or right-hand lanes.

Make sure that you move back to the left-hand lane when you've finished overtaking. Don't stay in the middle or right-hand lanes if the left-hand lane is free.

Question 9.23

The left-hand lane of a motorway should be used for

Mark one answer

- [ ] breakdowns and emergencies only
- [ ] overtaking slower traffic in the other lanes
- [ ] slow vehicles only
- [ ] normal driving

Answer

✖ **normal driving**

You should keep to the left lane whenever possible for normal driving.

Question 9.24

What is the right-hand lane used for on a three-lane motorway?

Mark one answer

- [ ] Emergency vehicles only
- [ ] Overtaking
- [ ] Vehicles towing trailers
- [ ] Coaches only

Answer

✖ **Overtaking**

You should keep to the left and only use the right-hand lane if you're passing slower-moving traffic.

Which of these IS NOT allowed to travel in the right-hand lane of a three-lane motorway?

Mark one answer

- ☒ A small delivery van
- ☒ A motorcycle
- ☒ A vehicle towing a trailer
- ☒ A motorcycle and side-car

Answer

☒ **A vehicle towing a trailer**

A vehicle with a trailer is restricted to 60 mph. For this reason it isn't allowed in the right-hand lane as it might hold up faster-moving traffic that wishes to overtake in that lane.

Question 9.26

For what reason may you use the right-hand lane of a motorway?

Mark one answer

- ☒ For keeping out of the way of lorries
- ☒ For driving at more than 70 mph
- ☒ For turning right
- ☒ For overtaking other vehicles

Answer

☒ **For overtaking other vehicles**

The right-hand lanes of the motorway are for overtaking. Sometimes you may be directed into a right-hand lane as a result of roadworks or an accident. Be guided by the signs or police directing the traffic.

Question 9.27

On motorways you should never overtake on the left UNLESS

Mark one answer

- ☒ you can see well ahead that the hard shoulder is clear
- ☒ the traffic in the right-hand lane is signalling right
- ☒ you warn drivers behind by signalling left
- ☒ there is a queue of traffic to your right that is moving more slowly

Answer

☒ **there is a queue of traffic to your right that is moving more slowly**

Only overtake on the left if traffic is moving slowly in queues and the traffic on the right is moving slower.

Question 9.28

On a motorway you may ONLY stop on the hard shoulder

Mark one answer

- ☒ in an emergency
- ☒ If you feel tired and need to rest
- ☒ if you accidentally go past the exit that you wanted to take
- ☒ to pick up a hitch-hiker

Question 9.29

You are travelling on a motorway. You decide you need a rest. You should

Mark two answers

- ☒ stop on the hard shoulder
- ☒ go to a service area
- ☒ park on the slip road
- ☒ park on the central reservation
- ☒ leave at the next exit

Answer

☒ **in an emergency**

Don't stop on the hard shoulder to

- have a rest or a picnic
- pick up hitch-hikers
- answer a mobile phone
- check a road map.

Never reverse along the hard shoulder if you accidentally go past the exit you wanted.

Answers

☒ **go to a service area**
☒ **leave at the next exit**

Stopping on the motorway in any circumstances other than an emergency or traffic queue will cause a major hazard. You should plan your journey so that you have a rest about every two hours. Stop where you are able to get out of the car for some fresh air and something to eat and drink.

Question 9.30

You are driving on a motorway. The car ahead shows its hazard lights for a short time. This tells you that

Mark one answer

☒ the driver wants you to overtake

☒ the other car is going to change lanes

☒ traffic ahead is slowing or stopping suddenly

☒ there is a police speed check up ahead

Answer

☒ **traffic ahead is slowing or stopping suddenly**

There may be an accident or queuing due to roadworks. Look well ahead, not just at the car in front, and you'll get an earlier warning of any hazard.

Question 9.31

You are driving on a motorway. You have to slow down quickly due to a hazard. You should

Mark one answer

☒ switch on your hazard lights

☒ switch on your headlights

☒ sound your horn

☒ flash your headlights

Answer

☒ **switch on your hazard lights**

The traffic behind you will be given an extra warning, in addition to your brake lights. Switch them off again as the queue forms behind you.

Question 9.32

Which vehicles are normally fitted with amber flashing beacons on the roof?

Mark two answers

☒ Doctor's car

☒ Bomb disposal team

☒ Blood transfusion team

☒ Breakdown recovery vehicles

☒ Coastguard

☒ Maintenance vehicles

Answers

☒ **Breakdown recovery vehicles**

☒ **Maintenance vehicles**

These vehicles are often carrying out tasks on the hard shoulder. If you see an amber beacon ahead, be prepared in case you have to give them more room by moving into the middle lane.

Question 9.33

You break down on a motorway. You need to call for help. Why may it be better to use an emergency roadside telephone rather than a mobile phone?

Mark one answer

- [ ] It connects you to a local garage
- [ ] Using a mobile phone will distract other drivers
- [ ] It allows easy location by the emergency services
- [ ] Mobile phones do not work on motorways

Answer

- [x] **It allows easy location by the emergency services**

On a motorway it is best to use a roadside emergency telephone so that the emergency services are able to locate you easily.

Question 9.34

Your vehicle breaks down on the hard shoulder of a motorway. You decide to use your mobile phone to call for help. You should

Mark one answer

- [ ] stand at the rear of the vehicle while making the call
- [ ] try to repair the vehicle yourself
- [ ] get out of the vehicle by the right hand door
- [ ] check your location from the marker posts on the left

Answer

- [x] **check your location from the marker posts on the left**

In the case of an emergency, time can be of the essence. The emergency services need to know your exact location. Look at the number on the marker posts on the edge of the hard shoulder before you phone, and tell the services this number; it will help them to locate you. Be ready to describe where you are, for example, by reference to the last junction you passed.

You get a puncture on the motorway. You manage to get your vehicle onto the hard shoulder. You should

Mark one answer

☒ change the wheel yourself immediately

☒ use the emergency telephone and call for assistance

☒ try to wave down another vehicle for help

☒ only change the wheel if you have a passenger to help you

Answer

✖ **use the emergency telephone and call for assistance**

Due to the danger from passing traffic you shouldn't attempt repairs on the hard shoulder, especially if you have to change an offside wheel.

The emergency telephones on a motorway are connected to the

Mark one answer

☒ ambulance service

☒ police control

☒ fire brigade

☒ breakdown service

Answer

✖ **police control**

The controller will ask you

- the make and colour of your vehicle
- whether you are a member of an emergency breakdown service
- the number shown on the emergency telephone casing
- whether you are travelling alone.

Question 9.37

How should you use the emergency telephone on a motorway?

Mark one answer

- [ ] Stay close to the carriageway
- [ ] Face the oncoming traffic
- [ ] Keep your back to the traffic
- [ ] Keep your head in the kiosk

Answer

 Face the oncoming traffic

Traffic is passing you at speed. The draught from a large lorry could unsteady you, so be prepared. By facing the oncoming traffic you can spot this in advance, as well as other hazards approaching.

Question 9.38

What should you use the hard shoulder of a motorway for?

Mark one answer

- [ ] Stopping in an emergency
- [ ] Leaving the motorway
- [ ] Stopping when you are tired
- [ ] Joining the motorway

Answer

 Stopping in an emergency

Don't use the hard shoulder for stopping other than for emergencies. Drive to the next exit or service station if you're able to do so safely.

Question 9.39

After a breakdown you need to rejoin the main carriageway of a motorway from the hard shoulder. You should

Mark one answer

[X] move out onto the carriageway then build up your speed

[X] move out onto the carriageway using your hazard lights

[X] gain speed on the hard shoulder before moving out onto the carriageway

[X] wait on the hard shoulder until someone flashes their headlights at you

Answer

[X] **gain speed on the hard shoulder before moving out onto the carriageway**

Wait for a safe gap in the traffic before you move out. Indicate your intention; but don't force your way into the traffic

Question 9.40

A crawler lane on a motorway is found

Mark one answer

[X] on a steep gradient

[X] before a service area

[X] before a junction

[X] along the hard shoulder

Answer

 on a steep gradient

There are likely to be slow moving large vehicles which might slow the progress of other traffic. This extra lane is provided for these vehicles, enabling the faster moving traffic to flow. If the crawler lane is free then use it as you would a normal left-hand lane.

Question 9.41

Your vehicle has broken down on a motorway. You are not able to stop on the hard shoulder. What should you do FIRST?

Mark one answer

[X] Switch on your hazard warning lights

[X] Stop following traffic and ask for help

[X] Attempt to repair your vehicle quickly

[X] Place a warning triangle in the road

Answer

 Switch on your hazard warning lights

Use your hazard warning lights to warn others. Don't try to repair the vehicle.

Question 9.42

When may you stop on a motorway?

Mark three answers

- ☒ If you have to read a map
- ☒ When you are tired and need a rest
- ☒ If red lights show above every lane
- ☒ When told to by the police
- ☒ If a child in the car feels ill
- ☒ In an emergency or a breakdown

Answers

- ☒ **If red lights show above every lane**
- ☒ **When told to by the police**
- ☒ **In an emergency or a breakdown**

You may only stop on the carriageway of a motorway

- when told to do so by the police
- when flashing red lights show above every lane
- in a traffic jam
- in an emergency or breakdown.

Question 9.43

You are allowed to stop on a motorway when you

Mark one answer

- ☒ need to walk and get fresh air
- ☒ wish to pick up hitch-hikers
- ☒ are told to do so by flashing red lights
- ☒ need to use a mobile telephone

Answer

- ☒ **are told to do so by flashing red lights**

If any of the other lanes show a green arrow you may move into that lane and continue if it is safe to do so. If there are red lights above every lane you must stop.

Question 9.44

You are driving on a motorway. There are red flashing lights above every lane. You must

Mark one answer

- ☒ pull onto the hard shoulder
- ☒ slow down and watch for further signals
- ☒ leave at the next exit
- ☒ stop and wait

Answer

- ☒ **stop and wait**

Flashing red lights above every lane mean you must not go on any further. You'll also see a red cross illuminated. Stop and wait. Don't

- change lanes
- continue
- pull onto the hard shoulder (unless in an emergency).

Question 9.45

You are driving in the right-hand lane on a motorway. You see these overhead signs. This means

Answer

 move to the left and reduce your speed to 50 mph

You must obey this sign. There might not be any visible signs of a problem ahead. However, there might be queuing traffic, fog or another hazard ahead.

Mark one answer

☒ move to the left and reduce your speed to 50 mph

☒ there are roadworks 50 metres (55 yards) ahead

☒ use the hard shoulder until you have passed the hazard

☒ leave the motorway at the next exit

Question 9.46

The minimum safe time gap to keep between you and the vehicle in front in good conditions is at least

Mark one answer

☒ four seconds

☒ one second

☒ three seconds

☒ two seconds

Answer

 two seconds

Driving too close to the vehicle in front can cause accidents, potentially involving many vehicles and causing serious injury. As you drive at higher speeds you must increase your separation distance from the car in front. One way to judge this is to use the 'two-second rule'. Pick an object some distance ahead, such as a lamppost or a bridge. As the vehicle in front passes it begin to say 'Only a fool breaks the Two-Second Rule.' If you pass the object before you finish saying it, you're too close. Drop back and try again.

DSA THEORY TEST for car drivers and motorcyclists

Question 9.47

When driving through a contraflow system on a motorway you should

Mark one answer

- [ ] ensure that you do not exceed 30 mph, for safety
- [ ] keep a good distance from the vehicle ahead, for safety
- [ ] switch lanes to keep the traffic flowing
- [ ] drive close to the vehicle ahead to reduce queues

Answer

✗ **keep a good distance from the vehicle ahead, for safety**

There's likely to be a speed restriction in force. Keep to it. Don't

- switch lanes
- drive too close to other traffic.

There will be no permanent barrier between you and the traffic coming towards you. Be extra cautious.

Question 9.48

You are intending to leave the motorway at the next exit. Before you reach the exit you should normally position your vehicle

Mark one answer

- [ ] in the middle lane
- [ ] in the left-hand lane
- [ ] on the hard shoulder
- [ ] in any lane

Answer

✗ **in the left-hand lane**

You'll see the first sign one mile from the exit. If you're travelling at 60 miles an hour in the right-hand lane you'll only have about 50 seconds before you reach the countdown markers. There's another sign at the half-mile point. Think about what you need to do to be in the left-hand lane in good time. Don't cut across traffic at the last moment.

What do these motorway signs show?

Answer

 They are countdown markers to the next exit

The exit from a motorway is indicated by countdown markers. These are positioned 90 metres (100 yards) apart, the first being 270 metres (300 yards) from the slip road. Try to get yourself into the left lane in good time.

Mark one answer

☒ They are countdown markers to a bridge

☒ They are distance markers to the next telephone

☒ They are countdown markers to the next exit

☒ They warn of a police control ahead

Question 9.50

At night, when leaving a well-lit motorway service area, you should

Mark one answer

☒ drive for some time using only your sidelights

☒ give your eyes time to adjust to the darkness

☒ switch on your interior light until your eyes adjust

☒ close your eyes for a moment before leaving the slip road

Answer

 give your eyes time to adjust to the darkness

You should have your eyesight checked regularly. If you can't see well at night it could be that your eyes are to blame. Night driving might show up a need for a check with an optician.

Question 9.51

You are driving on a motorway. By mistake, you go past the exit that you wanted to take. You should

Mark one answer

 carefully reverse on the hard shoulder

 carry on to the next exit

 carefully reverse in the left-hand lane

 make a U-turn at the next gap in the central reservation

Answer

✖ **carry on to the next exit**

Don't

• reverse anywhere

• make a U-turn. This is highly dangerous, as high-speed traffic might not be able to take evasive action.

Question 9.52

On a motorway the amber reflective studs can be found between

Mark one answer

 the hard shoulder and the carriageway

 the acceleration lane and the carriageway

 the central reservation and the carriageway

 each pair of the lanes

Answer

✖ **the central reservation and the carriageway**

On motorways reflective studs are fitted into the road to help you

• in the dark

• in conditions of poor visibility.

The reflective studs are coloured. These will help you to know which lane you're in and where slip roads join or leave the motorway.

What colour are the reflective studs between the lanes on a motorway?

Answer

 White

These are especially useful in bad weather when visibility is restricted. The light from your headlights is reflected back, highlighting the markings between the lanes.

Mark one answer

 Green

 Amber

 White

Red

You are driving on a three-lane motorway. There are red reflective studs on your left and white ones to your right. Where are you?

Answer

 In the left-hand lane

The colours of the reflective studs on the motorway and their locations are

- Red – between the hard shoulder and the carriageway.
- White – lane markings.
- Amber – between the edge of the carriageway and the central reservation.
- Green – along slip road exits and entrances.
- Bright Green/Yellow – roadworks and contraflow systems.

Mark one answer

In the right-hand lane

 In the middle lane

On the hard shoulder

 In the left-hand lane

Question 9.55

What colour are the reflective studs between a motorway and its slip road?

Mark one answer

- ☒ Amber
- ☒ White
- ☒ Green
- ☒ Red

Question 9.56

You are travelling on a motorway. What colour are the reflective studs on the left of the carriageway?

Mark one answer

- ☒ Green
- ☒ Red
- ☒ White
- ☒ Amber

Answer

 Green

These will help you when driving in conditions of poor visibility or in the dark.

Answer

 Red

When you have passed your practical test, ask your instructor about lessons on the motorway. Good professional instruction will help you to become a confident and safe motorway driver.

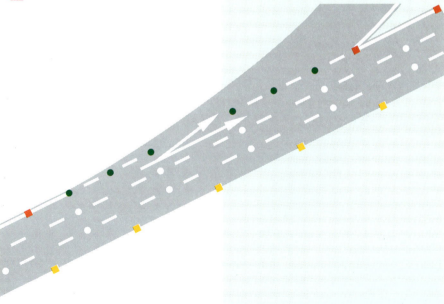

This section looks at rules of the road

The questions will ask you about

- speed limits
- lane discipline
- parking
- lighting.

You are riding slowly in a town centre. Before turning left you should glance over your left shoulder to

Mark one answer

- [ ] check for cyclists
- [ ] help keep your balance
- [ ] look for traffic signs
- [ ] check for potholes

Answer

 check for cyclists

When riding slowly you must remember cyclists. They can travel quickly and fit through surprisingly narrow spaces. Before you turn left in slow-moving traffic it's important to check that a cyclist isn't trying to overtake on your left.

You may drive over a footpath

Mark one answer

- [ ] to overtake slow-moving traffic
- [ ] when the pavement is very wide
- [ ] if no pedestrians are near
- [ ] to get into a property

Answer

 to get into a property

When you're crossing the pavement watch out for pedestrians and cyclists in both directions.

What is the meaning of this sign?

Mark one answer

- [ ] Local speed limit applies
- [ ] No waiting on the carriageway
- [ ] National speed limit applies
- [ ] No entry to vehicular traffic

Answer

 National speed limit applies

This sign doesn't tell you the speed limit in figures. You should know the speed limit for the type of road that you're on. Study your copy of *The Highway Code*.

Question 10.4

What is the national speed limit on a single-carriageway road for cars and motorcycles?

Mark one answer

- ☒ 70 mph
- ☒ 60 mph
- ☒ 50 mph
- ☒ 30 mph

Answer

☒ **60 mph**

Exceeding the speed limit is dangerous and can result in you receiving penalty points on your licence. It isn't worth it. Know the speed limit of the road that you're driving on by observing the road signs.

Question 10.5

What is the national speed limit for cars and motorcycles on a dual carriageway?

Mark one answer

- ☒ 30 mph
- ☒ 50 mph
- ☒ 60 mph
- ☒ 70 mph

Answer

☒ **70 mph**

Ensure that you know the speed limit for the road that you're driving on. The speed limit on a dual carriageway or motorway is 70 mph for cars and motorcycles, unless there are signs to indicate otherwise. The speed limits for different vehicles are listed in *The Highway Code*.

Question 10.6

A single carriageway road has this sign. What is the maximum permitted speed for a car towing a trailer?

Mark one answer

- ☒ 30 mph
- ☒ 40 mph
- ☒ 50 mph
- ☒ 60 mph

Answer

☒ **50 mph**

When towing trailers, speed limits are also lower on dual carriageways and motorways. On these roads vehicles towing a trailer are restricted to 60 mph.

Question 10.7

You are driving along a road that has no traffic signs. There are street lights. What is the speed limit?

Mark one answer

- [ ] 20 mph
- [ ] 30 mph
- [ ] 40 mph
- [ ] 60 mph

Answer

✗ 30 mph

If you aren't sure of the speed limit it can be indicated by the presence of street lights. If there is street lighting the speed limit will be 30 mph, unless otherwise indicated.

Question 10.8

There are no speed limit signs on the road. How is a 30 mph limit indicated?

Mark one answer

- [ ] By hazard warning lines
- [ ] By street lighting
- [ ] By pedestrian islands
- [ ] By double or single yellow lines

Answer

✗ By street lighting

This usually indicates a 30 mph speed limit when there are no signs to show other limits.

Question 10.9

Where you see street lights but no speed limit signs the limit is usually

Mark one answer

- [ ] 30 mph
- [ ] 40 mph
- [ ] 50 mph
- [ ] 60 mph

Answer

✗ 30 mph

If you are travelling faster than the limit, slow down before you reach the lights. Check your mirror and ease off the accelerator.

You see this sign ahead of you. It means

Mark one answer

 start to slow down to 30 mph after passing it

you are leaving the 30 mph speed limit area

do not exceed 30 mph after passing it

the minimum speed limit ahead is 30 mph

Answer

 do not exceed 30 mph after passing it

Adjust your speed in good time. Don't
* brake sharply
* wait until you're beyond the limit sign before slowing down.

If you see a 30 mph limit ahead it means

Mark one answer

 that the restriction applies only during the working day

that you must not exceed this speed

that it is a guide and you are allowed to drive 10% faster

that you must keep your speed up to 30 mph

Answer

X **that you must not exceed this speed**

Because the sign is round it gives you an order. You must obey it. In a built-up area there are many hazards that call for reduced speed, such as
* pedestrians
* cyclists
* junctions
* busy traffic situations.

Question 10.12

What does a speed limit sign like this mean?

Mark one answer

- [ ] It is safe to drive at the speed shown
- [ ] The speed shown is the advised maximum
- [ ] The speed shown allows for various road and weather conditions
- [ ] You must not exceed the speed shown

Answer

✖ **You must not exceed the speed shown**

Speed limit signs are there for a reason. There may be a large number of side roads. The lower speed limit makes emerging from these safer.

Question 10.13

You are towing a small caravan on a dual carriageway. You must not exceed

Mark one answer

- [ ] 50 mph
- [ ] 40 mph
- [ ] 70 mph
- [ ] 60 mph

Answer

✖ **60 mph**

Due to the increased weight and width of the combined vehicles you will need to plan well ahead. Be extra careful in wet or windy weather. Strong winds might cause the caravan to snake from side to side. The speed limit is reduced for vehicles towing trailers or caravans to lessen the risk of this.

Question 10.14

What does this sign mean?

Mark one answer

☒	Minimum speed 30 mph
☒	End of maximum speed
☒	End of minimum speed
☒	Maximum speed 30 mph

Answer

☒ End of minimum speed

A red slash through this sign indicates that the restriction has ended.

Question 10.15

You are driving along a street with parked vehicles on the left-hand side. For which THREE reasons should you keep your speed down?

Mark three answers

☒	So that oncoming traffic can see you more clearly
☒	You may set off car alarms
☒	Vehicles may be pulling out
☒	Drivers' doors may open
☒	Children may run out from between the vehicles

Answers

☒ Vehicles may be pulling out

☒ Drivers' doors may open

☒ Children may run out from between the vehicles

Care must be taken where there are parked vehicles in a built-up area. Beware of

- vehicles pulling out, especially motorcycles and cycles which are small and difficult to see
- pedestrians, especially children, who may run out from between cars
- drivers opening vehicle doors.

DSA THEORY TEST for car drivers and motorcyclists

Question 10.16

You meet an obstruction on your side of the road. You should

Mark one answer

- [ ] drive on; it is your right of way
- [ ] give way to oncoming traffic
- [ ] wave oncoming vehicles through
- [ ] accelerate to get past first

Answer

✗ give way to oncoming traffic

If you have to pass a parked vehicle on your side of the road, take care. Give way to oncoming traffic if there isn't enough room for you both to continue safely.

Question 10.17

There is a tractor ahead of you. You wish to overtake but you are NOT sure if it is safe to do so. You should

Mark one answer

- [ ] follow another overtaking vehicle through
- [ ] sound your horn to the slow vehicle to pull over
- [ ] speed through but flash your lights to oncoming traffic
- [ ] not overtake if you are in doubt

Answer

✗ not overtake if you are in doubt

Always ask yourself if you really need to overtake. Can you see well down the road? If the answer is no, DON'T GO.

Which three of the following are most likely to take an unusual course at roundabouts?

Mark three answers

☒ Horse riders

☒ Milk floats

☒ Delivery vans

☒ Long vehicles

☒ Estate cars

☒ Cyclists

Answers

☒ **Horse riders**

☒ **Long vehicles**

☒ **Cyclists**

Long vehicles might have to take a slightly different position when approaching the roundabout or going around it. This is to stop the rear of the vehicle cutting in and mounting the kerb. Horse riders and cyclists might also stay in the left-hand lane although they are turning right. Be aware of this and allow them room.

You are leaving your vehicle parked on a road. When may you leave the engine running?

Mark one answer

☒ If you will be parked for less than five minutes

☒ If the battery is flat

☒ When in a 20 mph zone

☒ Not on any occasion

Answer

☒ **Not on any occasion**

When you leave your vehicle parked on a road

- apply the handbrake
- switch off the engine
- make sure that there aren't any valuables visible
- shut all the windows
- lock the vehicle
- use an anti-theft device if you have one.

In which FOUR places must you NOT park or wait?

Mark four answers

☒ On a dual carriageway

☒ At a bus stop

☒ On the slope of a hill

☒ Opposite a traffic island

☒ In front of someone else's drive

☒ On the brow of a hill

Answers

☒ **At a bus stop**

☒ **Opposite a traffic island**

☒ **In front of someone else's drive**

☒ **On the brow of a hill**

Care and thought should be taken when parking your own vehicle. Don't park

- on a footpath, pavement or cycle track
- near a school entrance
- on the approach to a zebra crossing (except in an authorised parking place)
- opposite another parked vehicle.

Question 10.21

What is the nearest you may park your vehicle to a junction?

Mark one answer

- [ ] 10 metres (32 feet)
- [ ] 12 metres (39 feet)
- [ ] 15 metres (49 feet)
- [ ] 20 metres (66 feet)

Answer

✗ 10 metres (32 feet)

Don't park within 10 metres (32 feet) of a junction (unless in an authorized parking place) or

- where you would force other traffic to enter a tram lane
- where the kerb has been lowered to help wheelchair users
- in front of an entrance to a property
- where your vehicle might obstruct a tram.

Question 10.22

You are finding it difficult to find a parking place in a busy town. You can see there is space on the zigzag lines of a zebra crossing. Can you park there?

Mark one answer

- [ ] No, unless you stay with your car
- [ ] Yes, in order to drop off a passenger
- [ ] Yes, if you do not block people from crossing
- [ ] No, not in any circumstances

Answer

✗ No, not in any circumstances

It's an offence to park there. You will be causing an obstruction by obscuring the view of both pedestrians and drivers.

Question 10.23

In which TWO places must you NOT park?

Mark two answers

- [ ] Near a school entrance
- [ ] Near a police station
- [ ] In a side road
- [ ] At a bus stop
- [ ] In a one-way street

Answers

✗ Near a school entrance
✗ At a bus stop

It may be tempting to park where you shouldn't while you run a quick errand. Careless parking is a selfish act and could endanger other road users.

Question 10.24

In which THREE places must you NOT park your vehicle?

Mark three answers

- [ ] Near the brow of a hill
- [ ] At or near a bus stop
- [ ] Where there is no pavement
- [ ] Within 10 metres (32 feet) of a junction
- [ ] On a 40 mph road

Answers

- [x] **Near the brow of a hill**
- [x] **At or near a bus stop**
- [x] **Within 10 metres (32 feet) of a junction**

Other traffic will have to pull out to pass you. This might mean they have to use the other side of the road where there might be oncoming traffic.

Parking near a junction could restrict the view for emerging vehicles.

Question 10.25

On a clearway you must NOT stop

Mark one answer

- [ ] at any time
- [ ] when it is busy
- [ ] in the rush hour
- [ ] during daylight hours

Answer

- [x] **at any time**

Clearways are in place so that traffic can flow without the obstruction of parked vehicles. Just one parked vehicle will cause an obstruction for all other traffic. You should not even stop to pick up or set down passengers.

Question 10.26

You are driving on an urban clearway. You may stop only to

Mark one answer

- [ ] set down and pick up passengers
- [ ] use a mobile telephone
- [ ] ask for directions
- [ ] load or unload goods

Answer

- [x] **set down and pick up passengers**

These may be provided in built up areas and times of operation will be clearly signed. You should stop only for a time that is reasonable to pick up and set down passengers. You should make sure that you are not causing an obstruction for other traffic before you stop.

Question 10.27

You want to park and you see this sign. On the days and times shown you should

Mark one answer

☒ park in a bay and not pay

☒ park on yellow lines and pay

☒ park on yellow lines and not pay

☒ park in a bay and pay

Answer

✖ **park in a bay and pay**

Parking restrictions vary from town to town. Look at the signs carefully. Parking in the wrong place could cause an obstruction and you could be fined.

Question 10.28

What is the meaning of this sign?

Mark one answer

☒ No entry

☒ Waiting restrictions

☒ National speed limit

☒ School crossing patrol

Answer

✖ **Waiting restrictions**

Don't cause an obstruction by stopping or waiting where there are restrictions. You should know the meaning of road signs. Buy a copy of *Know Your Traffic Signs* (The Stationery Office) and study it.

What MUST you have to park in a disabled space?

Mark one answer

- [x] An orange badge
- [x] A wheelchair
- [x] An advanced driver certificate
- [x] A modified vehicle

Answer

✗ An orange badge

Don't park in a space reserved for disabled people unless you or your passenger are a disabled badge-holder. The badge must be displayed on your vehicle in the bottom left-hand corner of the windscreen.

You are looking for somewhere to park your vehicle. The area is full EXCEPT for spaces marked 'disabled use'. You can

Mark one answer

- [x] use these spaces when elsewhere is full
- [x] park if you stay with your vehicle
- [x] use these spaces, disabled or not
- [x] not park there unless permitted

Answer

✗ not park there unless permitted

Don't be selfish. Find somewhere else to park, even if it means that you have to walk further.

Your vehicle is parked on the road at night. When must you use sidelights?

Mark one answer

- [x] Where there are continuous white lines in the middle of the road
- [x] Where the speed limit exceeds 30 mph
- [x] Where you are facing oncoming traffic
- [x] Where you are near a bus stop

Answer

✗ Where the speed limit exceeds 30 mph

When parking at night, park in the direction of the traffic. This will enable other road users to see the reflectors on the rear of your vehicle.

Use your sidelights if the speed limit is over 30 mph or you're parking a vehicle over 1,525 kg (1.5 tons).

Question 10.32

You park overnight on a road with a 40 mph speed limit. You should

Mark one answer

☒ park facing the traffic

☒ park with sidelights on

☒ park with dipped headlights on

☒ park near a street light

Answer

❌ **park with sidelights on**

Make sure that other road users can see your vehicle. Park in the direction of the traffic flow so that your vehicle isn't mistaken for a moving oncoming car.

Question 10.33

You can park on the right-hand side of a road at night

Mark one answer

☒ in a one-way street

☒ with your sidelights on

☒ more than 10 metres (32 feet) from a junction

☒ under a lamp-post

Answer

❌ **in a one-way street**

Vehicles are fitted with red rear reflectors that show up when headlights shine on them. These are useful when cars are parked at night, but will only reflect if the vehicles are parked in the same direction as the traffic passing alongside. Normally you should park on the left, but if you're in a one-way street the right-hand side is OK too.

Question 10.34

On a three-lane dual carriageway the right-hand lane can be used for

Mark one answer

☒ overtaking only, never turning right

☒ overtaking or turning right

☒ fast-moving traffic only

☒ turning right only, never overtaking

Answer

❌ **overtaking or turning right**

Use the left-hand lane at other times. When overtaking on a dual carriageway, be on the lookout for vehicles ahead that are turning right. They're likely to be slowing or stopped. You need to see them in good time so that you can take appropriate action.

Question 10.35

You are driving at night with full-beam headlights on. A vehicle is overtaking you. You should dip your lights

Mark one answer

- [ ] some time after the vehicle has passed you
- [ ] before the vehicle starts to pass you
- [ ] only if the other driver dips his headlights
- [ ] as soon as the vehicle passes you

Answer

✗ as soon as the vehicle passes you

Your lights on full beam could dazzle the driver in front. Make sure that your light beam falls short of the vehicle in front.

Question 10.36

You are riding on a busy dual carriageway. When changing lanes you should

Mark one answer

- [ ] rely totally on mirrors
- [ ] always increase your speed
- [ ] signal so others will give way
- [ ] use mirrors and shoulder checks

Answer

✗ use mirrors and shoulder checks

Before you change lanes you need to see if there's a safe gap to move across into. You have areas behind and to the side which are not covered by your mirrors. As well as using your mirrors you need to make a shoulder check to see if any vehicle is in this blind area before changing direction.

Question 10.37

You are driving on a two-lane dual carriageway. For which TWO of the following would you use the right-hand lane?

Mark two answers

- [ ] Turning right
- [ ] Normal driving
- [ ] Driving at the minimum allowed speed
- [ ] Constant high speed driving
- [ ] Overtaking slower traffic
- [ ] Mending punctures

Answers

✗ Turning right
✗ Overtaking slower traffic

If you overtake on a dual carriageway move back into the left-hand lane as soon as it's safe. Don't cut in across the path of the vehicle you've just passed.

Question 10.38

You are driving in the right hand lane of a dual carriageway. You see signs showing that the right-hand lane is closed 800 yards ahead. You should

GET IN LANE

800 yards

Mark one answer

- [ ] keep in that lane until you reach the queue
- [ ] move to the left immediately
- [ ] wait and see which lane is moving faster
- [ ] move to the left in good time

Answer

❌ **move to the left in good time**

Keep a lookout for traffic signs. If you're directed to change lanes, do so in good time. Don't

- push your way into traffic in another lane
- leave changing lanes until the last moment.

Question 10.39

You are entering an area of roadworks. There is a temporary speed limit displayed. You must

Mark one answer

- [ ] not exceed the speed limit
- [ ] obey the limit only during rush hour
- [ ] accept the speed limit as advisable
- [ ] obey the limit except for overnight

Answer

❌ **not exceed the speed limit**

Where there are extra hazards, such as roadworks it's often necessary to slow traffic down by imposing a temporary speed limit. These speed limits aren't advisory – they must be adhered to.

Question 10.40

While driving, you approach roadworks. You see a temporary maximum speed limit sign. You must

Mark one answer

- [ ] comply with the sign during the working day
- [ ] comply with the sign at all times
- [ ] comply with the sign when the lanes are narrow
- [ ] comply with the sign during the hours of darkness

Answer

❌ **comply with the sign at all times**

The sign has been put there to allow traffic to deal with the hazard at a low speed. Reduce the risk and don't exceed the limit.

Question 10.41

You may drive a motor car in this bus lane

Mark one answer

- [ ] outside its operation hours
- [ ] to get to the front of a traffic queue
- [ ] at no times at all
- [ ] to overtake slow moving traffic

Answer

❌ **outside its operation hours**

Make full use of bus lanes if it's permitted. This can often be at times other than rush hours. Check the sign. Times will differ from place to place.

Question 10.42

As a car driver which THREE lanes are you NOT normally allowed to use?

Mark three answers

- [ ] Crawler lane
- [ ] Bus lane
- [ ] Overtaking lane
- [ ] Acceleration lane
- [ ] Cycle lane
- [ ] Tram lane

Answers

❌ **Bus lane**
❌ **Cycle lane**
❌ **Tram lane**

Look out for signs or road markings that tell you which lane to use. Some lanes can only be used by certain road users. This might be to allow the traffic to flow, or to protect vulnerable road users.

Question 10.43

You are driving on a road that has a cycle lane. The lane is marked by a broken white line. This means that

Mark two answers

- [ ] you should not drive in the lane unless it is unavoidable
- [ ] you should not park in the lane unless it is unavoidable
- [ ] you can drive in the lane at any time
- [ ] the lane must be used by motorcyclists in heavy traffic

Answers

- ✗ **you should not drive in the lane unless it is unavoidable**
- ✗ **you should not park in the lane unless it is unavoidable**

Where signs or road markings show lanes are for cyclists only, leave them free. You should not drive or park in the lane unless it is unavoidable.

Question 10.44

You are driving along a road that has a cycle lane. The lane is marked by a solid white line. This means that during its period of operation

Mark one answer

- [ ] the lane may be used for parking your car
- [ ] you may drive in that lane at any time
- [ ] the lane may be used when necessary
- [ ] you must not drive in that lane

Answer

- ✗ **you must not drive in that lane**

Leave the lane free for cyclists. At other times, when the lane is not in operation, you should be aware that there still might be cyclists about. Give them room and don't pass too closely.

Question 10.45

A cycle lane is marked by a solid white line. You must not drive or park in it

Mark one answer

- [ ] at any time
- [ ] during the rush hour
- [ ] if a cyclist is using it
- [ ] during its period of operation

Answer

- ✗ **during its period of operation**

The cycle lanes are there for a reason. Keep them free and allow the cyclists to use them. Parking in the lane will force cyclists into the path of traffic on the main carriageway. This could be hazardous for both the cyclists and other road users.

As a motorcycle rider which TWO lanes must you NOT use?

Mark two answers

- [ ] Crawler lane
- [ ] Overtaking lane
- [ ] Acceleration lane
- [ ] Cycle lane
- [ ] Tram lane

Answers

☒ **Cycle lane**

☒ **Tram lane**

In some towns motorcycles are permitted to use bus lanes. Check the signs carefully.

You are approaching a busy junction. There are several lanes with road markings. At the last moment you realise that you are in the wrong lane. You should

Mark one answer

- [ ] continue in that lane
- [ ] force your way across
- [ ] stop until the area has cleared
- [ ] use clear arm signals to cut across

Answer

☒ **continue in that lane**

There are times where road markings can be obscured by queuing traffic, or you might be unsure of your correct lane. Don't cut across lanes or bully other drivers to let you in. Follow the lane you're in and find somewhere safe to turn around if you need to.

Where may you overtake on a one-way street?

Mark one answer

- [ ] Only on the left-hand side
- [ ] Overtaking is not allowed
- [ ] Only on the right-hand side
- [ ] Either on the right or the left

Answer

☒ **Either on the right or the left**

You can overtake other traffic on either side when travelling in a one-way street. Make full use of your mirrors and ensure that it's clear all around before you attempt to overtake. Look for signs and road markings and use the most suitable lane for your destination.

Question 10.49

You are going along a single-track road with passing places only on the right. The driver behind wishes to overtake. You should

Mark one answer

- [ ] speed up to get away from the following driver
- [ ] switch on your hazard warning lights
- [ ] wait opposite a passing place on your right
- [ ] drive into a passing place on your right

Question 10.50

You are on a road that is only wide enough for one vehicle. There is a car coming towards you. Which TWO of these would be correct?

Mark two answers

- [ ] Pull into a passing place on your right
- [ ] Force the other driver to reverse
- [ ] Pull into a passing place if your vehicle is wider
- [ ] Pull into a passing place on your left
- [ ] Wait opposite a passing place on your right
- [ ] Wait opposite a passing place on your left

Answer

✗ wait opposite a passing place on your right

Some roads are only wide enough for one vehicle. Often this type of road has special passing places where the road is widened for a short distance.

If there's a car coming toward you, pull into a passing place on your left or stop opposite one on your right. Don't

- force other vehicles to reverse
- pull into the passing place on the right.

Answers

✗ Pull into a passing place on your left
✗ Wait opposite a passing place on your right

If you meet another vehicle in a narrow road and the passing place is on the right, pull up opposite it. This will allow the oncoming vehicle to pull into it and pass you safely.

Question 10.51

Signals are normally given by direction indicators and

Mark one answer

- [ ] brake lights
- [ ] side lights
- [ ] fog lights
- [ ] interior lights

Answer

❌ **brake lights**

Your brake lights will give an indication to traffic behind that you're slowing down. Good anticipation will allow you time to check your mirrors before slowing. If you're intending to change direction you should use your direction indicators before you brake.

Question 10.52

When going straight ahead at a roundabout you should

Mark one answer

- [ ] indicate left before leaving the roundabout
- [ ] not indicate at any time
- [ ] indicate right when approaching the roundabout
- [ ] indicate left when approaching the roundabout

Answer

❌ **indicate left before leaving the roundabout**

When you want to go ahead at a roundabout indicate left just after you pass the exit before the one you wish to take. Don't

- signal right on approach
- signal left on approach.

Question 10.53

Which vehicle might have to use a different course to normal at roundabouts?

Mark one answer

- [ ] Sports car
- [ ] Van
- [ ] Estate car
- [ ] Long vehicle

Answer

❌ **Long vehicle**

A long vehicle may have to straddle lanes either on or approaching a roundabout so that the rear wheels don't cut in over the kerb. Stay well back and give it room.

Question 10.54

You are going straight ahead at a roundabout. How should you signal?

Mark one answer

☒ Signal right on the approach and then left to leave the roundabout

☒ Signal left as you leave the roundabout

☒ Signal left on the approach to the roundabout and keep the signal on until you leave

☒ Signal left just after you pass the exit before the one you will take

Answer

✖ **Signal left just after you pass the exit before the one you will take**

To go straight ahead at a roundabout you should normally approach in the left-hand lane. Where there are road markings, use the lane indicated. Ensure that you signal correctly and in good time; other road users need to know your intentions.

Question 10.55

You are turning right at a large roundabout. Just before you leave the roundabout you should

Mark one answer

☒ take a 'lifesaver' glance over your left shoulder

☒ take a 'lifesaver' glance over your right shoulder

☒ put on your right indicator

☒ cancel the left indicator

Answer

✖ **take a 'lifesaver' glance over your left shoulder**

You must be aware of what's happening behind and alongside you. A final, quick rearward glance will give you the chance to react if it isn't safe to make the manoeuvre.

Question 10.56

At a crossroads there are no signs or road markings. Two vehicles approach. Which has priority?

Mark one answer

☒ Neither vehicle

☒ The vehicle travelling the fastest

☒ The vehicle on the widest road

☒ Vehicles approaching from the right

Answer

✖ **Neither vehicle**

At a crossroads where there are no 'give way' signs or road markings BE VERY CAREFUL. No vehicle has priority, even if the size of the roads are different.

Who has priority at an unmarked crossroads?

Mark one answer

- [ ] The driver of the larger vehicle
- [ ] No one
- [ ] The driver who is going faster
- [ ] The driver on the wider road

Answer

✗ No one

Practise good observation in all directions before you emerge or make a turn.

Question 10.58

When filtering through slow moving or stationary traffic you should

Mark three answers

- [ ] watch for hidden vehicles emerging from side roads
- [ ] continually use your horn as a warning
- [ ] look for vehicles changing course suddenly
- [ ] always ride with your hazard lights on
- [ ] stand up on the footrests for a good view ahead
- [ ] look for pedestrians walking between vehicles

Answers

✗ watch for hidden vehicles emerging from side roads

✗ look for vehicles changing course suddenly

✗ look for pedestrians walking between vehicles

Other road users may not expect or look for motorcycles filtering through slow-moving or stationary traffic. The view all around will be reduced by the vehicles and you will need to watch for

- pedestrians walking between the vehicles
- vehicles suddenly changing direction
- vehicles pulling out of side roads.

Question 10.59

You are intending to turn right at a junction. An oncoming driver is also turning right. It will normally be safer to

Mark one answer

☒ keep the other vehicle to your RIGHT and turn behind it (offside to offside)

☒ keep the other vehicle to your LEFT and turn in front of it (nearside to nearside)

☒ carry on and turn at the next junction instead

☒ hold back and wait for the other driver to turn first

Answer

✖ **keep the other vehicle to your RIGHT and turn behind it (offside to offside)**

At some junctions the layout may make it difficult to turn this way. Be prepared to pass nearside to nearside, but take extra care. Your view ahead will be obscured by the vehicle turning in front of you.

Question 10.60

You are both turning right at these crossroads. It is safer to keep the car to your right so you can

Mark one answer

☒ see approaching traffic

☒ keep close to the kerb

☒ keep clear of following traffic

☒ make oncoming vehicles stop

Answer

✖ **see approaching traffic**

When turning right at this crossroads you should keep the oncoming car on your right. This will give you a clear view of the road ahead and any oncoming traffic.

The dual carriageway you are turning right onto has a narrow central reserve. You should

Mark one answer

☒ proceed to central reserve and wait

☒ wait until the road is clear in both directions

☒ stop in the first lane so that other vehicles give way

☒ emerge slightly to show your intentions

Answer

☒ **wait until the road is clear in both directions**

If you treat this carriageway as two separate roads you could cause an obstruction to traffic in both directions.

Question 10.62

While driving, you intend to turn left into a minor road. On the approach you should

Mark one answer

☒ keep just left of the middle of the road

☒ keep in the middle of the road

☒ swing out wide just before turning

☒ keep well to the left of the road

Answer

☒ **keep well to the left of the road**

Don't swing out into the centre of the road in order to make the turn. This could endanger oncoming traffic and mislead other road users of your intentions.

Question 10.63

You may only enter a box junction when

Mark one answer

☒ there are less than two vehicles in front of you

☒ the traffic lights show green

☒ your exit road is clear

☒ you need to turn left

Answer

☒ **your exit road is clear**

Box junctions are marked on the road to prevent the road becoming blocked. Don't enter the box unless your exit road is clear. You may only wait in the box if your exit road is clear but oncoming traffic is preventing you from completing the turn.

You may wait in a yellow box junction when

Mark one answer

☒ oncoming traffic is preventing you from turning right

☒ you are in a queue of traffic turning left

☒ you are in a queue of traffic to go ahead

☒ you are on a roundabout

Answer

☒ **oncoming traffic is preventing you from turning right**

The purpose of this road marking is to keep the centre of the junction clear of queuing traffic when the lights change priority. Don't stop in it if you aren't turning right.

You want to turn right at a box junction. There is oncoming traffic. You should

Mark one answer

☒ wait in the box junction if your exit is clear

☒ wait before the junction until it is clear of all traffic

☒ drive on: you cannot turn right at a box junction

☒ drive slowly into the box junction when signalled by oncoming traffic

Answer

☒ **wait in the box junction if your exit is clear**

As the lights change priority the oncoming traffic will stop, allowing you to proceed.

On which THREE occasions MUST you stop your vehicle?

Mark three answers

- [x] When involved in an accident
- [x] At a red traffic light
- [x] When signalled to do so by a police officer
- [x] At a junction with ~~double broken white lines~~
- [x] At a pelican crossing when the amber light is flashing and no pedestrians are crossing

Answers

- [x] **When involved in an accident**
- [x] **At a red traffic light**
- [x] **When signalled to do so by a police officer**

Don't stop or hold up traffic unnecessarily. However you MUST stop when signalled to do so by

- a police officer
- a school crossing patrol
- a red traffic light

or when you have had an accident.

You MUST stop when signalled to do so by which THREE of these?

Mark three answers

- [x] A police officer
- [x] A pedestrian
- [x] A school crossing patrol
- [x] A bus driver
- [x] A red traffic light

Answers

- [x] **A police officer**
- [x] **A school crossing patrol**
- [x] **A red traffic light**

Looking well ahead and 'reading' the road will help you to anticipate hazards. This will allow you to stop safely if asked to do so by a person or a road sign.

At roadworks which of the following can control traffic flow?

Mark three answers

- [x] A STOP–GO board
- [x] Flashing amber lights
- [x] A policeman
- [x] Flashing red lights
- [x] Temporary traffic lights

Answers

- [x] **A STOP–GO board**
- [x] **A policeman**
- [x] **Temporary traffic lights**

As you approach the warning signs you should be considering what actions you need to take. You might have to slow right down or stop. Obey any instructions you are given and don't try to beat any lights by driving up to them quickly.

Question 10.69

You are waiting at a level crossing. The red warning lights continue to flash after a train has passed by. What should you do?

Mark one answer

- [ ] Get out and investigate
- [ ] Telephone the signal operator
- [ ] Continue to wait
- [ ] Drive across carefully

Answer

✗ Continue to wait

At a level crossing flashing red lights mean you should stop. If the train passes but the lights keep flashing, wait – there may be another train coming.

Question 10.70

You are driving over a level crossing. The warning lights come on and a bell rings. What should you do?

Mark one answer

- [ ] Get everyone out of the vehicle immediately
- [ ] Stop and reverse back to clear the crossing
- [ ] Keep going and clear the crossing
- [ ] Stop immediately and use your hazard warning lights

Answer

✗ Keep going and clear the crossing

Keep going – don't stop on the crossing. If the warning lights come on as you're approaching the crossing, stop. Don't try to dart across before the train comes.

You are waiting at a level crossing. A train has passed but the lights keep flashing. You must

Mark one answer

- ☒ carry on waiting
- ☒ 'phone the signal operator
- ☒ edge over the stop line and look for trains
- ☒ park your vehicle and investigate

Answer

✖ **carry on waiting**

If the lights at a level crossing continue to flash after a train has passed, wait – there might be another train coming. Time seems to pass slowly when you're held up in a queue. Be patient and wait until the lights stop flashing.

You will see these markers when approaching

Mark one answer

- ☒ the end of a motorway
- ☒ a concealed level crossing
- ☒ a concealed speed limit sign
- ☒ the end of a dual carriageway

Answer

✖ **a concealed level crossing**

There may be a bend before a level crossing, in which case you won't be able to see barriers or waiting traffic ahead. These signs give you an early warning that you may find these hazards just around the bend.

Question 10.73

Someone is waiting to cross at a zebra crossing. They are standing on the pavement. You should normally

Mark one answer

- go on quickly before they step onto the crossing
- stop before you reach the zigzag lines and let them cross
- stop, let them cross, wait patiently
- ignore them as they are still on the pavement

Answer

✗ stop, let them cross, wait patiently

The pedestrian is showing an intention to cross. If you are looking well down the road you will give yourself enough time to slow down and stop correctly. Don't forget to check your mirrors before slowing down.

Question 10.74

At toucan crossings, apart from pedestrians, you should be aware of

Mark one answer

- emergency vehicles emerging
- buses pulling out
- trams crossing in front
- cyclists riding across

Answer

✗ cyclists riding across

The use of cycles is being encouraged and more toucan crossings are being installed. These crossings enable pedestrians and cyclists to cross the path of other traffic. Watch out as cyclists will approach the crossing faster than a pedestrian.

Who can use a toucan crossing?

Mark two answers

- [x] Trains
- [x] Cyclists
- [x] Buses
- [x] Pedestrians
- [x] Trams

Answers

- [x] Cyclists
- [x] Pedestrians

Toucan crossings are similar to pelican crossings. Cyclists share the crossing with pedestrians without the need to dismount. They're shown a green cycle when it's safe to cross.

Question 10.76

At a pelican crossing, what does a flashing amber light mean?

Mark one answer

- [x] You must not move off until the lights stop flashing
- [x] You must give way to pedestrians still on the crossing
- [x] You can move off, even if pedestrians are still on the crossing
- [x] You must stop because the lights are about to change to red

Answer

- [x] **You must give way to pedestrians still on the crossing**

If the road is clear then proceed. The green light will show after the flashing amber.

Question 10.77

You are waiting at a pelican crossing. The red light changes to flashing amber. This means you must

Mark one answer

- [x] wait for pedestrians on the crossing to clear
- [x] move off immediately without any hesitation
- [x] wait for the green light before moving off
- [x] get ready and go when the continuous amber light shows

Answer

- [x] **wait for pedestrians on the crossing to clear**

This light allows time for the pedestrians already on the crossing to get to the other side in their own time, without undue hurry. Don't rev your engine or start to move off while they are still crossing.

Question 10.78

You are on a busy main road and find that you are travelling in the wrong direction. What should you do?

Mark one answer

☒ Turn into a side road on the right and reverse into the main road

☒ Make a U-turn in the main road

☒ Make a 'three-point' turn in the main road

☒ Turn round in a side road

Answer

☒ **Turn round in a side road**

Don't

- turn in a busy street
- reverse into a main road.

Find a quiet side road. Choose a place where you won't obstruct an entrance or exit, and look out for pedestrians and cyclists as well as other traffic.

Question 10.79

You may remove your seat belt when carrying out a manoeuvre that involves

Mark one answer

☒ reversing

☒ a hill start

☒ an emergency stop

☒ driving slowly

Answer

 reversing

Don't forget to click your seat belt back on when you've finished reversing.

Question 10.80

You must not reverse

Mark one answer

☒ for longer than necessary

☒ for more than a car's length

☒ into a side road

☒ in a built-up area

Answer

☒ **for longer than necessary**

You may decide to turn your vehicle around by reversing into an opening or side road. When you reverse, always look behind and watch for pedestrians. Don't

- reverse for longer than is necessary
- reverse from a side road into a main road.

You are parked in a busy high street. What is the safest way to turn your vehicle around to go the opposite way?

Mark one answer

- [ ] Find a quiet side road to turn round in
- [ ] Drive into a side road and reverse into the main road
- [ ] Get someone to stop the traffic
- [ ] Do a U-turn

Answer

✗ Find a quiet side road to turn round in

You should carry out the manoeuvre without causing a hazard to other vehicles.

Question 10.82

When you are NOT sure that it is safe to reverse your vehicle you should

Mark one answer

- [ ] use your horn
- [ ] rev your engine
- [ ] get out and check
- [ ] reverse slowly

Answer

✗ get out and check

If you can't see all around your vehicle, get out and have a look. You could also ask someone outside the vehicle to guide you. A small child could easily be hidden directly behind you. Don't take risks.

Question 10.83

When may you reverse from a side road into a main road?

Mark one answer

- [ ] Only if both roads are clear of traffic
- [ ] Not at any time
- [ ] At any time
- [ ] Only if the main road is clear of traffic

Answer

✗ Not at any time

Don't reverse into a main road from a side road. The main road is likely to be busy and the traffic on it moving quickly. Cut down the risks by using a quiet side road to reverse into.

Question 10.84

You are reversing your vehicle into a side road. When would the greatest hazard to passing traffic occur?

Mark one answer

- [ ] After you've completed the manoeuvre
- [ ] Just before you actually begin to manoeuvre
- [ ] After you've entered the side road
- [ ] When the front of your vehicle swings out

Answer

✗ **When the front of your vehicle swings out**

Always check road and traffic conditions in all directions. Act on what you see and wait if you need to.

This section looks at road and traffic signs.

The questions will ask you about

- road signs
- speed limits
- road markings
- regulations.

Question 11.1

You MUST obey signs giving orders. These signs are mostly in

Mark one answer

- green rectangles
- red triangles
- blue rectangles
- red circles

Answer

❌ **red circles**

Traffic signs can be divided into three classes – those giving orders, those warning and those informing. On the road each class of sign has a different shape.

Question 11.2

Traffic signs giving orders are generally which shape?

Mark one answer

Answer

❌

Road signs in the shape of a circle give orders. Those with a red circle are mostly prohibitive. The stop sign is octagonal to give it greater prominence. These signs must always be obeyed.

Question 11.3

Which type of sign tells you NOT to do something?

Mark one answer

Answer

❌

Signs in the shape of a circle mean that you aren't allowed to do something. Study *Know Your Traffic Signs* to ensure that you understand the order you're given.

Question 11.4

What does this sign mean?

Mark one answer

 Maximum speed limit with traffic calming

☒ Minimum speed limit with traffic calming

☒ '20 cars only' parking zone

☒ Only 20 cars allowed at any one time

Question 11.5

Which sign means no motor vehicles are allowed?

Mark one answer

Answer

✗ **Maximum speed limit with traffic calming**

If you're driving in areas where there are likely to be pedestrians such as

- outside schools
- near parks
- residential areas
- shopping areas

be extra cautious and keep your speed down. Many local authorities have taken measures to slow traffic down by creating traffic calming measures such as speed humps. They're there for a reason: slow down.

Answer

Certain areas are set aside for pedestrians to walk free of traffic.

Which of these signs means no motor vehicles?

Mark one answer

Answer

✗

If you are driving a motor vehicle or riding a motorcycle you must not enter. This area has been especially designated for pedestrians.

What does this sign mean?

Mark one answer

- ☒ New speed limit 20 mph
- ☒ No vehicles over 30 tonnes
- ☒ Minimum speed limit 30 mph
- ☒ End of 20 mph zone

Answer

✗ **End of 20 mph zone**

Where you see this sign the 20 mph restriction ends. Only increase your speed if it's safe to do so. Check all around and well down the road before increasing your speed.

This traffic sign means there is

Answer

✗ **a compulsory maximum speed limit**

In this picture the traffic is slow moving, which could be due to road works or another temporary obstruction. The sign gives you an early warning of a speed restriction. If you are travelling at a higher speed, slow down in good time.

Mark one answer

☒ a compulsory maximum speed limit

☒ an advised maximum speed limit

☒ a compulsory minimum speed limit

☒ an advised separation distance

Question 11.9

What does this sign mean?

Answer

✗ **No motor vehicles**

Traffic may be prohibited from certain roads. A sign will indicate which types of vehicles aren't allowed to use it. Make sure that you know which signs apply to the vehicle you're using.

Mark one answer

☒ No overtaking

☒ No motor vehicles

☒ Clearway (no stopping)

☒ Cars and motorcycles only

Question 11.10

What does this sign mean?

Answer

✗ **No entry**

Not knowing the meaning of a road sign could lead you into a dangerous situation.

Mark one answer

☒ No parking

☒ No road markings

☒ No through road

☒ No entry

Question 11.11

What does this sign mean?

Mark one answer

☒ Bend to the right

☒ Road on the right closed

☒ No traffic from the right

☒ No right turn

Question 11.12

Which sign means 'no entry'?

Mark one answer

Answer

✖ **No right turn**

The road on the right might be a no entry or the sign could be there to allow the traffic on the main road to flow by stopping cars from queuing to turn right.

Answer

✖

Look out for traffic signs as you drive. Disobeying or not seeing a sign could not only be dangerous, but also an offence; you could be fined.

Question 11.13

What does this sign mean?

Mark one answer

 Route for trams only

 Route for buses only

 Parking for buses only

 Parking for trams only

Answer

 Route for trams only

Avoid blocking tram routes. Trams are fixed on their route and can't dodge around other vehicles and pedestrians. Modern trams travel quickly and are quiet, so you might not hear them approaching.

Question 11.14

Which type of vehicle does this sign apply to?

Mark one answer

 Wide vehicles

 Long vehicles

 High vehicles

 Heavy vehicles

Answer

 High vehicles

The triangular shapes at the top and bottom of the sign mean that the sign is showing you the restricted height.

Question 11.15

Which sign means NO motor vehicles allowed?

Mark one answer

Answer

This sign is used to enable pedestrians to walk free from traffic. It's often found in shopping areas.

Question 11.16

What does this sign mean?

Mark one answer

- ☒ You have priority
- ☒ No motor vehicles
- ☒ Two-way traffic
- ☒ No overtaking

Answer

☒ **No overtaking**

Road signs that show no overtaking will be placed in locations where passing the vehicle in front is dangerous. If you see this sign, don't attempt to overtake. The sign is there for a reason and you must obey it.

Question 11.17

What does this sign mean?

Mark one answer

 Keep in one lane

 Give way to oncoming traffic

 Do not overtake

 Form two lanes

Question 11.18

Which sign means no overtaking?

Mark one answer

Question 11.19

What does this sign mean?

Mark one answer

Waiting restrictions apply

Waiting permitted

National speed limit applies

Clearway (no stopping)

Answer

 Do not overtake

If you're behind a slow-moving vehicle, be patient. Wait until the restriction no longer applies and you can see that it is safe to overtake.

Answer

This sign indicates that overtaking here would be dangerous. Don't take risks.

Answer

Waiting restrictions apply

There will be a plate or additional sign to tell you when the restrictions apply.

Question 11.20

What does this sign mean?

Mark one answer

- You can park on the days and times shown
- No parking on the days and times shown
- No parking at all from Monday to Friday
- You can park at any time; the urban clearway ends

Answer

No parking on the days and times shown

Before you leave your vehicle parked at the side of the road, check that the space isn't restricted. Parking times vary from place to place, so always check the sign before securing and leaving your car.

Question 11.21

What does this sign mean?

Mark one answer

- End of restricted speed area
- End of restricted parking area
- End of clearway
- End of cycle route

Answer

End of restricted parking area

Even though there are no restrictions, make sure that you park where you won't cause an obstruction or endanger other road users.

Question 11.22

Which sign means 'no stopping'?

Mark one answer

Answer

Stopping where you see this sign is likely to cause congestion. Allow the traffic to flow by obeying the signs.

Question 11.23

What does this sign mean?

Mark one answer

- [ ] Roundabout
- [ ] Crossroads
- [ ] No stopping
- [ ] No entry

Answer

✖ **No stopping**

This sign is in place to ensure a clear route for traffic. Don't stop except in an emergency.

Question 11.24

You see this sign ahead. It means

Mark one answer

- [ ] national speed limit applies
- [ ] waiting restrictions apply
- [ ] no stopping
- [ ] no entry

Answer

✖ **no stopping**

There are stretches of road where you aren't allowed to stop (unless in an emergency). These are called 'clearways'. You'll see this sign. Stopping where these restrictions apply may be dangerous and could cause an obstruction. Restrictions might apply for several miles, and this may be indicated on the sign.

What does this sign mean?

Mark one answer

 Distance to parking place ahead

 Distance to public telephone ahead

 Distance to public house ahead

 Distance to passing place ahead

Answer

✗ Distance to parking place ahead

If you intend to stop and rest, note this early indication. This sign allows you time to ask any passengers if they need to stop for any reason.

What does this sign mean?

Mark one answer

 Vehicles may not park on the verge or footway

 Vehicles may park on the left-hand side of the road only

 Vehicles may park fully on the verge or footway

 Vehicles may park on the right-hand side of the road only

Answer

✗ Vehicles may park fully on the verge or footway

In order to keep roads free from parked cars there are some areas where you're allowed to park on the verge. Only do this where you see this sign. Parking on verges or kerbs in other areas could lead to a fine.

What does this traffic sign mean?

Mark one answer

☒ No overtaking allowed

☒ Give priority to oncoming traffic

☒ Two way traffic

☒ One-way traffic only

Answer

☒ **Give priority to oncoming traffic**

Priority signs are normally shown where the road is narrow and there isn't enough room for two vehicles to pass, such as

- a narrow bridge
- at roadworks
- a width restriction.

Make sure that you know who has priority. Comply with the sign and don't force your way through. Show courtesy and consideration to other road users.

Question 11.28

What is the meaning of this traffic sign?

Mark one answer

☒ End of two-way road

☒ Give priority to vehicles coming towards you

☒ You have priority over vehicles coming towards you

☒ Bus lane ahead

Answer

☒ **You have priority over vehicles coming towards you**

Don't force your way through. Show courtesy and consideration to other road users. Although you have priority, make sure oncoming traffic is going to give way.

Question 11.29

Which sign means 'traffic has priority over oncoming vehicles'?

Mark one answer

Answer

Even though you may have priority, give way if proceeding is likely to cause an accident, congestion or confrontation.

Question 11.30

What MUST you do when you see this sign?

Mark one answer

- ☒ Stop, ONLY if traffic is approaching
- ☒ Stop, even if the road is clear
- ☒ Stop, ONLY if children are waiting to cross
- ☒ Stop, ONLY if a red light is showing

Answer

☒ **Stop, even if the road is clear**

A stop sign is shown on an octagonal-shaped background. The sign will be at a junction where visibility is restricted or there's heavy traffic.

IT MUST BE OBEYED. YOU MUST STOP.

Practice good all-round observation before moving off.

Question 11.31

What does this sign mean?

Mark one answer

- [ ] No overtaking
- [ ] You are entering a one-way street
- [ ] Two-way traffic ahead
- [ ] You have priority over vehicles from the opposite direction

Question 11.32

What shape is a STOP sign at a junction?

Mark one answer

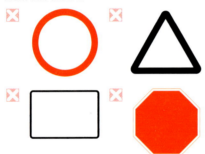

Answer

✗ **You have priority over vehicles from the opposite direction**

Don't force the issue. Slow down and give way to avoid confrontation or an accident.

Answer

✗

The 'Stop' sign is distinctive and the only sign of this shape. You must stop and make effective observation before proceeding.

Question 11.33

At a junction you see this sign partly covered by snow. What does it mean?

Mark one answer

- Cross roads
- Give way
- Stop
- Turn right

Answer

 Stop

The 'Stop' sign is the only sign this shape. This is to give it greater prominence. Although the snow has covered the wording you must still be able to recognise and obey this sign.

Question 11.34

Which shape is used for a GIVE WAY sign?

Mark one answer

Answer

Other warning signs are the same shape and colour, but the 'Give Way' sign points downwards. You must give way to traffic already on the major road.

What does this sign mean?

Mark one answer

- [X] Service area 30 miles ahead
- [X] Maximum speed 30 mph
- [X] Minimum speed 30 mph
- [X] Lay-by 30 miles ahead

Question 11.36

Which of these signs means turn left ahead?

Mark one answer

Question 11.37

At a mini-roundabout you should

Mark one answer

- [X] give way to traffic from the right
- [X] give way to traffic from the left
- [X] give way to traffic from the other way
- [X] stop even when clear

Answer

 Minimum speed 30 mph

This sign is shown where slow-moving vehicles would impede the flow of traffic. However, if you need to slow down to avoid a potential accident you should do so.

Answer

This sign gives a clear instruction. You should be looking out for signs as you drive. Prepare to negotiate a left-hand turn.

Answer

 give way to traffic from the right

Look out for other traffic as you approach. Vehicles entering the mini-roundabout from your left or ahead might prevent traffic on your right from proceeding. Watch for their signals and continue only if it's safe to do so.

Question 11.38

What does this sign mean?

Mark one answer

- Buses turning
- Ring road
- Mini-roundabout
- Keep right

Question 11.39

What does this sign mean?

Mark one answer

- Give way to oncoming vehicles
- Approaching traffic passes you on both sides
- Turn off at the next available junction
- Pass either side to get to the same destination

Answer

 Mini-roundabout

Look out for any direction signs and judge whether you need to signal your intentions. Do this in good time so that other road users approaching the roundabout can assess the situation.

Answer

 Pass either side to get to the same destination

These signs are often seen in one-way streets that have more than one lane. Use the route that's the most convenient and doesn't require a late change of direction.

What does this sign mean?

Mark one answer

- ☒ Route for trams
- ☒ Give way to trams
- ☒ Route for buses
- ☒ Give way to buses

Answer

 Route for trams

Take extra care when you first encounter trams. Look out for road markings and signs that alert you to them. Modern trams are very quiet and you may not hear them approaching.

What does a circular traffic sign with a blue background do?

Mark one answer

- ☒ Give warning of a motorway ahead
- ☒ Give directions to a car park
- ☒ Give motorway information
- ☒ Give an instruction

Answer

 Give an instruction

Signs with blue circles give a positive instruction. They will often be seen in towns or urban areas. For example, 'mini-roundabout' or 'pass either side'.

Question 11.42

Which of these signs means that you are entering a one-way street?

Mark one answer

Answer

If the road has two lanes you can use either lane and overtake on either side. Use the lane that's more convenient for your destination.

Question 11.43

Where would you see a contraflow bus and cycle lane?

Mark one answer

   On a dual carriageway

   On a roundabout

   On an urban motorway

   On a one-way street

Answer

 On a one-way street

'Contraflow' means that the bus or cycle lane is going in the opposite direction to the other lanes in the road. Don't drive in or straddle these lanes.

Question 11.44

What does this sign mean?

Mark one answer

   Bus station on the right

   Contraflow bus lane

   With-flow bus lane

   Give way to buses

Answer

 Contraflow bus lane

There will also be markings on the road surface to indicate the bus lane. Don't use this lane for parking or overtaking.

Question 11.45

What does this sign mean?

Mark one answer

- [X] With-flow bus and cycle lane
- [X] Contraflow bus and cycle lane
- [X] No buses and cycles allowed
- [X] No waiting for buses and cycles

Answer

X **With-flow bus and cycle lane**

In this case buses and cycles may travel in this lane in the same direction as other traffic. There may be times shown on the sign to indicate when the lane is in use.

Question 11.46

What does a sign with a brown background show?

Mark one answer

- [X] Tourist directions
- [X] Primary roads
- [X] Motorway routes
- [X] Minor routes

Answer

X **Tourist directions**

Signs with a brown background give directions to places of interest. They will often be seen on the motorway directing you along the easiest route.

Question 11.47

This sign means

Mark one answer

- [X] tourist attraction
- [X] beware of trains
- [X] level crossing
- [X] beware of trams

Answer

X **tourist attraction**

These signs indicate places of interest and are designed to guide you by the easiest route. If you are a tourist you're likely to be unfamiliar with the area, so these signs are particularly useful.

Question 11.48

What are triangular signs for?

Mark one answer

- [X] To give warnings
- [X] To give information
- [X] To give orders
- [X] To give directions

Answer

[X] **To give warnings**

This type of sign will tell you about the road ahead and what to expect. Get into the habit of checking each sign that you pass. They will warn you of the hazards ahead.

Question 11.49

What does this sign mean?

Mark one answer

- [X] Turn left ahead
- [X] T-junction
- [X] No through road
- [X] Give way

Answer

[X] **T-junction**

Look well down the road and check the road signs as you drive. You'll then be able to anticipate any junction hazards.

Question 11.50

What does this sign mean?

Mark one answer

- [X] Multi-exit roundabout
- [X] Risk of ice
- [X] Six roads converge
- [X] Place of historical interest

Answer

[X] **Risk of ice**

It will take up to ten times longer to stop when it's icy. Consider this and drive carefully. Don't brake or steer harshly as your tyres could lose their grip on the road.

What does this sign mean?

Answer

❌ **Crossroads**

The priority through the junction is shown by the broader line. However, be aware of the danger when other traffic is crossing a major road.

Mark one answer

☒ Crossroads

☒ Level crossing with gate

☒ Level crossing without gate

☒ Ahead only

What does this sign mean?

Answer

❌ **Roundabout**

Prepare yourself for approaching hazards by checking signs as you drive.

Decide which exit you wish to take. Prepare to position your vehicle correctly as you approach the roundabout.

Mark one answer

☒ Ring road

☒ Mini-roundabout

☒ No vehicles

☒ Roundabout

Which FOUR of these would be indicated by a triangular road sign?

Answers

❌ **Road narrows**

❌ **Low bridge**

❌ **Children crossing**

❌ **T-junction**

Make use of the warning sign and be prepared for the hazard ahead.

Mark four answers

☒ Road narrows

☒ Ahead only

☒ Low bridge

☒ Minimum speed

☒ Children crossing

☒ T-junction

Question 11.54

What does this sign mean?

Mark one answer

 Cyclists must dismount

 Cycles are not allowed

 Cycle route ahead

 Cycle in single file

Question 11.55

Which sign means that pedestrians may be walking along the road?

Mark one answer

Answer

 Cycle route ahead

Where there's a cycle route ahead, a sign will show a bicycle in a red warning triangle. Watch out for children on bicycles and cyclists rejoining the main road.

Answer

Be extra cautious especially if there is a bend in the road and you're unable to see well ahead. When you pass pedestrians walking along the road, leave plenty of room. Consider that you might have to use the right-hand side of the road, so look well ahead along the road, as well as in your mirrors, before you pull out.

Question 11.56

Which of these signs warn you of a pedestrian crossing?

Mark one answer

Answer

Look well ahead and check the pavements and surrounding areas for pedestrians. Keep an eye on those who are walking towards the crossing. Check your mirrors for traffic behind, in case you have to slow down or stop.

Question 11.57

What does this sign mean?

Mark one answer

- ☒ No footpath ahead
- ☒ Pedestrians only ahead
- ☒ Pedestrian crossing ahead
- ☒ School crossing ahead

Answer

☒ **Pedestrian crossing ahead**

There are many signs relating to pedestrians. Study *The Highway Code* and *Know Your Traffic Signs*. Some of the signs look similar, but give different warnings. Make a mental note as you drive so that you're prepared for any potential hazard.

Question 11.58

What does this sign mean?

Mark one answer

- ☒ School crossing patrol
- ☒ No pedestrians allowed
- ☒ Pedestrian zone – no vehicles
- ☒ Pedestrian crossing ahead

Answer

☒ **Pedestrian crossing ahead**

Look well ahead and be ready to stop for any pedestrians crossing the road. Also check the pavements for anyone who looks like they might step off into the road.

Question 11.59

Which of these signs means there is a double bend ahead?

Mark one answer

Answer

Triangular signs give you a warning of hazards ahead. They're there to give you time to adjust your speed and drive accordingly.

Question 11.60

What does this sign mean?

Mark one answer

- Wait at the barriers
- Wait at the crossroads
- Give way to trams
- Give way to farm vehicles

Answer

 Give way to trams

Obey the 'Give Way' signs. Trams are unable to steer around you or change their specific route.

What does this sign mean?

Mark one answer

☒ End of dual carriageway

☒ Tall bridge

☒ Road narrows

☒ End of narrow bridge

Answer

❌ **End of dual carriageway**

Don't leave moving into the left-hand lane until the last moment. Early planning will prevent you having to rely on other traffic letting you in.

Question 11.67

What does this sign mean?

Mark one answer

☒ Two-way traffic ahead across a one-way street

☒ Traffic approaching you has priority

☒ Two-way traffic straight ahead

☒ Motorway contraflow system ahead

Answer

❌ **Two-way traffic straight ahead**

This sign may be at the end of a dual carriageway or a one-way street. The sign is there to warn you of oncoming traffic.

Question 11.68

What does this sign mean?

Mark one answer

☒ Crosswinds

☒ Road noise

☒ Airport

☒ Adverse camber

Answer

❌ **Crosswinds**

Where weather conditions are often bad, signs will give you a warning. A sign with a picture of a windsock will indicate there may be strong crosswinds. This sign is often found on exposed roads.

Question 11.69

What does this traffic sign mean?

Mark one answer

- [ ] Slippery road ahead
- [ ] Tyres liable to punctures ahead
- [ ] Danger ahead
- [ ] Service area ahead

Answer

✗ Danger ahead

A sign showing an exclamation mark (!) will alert you to the likelihood of danger ahead. Be ready for any situation that requires you to reduce your speed.

Question 11.70

You are about to overtake when you see this sign. You should

Mark one answer

- [ ] overtake the other driver as quickly as possible
- [ ] move to the right to get a better view
- [ ] switch your headlights on before overtaking
- [ ] hold back until you can see clearly ahead

Answer

✗ hold back until you can see clearly ahead

You won't be able to see any hazards that might be out of sight in the dip. Imagine there might be

- cyclists
- horse riders
- parked vehicles
- pedestrians.

There might also be oncoming traffic to deal with.

What does this sign mean?

Mark one answer

☒ Level crossing with gate or barrier

☒ Gated road ahead

☒ Level crossing without gate or barrier

☒ Cattle grid ahead

Answer

✗ **Level crossing with gate or barrier**

Some crossings have gates but no attendant or signals. You should

• stop

• look both ways

• listen and make sure that there is no train approaching.

If there is a telephone, contact the signal operator to make sure that it's safe to cross.

What does this sign mean?

Mark one answer

☒ No trams ahead

☒ Oncoming trams

☒ Trams crossing ahead

☒ Trams only

Answer

✗ **Trams crossing ahead**

This is a warning sign. Watch out for trams. If you are not used to driving in a town where there are trams, be especially careful at junctions. Watch out for road signs.

What does this sign mean?

Mark one answer

☒ Adverse camber

☒ Steep hill downwards

☒ Uneven road

☒ Steep hill upwards

Answer

✗ **Steep hill downwards**

This warning sign will give you an early indication. Prepare to alter your speed and gear. Looking at the sign from left to right will show you whether it's up or downhill.

Question 11.74

What does this sign mean?

Mark one answer

- Quayside or river bank
- Steep hill downwards
- Slippery road
- Road liable to flooding

Answer

✖ **Quayside or river bank**

Be aware that the road surface in this location is likely to be wet and slippery.

Question 11.75

What does this sign mean?

Mark one answer

- Uneven road surface
- Bridge over the road
- Road ahead ends
- Water across the road

Answer

✖ **Water across the road**

This sign is found where a shallow stream crosses the road. Heavy rainfall could increase the flow of water. If the water looks too deep or the stream has swelled over a large distance, stop and find another route.

Question 11.76

What does this sign mean?

Mark one answer

- Humpback bridge
- Traffic calming hump
- Low bridge
- Uneven road

Answer

✖ **Humpback bridge**

Slow right down. Driving over a humpback bridge too fast could cause your wheels to leave the road surface and result in a loss of control.

What does this sign mean?

Mark one answer

 Turn left for parking area

Turn left for parking area

No through road on the left

No entry for traffic turning left

Turn left for ferry terminal

Answer

 No through road on the left

Signs are there to help you to drive and to help you to avoid making late decisions. If you intend to take a left turn, this sign shows you that you can't get through to another route.

What does this sign mean?

Mark one answer

T-junction

No through road

Telephone box ahead

Toilet ahead

Answer

 No through road

You will not be able to find a through route to another road. Only use this road for access.

Which sign means 'no through road'?

Mark one answer

Answer

This sign is found at the entrance to the road.

Question 11.80

Which of the following signs informs you that you are coming to a No Through Road?

Mark one answer

Answer

This sign is found at the entrance to the road.

Question 11.81

What does this sign mean?

Mark one answer

☒ Direction to park and ride car park

☒ No parking for buses or coaches

☒ Directions to bus and coach park

☒ Parking area for cars and coaches

Answer

☒ **Direction to park and ride car park**

To reduce congestion, some cities and towns provide a park and ride scheme. This allows you to park in a designated area and ride by bus into the centre. This is usually cheaper and easier than car parking in the centre.

Question 11.82

You are driving through a tunnel and you see this sign. What does it mean?

Mark one answer

- Direction to emergency pedestrian exit
- Beware of pedestrians, no footpath ahead
- No access for pedestrians
- Beware of pedestrians crossing ahead

Answer

 Direction to emergency pedestrian exit

If you find yourself having to evacuate a tunnel, do so as quickly as you can. Follow the signs, which will direct you to the nearest exit point. If there's a lot of people, don't panic, but try to leave in a calm and orderly manner.

Question 11.83

Which is the sign for a ring road?

Mark one answer

Answer

Ring roads are designed to relieve congestion in towns and cities.

Question 11.84

What does this sign mean?

Mark one answer

- Route for lorries
- Ring road
- Rest area
- Roundabout

Answer

 Ring road

Signs are also designed to give you advice. Ring road signs direct traffic around major towns and cities. Ring roads help the traffic to flow and ease congestion in town centres.

What does this sign mean?

Mark one answer

- ⊠ Hilly road
- ⊠ Humps in road
- ⊠ Holiday route
- ⊠ Hospital route

Answer

✖ **Holiday route**

In some areas where the volume of traffic increases during the summer months, signs show a route that diverts traffic away from town centres. This helps the traffic to flow, decreasing queues.

What does this sign mean?

Mark one answer

- ⊠ The right-hand lane ahead is narrow
- ⊠ Right-hand lane for buses only
- ⊠ Right hand lane for turning right
- ⊠ The right-hand lane is closed

Answer

✖ **The right-hand lane is closed**

Temporary signs may tell you about roadworks or lane restrictions. Look well ahead. If you have to change lanes, do so in good time.

What does this sign mean?

Mark one answer

- ☒ Change to the left lane
- ☒ Leave at the next exit
- ☒ Contraflow system
- ☒ One-way street

To avoid an accident when entering a contraflow system, you should

Mark three answers

- ☒ reduce speed in good time
- ☒ switch lanes anytime to make progress
- ☒ choose an appropriate lane early
- ☒ keep the correct separation distance
- ☒ increase speed to pass through quickly
- ☒ follow other motorists closely to avoid long queues

Answer

✗ Contraflow system

If you use the right-hand lane, you'll be travelling with no permanent barrier between your vehicle and the traffic coming towards you. Observe speed limits and keep a good distance from the car ahead.

Answers

✗ reduce speed in good time
✗ choose an appropriate lane early
✗ keep the correct separation distance

In a contraflow system you will be travelling close to oncoming traffic and sometimes in narrow lanes. You should

- obey the temporary signs governing speed limits
- get into the correct lane in good time
- keep a safe separation distance from the vehicle ahead.

Question 11.89

What does this sign mean?

Mark one answer

- ✗ Leave motorway at next exit
- ✗ Lane for heavy and slow vehicles
- ✗ All lorries use the hard shoulder
- ✗ Rest area for lorries

Answer

 Lane for heavy and slow vehicles

Where there's a long, steep, uphill gradient on a motorway there may be a crawler lane. This type of lane helps the traffic to flow by diverting the slower heavy vehicles into an extra lane on the left.

Question 11.90

You see this traffic light ahead. Which light(s) will come on next?

Mark one answer

- ✗ Red alone
- ✗ Red and amber together
- ✗ Green and amber together
- ✗ Green alone

Answer

 Red alone

At junctions controlled by traffic lights you must stop behind the white line until the lights change to green. Don't

- move forward when the red and amber lights are showing together
- proceed when the light is green if your exit road is blocked.

If you're approaching traffic lights that are visible from a distance and the light has been green for some time, it's likely to change. Try to anticipate this. Be ready to slow down and stop.

You are approaching a red traffic light. The signal will change from red to

Mark one answer

☒ red and amber, then green

☒ green, then amber

☒ amber, then green

☒ green and amber, then green

Answer

✖ **red and amber, then green**

If you know which light is going to show next you can plan your approach accordingly. This will prevent excessive braking or hesitation at the junction.

A red traffic light means

Mark one answer

☒ you should stop unless turning left

☒ stop, if you are able to brake safely

☒ you must stop and wait behind the stop line

☒ proceed with caution

Answer

✖ **you must stop and wait behind the stop line**

Learn the sequence of traffic lights.

- RED means stop and wait behind the stop line.

- RED-AND-AMBER also means stop. Don't go until the green light shows.

- GREEN means you may go if your way is clear. Don't proceed if your exit road is blocked, and don't block the junction. Look out for pedestrians.

- AMBER means stop at the stop line. You may continue if the amber light appears after you've crossed the stop line or you're so close to it that to pull up might cause an accident.

Question 11.93

At traffic lights, amber on its own means

Mark one answer

- [ ] prepare to go
- [ ] go if the way is clear
- [ ] go if no pedestrians are crossing
- [ ] stop at the stop line

Answer

✗ **stop at the stop line**

If the lights have been on green for a while they're likely to change to amber and then red as you approach. Anticipate this so that you're able to stop in time.

Question 11.94

A red traffic light means

Mark one answer

- [ ] you must stop behind the white stop line
- [ ] you may drive straight on if there is no other traffic
- [ ] you may turn left if it is safe to do so
- [ ] you must slow down and prepare to stop if traffic has started to cross

Answer

✗ **you must stop behind the white stop line**

The white line is positioned so that pedestrians have room to cross in front of waiting vehicles. If pedestrians are crossing, make sure your handbrake is on.

You are approaching traffic lights. Red and amble are showing. This means

Mark one answer

☒ pass the lights if the road is clear

☒ there is a fault with the lights – take care

☒ wait for the green light before you pass the lights

☒ the lights are about to change to red

Answer

❌ **wait for the green light before you pass the lights**

Other traffic might still be clearing the junction. Don't take risks.

You are at a junction controlled by traffic lights. When should you NOT proceed at green?

Mark one answer

☒ When pedestrians are waiting to cross

☒ When your exit from the junction is blocked

☒ When you think the lights may be about to change

☒ When you intend to turn right

Answer

❌ **When your exit from the junction is blocked**

As you approach the lights, look into the road you wish to take. Only proceed if your exit road is clear. If the road is blocked, hold back, even if you have to wait for the next green signal.

Question 11.97

You are in the left-hand lane at traffic lights. You are waiting to turn left. At which of these traffic lights must you NOT move on?

Mark one answer

Answer

At some junctions there may be a separate signal for each lane. These are called 'filter' lights. They're designed to help traffic flow at major junctions. Make sure that you're in the correct lane, and proceed if the green light shows.

Question 11.98

What does this sign mean?

Mark one answer

- [ ] Traffic lights out of order
- [ ] Amber signal out of order
- [ ] Temporary traffic lights ahead
- [ ] New traffic lights ahead

Answer

 Traffic lights out of order

Where traffic lights are out of order you might see this sign. Proceed with caution as nobody has priority at the junction.

Question 11.99

You see this sign at a crossroads. You should

Mark one answer

- [ ] maintain the same speed
- [ ] drive on with great care
- [ ] find another route
- [ ] telephone the police

Answer

✗ drive on with great care

Only do so if the road is clear. Treat the road as if it was an unmarked junction, that is, no one has priority.

Question 11.100

When traffic lights are out of order, who has priority?

Mark one answer

- [ ] Traffic going straight on
- [ ] Traffic turning right
- [ ] Nobody
- [ ] Traffic turning left

Answer

✗ Nobody

Treat the junction as an unmarked crossroads. Deal with the situation with caution.

Question 11.101

These flashing red lights mean STOP. In which THREE of the following places could you find them?

Mark three answers

- [ ] Pelican crossings
- [ ] Lifting bridges
- [ ] Zebra crossings
- [ ] Level crossings
- [ ] Motorway exits
- [ ] Fire stations

Answers

✗ Lifting bridges
✗ Level crossings
✗ Fire stations

Don't take risks by trying to beat the lights, even if it's clear. You must stop.

Question 11.102

What do these zigzag lines at pedestrian crossings mean?

Mark one answer

 No parking at any time

Parking allowed only for a short time

Slow down to 20 mph

Sounding horns is not allowed

Answer

 No parking at any time

The approach to hazards may be marked with signs on the road surface. The approach to a pedestrian crossing is marked with zigzag lines. Don't

* park on them
* overtake the leading vehicle when approaching the crossing.

Parking here will block the view for pedestrians and the approaching traffic.

Question 11.103

You are approaching a zebra crossing where pedestrians are waiting. Which arm signal might you give?

Mark one answer

Answer

A 'slowing down' signal will indicate your intentions to oncoming and following vehicles. Be aware that pedestrians might start to cross as soon as they see this signal.

The white line along the side of the road

Mark one answer

☒ shows the edge of the carriageway

☒ shows the approach to a hazard

☒ means no parking

☒ means no overtaking

Answer

☒ **shows the edge of the carriageway**

This is found at the edge of the road other than at junctions. This can be especially useful when visibility is restricted.

The white line painted in the centre of the road means

Mark one answer

☒ the area is hazardous and you must not overtake

☒ you should give priority to oncoming vehicles

☒ do not cross the line unless the road ahead is clear

☒ the area is a national speed limit zone

Answer

☒ **do not cross the line unless the road ahead is clear**

A long white line with short gaps is a warning line, so if you wish to overtake or need to turn, consider the risks.

When may you cross a double solid white line in the middle of the road?

Mark one answer

 To pass traffic that is queuing back at a junction

 To pass a car signalling to turn left ahead

 To pass a road maintenance vehicle travelling at 10 mph or less

 To pass a vehicle that is towing a trailer

Answer

 To pass a road maintenance vehicle travelling at 10 mph or less

Only overtake such a vehicle if you're sure that you can complete the manoeuvre safely. Keep well back before you overtake so that you have a clear view of the road. Double solid white lines indicate that there are hazards, such as bends in the road or junctions, so be extra cautious.

A white line like this along the centre of the road is a

Mark one answer

 bus lane marking

 hazard warning

 'give way' marking

 lane marking

Answer

 hazard warning

Make a note of hazard lines as you drive. Look well ahead and around so that you're prepared for any potential dangers.

You see this white arrow on the road ahead. It means

Mark one answer

- [×] entrance on the left
- [×] all vehicles turn left
- [×] keep left of the hatched markings
- [×] road bending to the left

Answer

× **keep left of the hatched markings**

Don't attempt to overtake here, there might be unseen hazards over the brow of the hill; keep to the left.

What does this road marking mean?

Mark one answer

- [×] Do not cross the line
- [×] No stopping allowed
- [×] You are approaching a hazard
- [×] No overtaking allowed

Answer

× **You are approaching a hazard**

Road markings will warn you of a hazard ahead. A single broken line, with long markings and short gaps, along the centre of the road is a hazard warning line. Don't cross it unless you can see that the road is clear WELL ahead.

Question 11.110

This marking appears on the road just before a

Mark one answer

 no entry sign

 give way sign

 stop sign

 no through road sign

Answer

✘ give way sign

You must give way to the traffic on the main road. This road marking might not be used at junctions where there is relatively little traffic. The give way rules still apply.

Question 11.111

Where would you see this road marking?

Mark one answer

 At traffic lights

 On road humps

 Near a level crossing

 At a box junction

Answer

✘ On road humps

Due to the dark colour of the road, changes in surface aren't easily seen. White triangles painted on the road surface give you an indication of where there are road humps.

Which is a hazard warning line?

Mark one answer

Answer

Look out for places where the single broken line on the road surface gets longer. This will mean there's a hazard ahead.

Question 11.113

At this junction there is a stop sign with a solid white line on the road surface. Why is there a stop sign here?

Mark one answer

☒ Speed on the major road is de-restricted

☒ It is a busy junction

☒ Visibility along the major road is restricted

☒ There are hazard warning lines in the centre of the road

Answer

☒ **Visibility along the major road is restricted**

If your view is restricted at a road junction you must stop. There may also be a 'Stop' sign. Don't emerge until you're sure there's no traffic approaching.

IF YOU DON'T KNOW, DON'T GO.

Question 11.114

You see this line across the road at the entrance to a roundabout. What does it mean?

Mark one answer

- [x] Give way to traffic from the right
- [x] Traffic from the left has right of way
- [x] You have right of way
- [x] Stop at the line

Answer

 Give way to traffic from the right

Slow down as you approach, checking the traffic as you do so. If you need to stop and give way, stay behind the broken line until it is safe to emerge onto the roundabout.

Question 11.115

Where would you find this road marking?

Mark one answer

- [x] At a railway crossing
- [x] At a junction
- [x] On a motorway
- [x] On a pedestrian crossing

Answer

 At a junction

This marking indicates the direction in which the traffic should flow.

Question 11.116

How will a police officer in a patrol vehicle normally get you to stop?

Mark one answer

- ☒ Flash the headlights, indicate left and point to the left
- ☒ Wait until you stop, then approach you
- ☒ Use the siren, overtake, cut in front and stop
- ☒ Pull alongside you, use the siren and wave you to stop

Answer

☒ **Flash the headlights, indicate left and point to the left**

You must obey signals given by the police. If a police officer in a patrol vehicle wants you to stop he or she will indicate this without causing danger to you or other traffic.

Question 11.117

There is a police car following you. The police officer flashes the headlights and points to the left. What should you do?

Mark one answer

- ☒ Turn at the next left
- ☒ Pull up on the left
- ☒ Stop immediately
- ☒ Move over to the left

Answer

☒ **Pull up on the left**

You must pull up on the left, as soon as it's safe to do so, and switch off your engine.

Question 11.118

You approach a junction. The traffic lights are not working. A police officer gives this signal. You should

Mark one answer

- ☒ turn left only
- ☒ turn right only
- ☒ stop level with the officer's arm
- ☒ stop at the stop line

Answer

☒ **stop at the stop line**

If police officers or traffic wardens are directing traffic you must obey them. They will use the arm signals shown in *The Highway Code*. Learn what these mean and act accordingly.

The driver of the car in front is giving this arm signal. What does it mean?

Mark one answer

- [ ] The driver is slowing down
- [ ] The driver intends to turn right
- [ ] The driver wishes to overtake
- [ ] The driver intends to turn left

Answer

✖ **The driver intends to turn left**

There might be an occasion where another driver uses an arm signal. This may be because the vehicle's indicators are obscured by other traffic. In order for such signals to be effective all drivers should know the meaning of them. Be aware that the 'left turn' signal might look similar to the 'slowing down' signal

The driver of this car is giving an arm signal. What is he about to do?

Mark one answer

- [ ] Turn to the right
- [ ] Turn to the left
- [ ] Go straight ahead
- [ ] Let pedestrians cross

Answer

✖ **Turn to the left**

This could be used where there is a complicated junction and you wish to make your intentions clear. For arm signals to be effective all road users should know their meaning.

Question 11.121

Which arm signal tells a following vehicle that you intend to turn left?

Mark one answer

Answer

There may be occasions when you need to give an arm signal. For example

- where other road users can't see your indicators
- in bright sunshine, when your indicators may be difficult to see
- to reinforce a signal at a complex road layout.

Make sure that they're clear, correct and decisive.

Question 11.122

How should you give an arm signal to turn left?

Mark one answer

Answer

There may be occasions where other road users are unable to see your indicators, such as in bright sunlight or at a busy complicated junction. In these cases a hand signal will help others to understand your intentions.

Question 11.123

You are signalling to turn right in busy traffic. How would you confirm your intention safely?

Mark one answer

- Sound the horn
- Give an arm signal
- Flash your headlamp
- Position over the centre line

Answer

❌ **Give an arm signal**

In some situations you may feel your indicators cannot be seen by other road users. If you feel you need to make your intention more clearly seen, give the arm signal shown in *The Highway Code*.

Question 11.124

How should you give an arm signal to turn left?

Mark one answer

Answer

❌

Arm signals are very effective during daylight, especially when you're wearing bright clothing. Practise giving arm signals when you're learning. You need to be able to keep full control of your machine with one hand off the handlebars.

Question 11.125

Your indicators are difficult to see due to bright sunshine. When using them you should

Mark one answer

- also give an arm signal
- sound your horn
- flash your headlamp
- keep both hands on the handlebars

Answer

❌ **also give an arm signal**

Arm signals are effective when you aren't sure that your indicators can be seen by other road users. Make sure that your signal is decisive, and return your hand to the handlebars before you turn.

Question 11.126

You are giving an arm signal ready to turn left. Why should you NOT continue with the arm signal while you turn?

Mark one answer

- Because you might hit a pedestrian on the corner
- Because you will have less steering control
- Because you will need to keep the clutch applied
- Because other motorists will think that you are stopping on the corner

Answer

 Because you will have less steering control

Don't maintain an arm signal when turning. You should have full control of your machine at all times.

Question 11.127

You want to turn right at a junction but you think that your indicators cannot be seen clearly. What should you do?

Mark one answer

- Get out and check if your indicators can be seen
- Stay in the left-hand lane
- Keep well over to the right
- Give an arm signal as well as an indicator signal

Answer

 Give an arm signal as well as an indicator signal

If you think that your indicators can't be seen clearly, make sure that your intention is clear by using an arm signal too.

Question 11.128

When may you sound the horn on your vehicle?

Mark one answer

- To give you right of way
- To attract a friend's attention
- To warn others of your presence
- To make slower drivers move over

Answer

✖ **To warn others of your presence**

Don't use the horn aggressively. You must not sound it

- when driving in a built-up area between 11.30 pm and 7 am
- when your vehicle is stationary

unless a moving vehicle poses a danger.

Question 11.129

You must not use your horn when your vehicle is stationary

Mark one answer

- ☒ unless a moving vehicle may cause you danger
- ☒ at any time whatsoever
- ☒ unless it is used only briefly
- ☒ except for signalling that you have just arrived

Answer

✗ unless a moving vehicle may cause you danger

Do this only if you think that there is a risk of an accident. Don't use it for attracting the attention of others for social reasons.

Question 11.130

When motorists flash their headlights at you it means

Mark one answer

- ☒ that there is a radar speed trap ahead
- ☒ that they are giving way to you
- ☒ that they are warning you of their presence
- ☒ that there is something wrong with your vehicle

Answer

✗ that they are warning you of their presence

If other drivers flash their headlights, it isn't a signal to show priority. The flashing of headlights has the same meaning as sounding the horn – it's a warning of their presence.

Question 11.131

Why should you make sure that you have cancelled your indicators after turning?

Mark one answer

- ☒ To avoid flattening the battery
- ☒ To avoid misleading other road users
- ☒ To avoid dazzling other road users
- ☒ To avoid damage to the indicator relay

Answer

✗ To avoid misleading other road users

If you haven't taken a sharp turn your indicators might not turn off automatically. Be aware of this if you've used them for slight deviations, such as passing parked vehicles.

You are waiting at a T-junction. A vehicle is coming from the right with the left signal flashing. What should you do?

Mark one answer

- [ ] Move out and accelerate hard
- [ ] Wait until the vehicle starts to turn in
- [ ] Pull out before the vehicle reaches the junction
- [ ] Move out slowly

Answer

❌ **Wait until the vehicle starts to turn in**

Other road users may give misleading signals. When you're waiting at a junction don't emerge until you're sure of their intentions. Pulling out safely calls for accurate judgement.

When may you use hazard warning lights when driving?

Mark one answer

- [ ] Instead of sounding the horn in a built-up area between 11.30 pm and 7 am
- [ ] On a motorway or unrestricted dual carriageway, to warn of a hazard ahead
- [ ] On rural routes, after a warning sign of animals
- [ ] On the approach to toucan crossings where cyclists are waiting to cross

Answer

❌ **On a motorway or unrestricted dual carriageway, to warn of a hazard ahead**

Where there's queuing traffic ahead and you have to slow down and maybe stop, showing your hazard warning lights will alert the traffic behind to the situation. Don't forget to switch them off as the queue forms behind you.

Question 11.134

Where would you see these road markings?

Mark one answer

- At a level crossing
- On a motorway slip road
- At a pedestrian crossing
- On a single-track road

Answer

✗ On a motorway slip road

You must not enter into the area marked except in an emergency.

Question 11.135

When may you NOT overtake on the left?

Mark one answer

- On a free-flowing motorway or dual carriageway
- When the traffic is moving slowly in queues
- On a one-way street
- When the car in front is signalling to turn right

Answer

✗ On a free-flowing motorway or dual carriageway

You may only overtake on the left

- when traffic is moving slowly in queues
- when a vehicle ahead is positioned to turn right and there's room to pass on the left
- in a one-way street.

Don't overtake on the left if the traffic on a dual carriageway is flowing freely. Other road users won't anticipate your action.

You are driving on a motorway. There is a slow-moving vehicle ahead. On the back you see this sign. You should

Mark one answer

☒ pass on the right

☒ pass on the left

☒ leave at the next exit

☒ drive no further

Answer

☒ **pass on the left**

If you have to change lanes in order to pass the vehicle, use your mirrors and signal. If it's safe to do so move over into the lane on your left. Look well down the road so that you can spot such hazards early, leaving you time to complete the manoeuvre safely.

Question 11.137

What does this motorway sign mean?

Mark one answer

☒ Change to the lane on your left

☒ Leave the motorway at the next exit

☒ Change to the opposite carriageway

☒ Pull up on the hard shoulder

Answer

☒ **Change to the lane on your left**

On the motorway, signs might show temporary warnings. This allows for different traffic or weather conditions and might indicate

• lane closures

• speed limits

• weather warnings.

Question 11.138

What does this motorway sign mean?

Mark one answer

 Temporary minimum speed 50 mph

 No services for 50 miles

 Obstruction 50 metres (164 feet) ahead

 Temporary maximum speed 50 mph

Answer

 Temporary maximum speed 50 mph

Look out for signs above your lane or on the central reservation. These will give you important information or warnings about the road ahead.

Due to the high speeds of motorway traffic these signs may light up some distance from any hazard. Don't ignore the signs just because the road looks clear to you.

Question 11.139

What does this sign mean?

Mark one answer

 Through traffic to use left lane

 Right-hand lane T-junction only

 Right-hand lane closed ahead

 11 tonne weight limit

Answer

 Right-hand lane closed ahead

Move over as soon as you see the sign and it's safe to do so. Don't stay in the lane which is closed ahead until the last moment to beat a queue of traffic.

Question 11.140

On a motorway this sign means

Mark one answer

- [ ] move over onto the hard shoulder
- [ ] overtaking on the left only
- [ ] leave the motorway at the next exit
- [ ] move to the lane on your left

Answer

❌ **move to the lane on your left**

Signs showing temporary warnings may be mounted on gantries over the motorway and might indicate

- lane closures
- speed limits
- weather warnings.

Question 11.141

What does '25' mean on this motorway sign?

Mark one answer

- [ ] The distance to the nearest town
- [ ] The route number of the road
- [ ] The number of the next junction
- [ ] The speed limit on the slip road

Answer

❌ **The number of the next junction**

Before you set out on your journey use a road map to plan your route. You should give yourself enough time to get into the correct lane for the exit that you wish to take. Uncertainty at road junctions can lead to danger.

Question 11.142

You are driving on a motorway. Red flashing lights appear above your lane only. What should you do?

Mark one answer

- [ ] Continue in that lane and await further information
- [ ] Go no further in that lane
- [ ] Drive onto the hard shoulder
- [ ] Stop and wait for an instruction to proceed

Answer

❌ **Go no further in that lane**

Flashing red lights above your lane show that your lane is closed. You should move into a clear lane in plenty of time.

Question 11.143

The right-hand lane of a three-lane motorway is

Mark one answer

- [ ] for lorries only
- [ ] an overtaking lane
- [ ] the right-turn lane
- [ ] an acceleration lane

Answer

 an overtaking lane

Motorways today can become very busy. If a vehicle in the right-hand lane is preventing traffic from overtaking, or is travelling at a slower speed than those on the nearside, bunching can occur. This means that drivers will begin to travel too close to the vehicle in front of them. If you aren't overtaking, use the left-hand lane.

Question 11.144

Where can you find reflective amber studs on a motorway?

Mark one answer

- [ ] Separating the slip road from the motorway
- [ ] On the left-hand edge of the road
- [ ] On the right-hand edge of the road
- [ ] Separating the lanes

Answer

 On the right-hand edge of the road

At night or in poor visibility reflective studs on the road will help you to judge your position on the carriageway.

Question 11.145

Where on a motorway would you find green reflective studs?

Mark one answer

- [ ] Separating driving lanes
- [ ] Between the hard shoulder and the carriageway
- [ ] At slip road entrances and exits
- [ ] Between the carriageway and the central reservation

Answer

 At slip road entrances and exits

Knowing the colours of the reflective studs on the road will help you in foggy conditions or when visibility is poor.

You are travelling along a motorway. You see this sign. You should

Mark one answer

☒ leave the motorway at the next exit

☒ turn left immediately

☒ change lane

☒ move onto the hard shoulder

Answer

 leave the motorway at the next exit

You'll see this sign if the motorway is closed ahead. When you see it prepare to get into the nearside lane so that you can take the exit safely. Don't leave it to the last moment.

You see these signs overhead on the motorway. They mean

Mark one answer

☒ leave the motorway at the next exit

☒ all vehicles use the hard shoulder

☒ sharp bend to the left ahead

☒ stop, all lanes ahead closed

Answer

 leave the motorway at the next exit

There has been an incident ahead and the motorway is closed. You must obey the sign. Make sure that you prepare to leave as soon as you see the warning sign. Don't leave it until the last moment and cut across other traffic.

What does this sign mean?

Mark one answer

 No motor vehicles

 End of motorway

No through road

End of bus lane

Answer

 End of motorway

When you leave the motorway make sure that you check your speedometer. You may be going faster than you realise. Slow down on the slip road. Look out for speed limit signs.

Which of these signs means that the national speed limit applies?

Mark one answer

Answer

You should know the speed limit for the road that you're travelling on and the vehicle that you're driving. Study your copy of *The Highway Code*, where the limits are clearly shown.

What is the maximum speed on a single carriageway road?

Mark one answer

 50 mph

 60 mph

 40 mph

70 mph

Answer

 60 mph

If you're travelling on a dual carriageway that becomes a single carriageway road, cut your speed gradually so that you aren't exceeding the limit as you enter. There might not be a sign to remind you of the limit, so learn the speed limits.

This section looks at the documents needed for drivers
and their vehicles.

The questions will ask you about

- licences

- insurance

- MOT test certificate.

Question 12.1

To drive on the road learners MUST

Mark one answer

☒ have NO penalty points on their licence

☒ have taken professional instruction

☒ have a signed, valid provisional licence

☒ apply for a driving test within 12 months

Answer

☒ have a signed, valid provisional licence

Before you drive on the road you must have a signed provisional licence for the category of vehicle that you're driving. As soon as you've received your licence, sign it. It isn't valid until you've done so.

Question 12.2

To supervise a learner driver you must

Mark two answers

☒ have held a full licence for at least 3 years

☒ be at least 21

☒ be an approved driving instructor

☒ hold an advanced driving certificate

Answers

☒ have held a full licence for at least 3 years

☒ be at least 21

Don't just take someone's word that they are qualified to supervise you. The person who sits alongside you while you are learning should be a responsible adult.

Question 12.3

Your driving licence must be signed by

Mark one answer

☒ a police officer

☒ a driving instructor

☒ your next of kin

☒ yourself

Answer

☒ yourself

Do this as soon as you receive it through the post. Don't drive until you've signed it.

Question 12.4

You have passed compulsory basic training (CBT). You want a direct access test. You must

Mark four answers

- [ ] be aged 21 or over
- [ ] not exceed 60 mph
- [ ] have an approved instructor with you
- [ ] remain in radio contact while learning
- [ ] only learn in daylight hours
- [ ] wear fluorescent or reflective clothing

Answers

- [X] **be aged 21 or over**
- [X] **have an approved instructor with you**
- [X] **remain in radio contact while learning**
- [X] **wear fluorescent or reflective clothing**

If you wish to learn to ride a motorcycle via the direct access route you must be at least 21 years old. When practising on the road you must

- have L plates fitted (D plates in Wales)
- be accompanied by an approved instructor in radio contact
- wear fluorescent or reflective safety clothing.

Question 12.5

You want a licence to ride a large motorcycle via direct access. You will

Mark one answer

- [ ] not require L plates if you have passed a car test
- [ ] require L plates only when learning on your own machine
- [ ] require L plates while learning with a qualified instructor
- [ ] not require L plates if you have passed a moped test

Answer

- [X] **require L plates while learning with a qualified instructor**

While training through the direct access scheme you must be accompanied by an instructor on another motorcycle and in radio contact. You will have to display L plates (D plates in Wales) on your motorcycle and follow all normal learner restrictions.

Question 12.6

You are a learner motorcyclist. The law states that you can carry a passenger when

Mark one answer

- [ ] your motorcycle is no larger than 125 cc
- [ ] your pillion passenger is a full licence-holder
- [ ] you have passed your test for a full licence
- [ ] you have had three years' experience of riding

Answer

- [X] **you have passed your test for a full licence**

When you're a learner motorcyclist you must comply with certain legal restrictions. The law states that you must

- display L plates (or D plates in Wales) to the front and rear on your machine
- not carry pillion passengers
- not use the motorway.

DSA THEORY TEST for car drivers and motorcyclists

NI

Question 12.7

What should you bring with you when taking your motorcycle test?

Mark three answers

- [ ] A service record book
- [ ] An insurance certificate
- [ ] A signed driving licence
- [ ] An MOT certificate
- [ ] A CBT certificate
- [ ] Signed photo identity

Answers

- [x] **A signed driving licence**
- [x] **A CBT certificate**
- [x] **Signed photo identity**

When you attend a motorcycle test your examiner will ask to see

- your driving licence
- your CBT certificate (except in Northern Ireland).
- signed photo ID.

NI

Question 12.8

Before taking a motorcycle test you need

Mark one answer

- [ ] a full moped licence
- [ ] a full car licence
- [ ] a Compulsory Basic Training (CBT) certificate
- [ ] 12 months riding experience

Answer

- [x] **a Compulsory Basic Training (CBT) certificate**

You can find out about a CBT course by asking your motorcycle dealer or by telephoning 0115 901 2595. In Northern Ireland the CBT scheme doesn't operate, so all reference to CBT isn't applicable.

NI

Question 12.9

Compulsory Basic Training (CBT) can only be carried out by

Mark one answer

- [ ] any Approved Driving Instructor (ADI)
- [ ] any road safety officer
- [ ] any DSA-approved training body
- [ ] any motorcycle main dealer

Answer

- [x] **any DSA-approved training body**

DSA approves bodies to provide training in a safe environment. Frequent checks are made to ensure a high standard of instruction. Taking a CBT course will provide you with the right start to your motorcycling life.

NI

Question 12.10

After passing your motorcycle test you must exchange the pass certificate for a full motorcycle licence within

Mark one answer

☒ six months

☒ one year

☒ two years

☒ five years

Answer

☒ **two years**

When you pass your practical motorcycle test you'll be issued with a pass certificate (form D10 – DL8 in Northern Ireland). You must exchange the certificate for a full licence within two years of passing your test. If you don't

- the certificate will lapse
- you'll have to retake your test if you wish to resume full motorcycle licence entitlement.

Question 12.11

For which TWO of these must you show your motor insurance certificate?

Mark two answers

☒ When you are taking your driving test

☒ When buying or selling a vehicle

☒ When a police officer asks you for it

☒ When you are taxing your vehicle

☒ When having an MOT inspection

Answers

☒ **When a police officer asks you for it**

☒ **When you are taxing your vehicle**

When you take out motor insurance you'll be issued with a Certificate of Insurance. This contains details explaining who and what is insured. You'll have to produce your Certificate of Insurance when you're paying your vehicle excise duty (road tax).

If a police officer asks for your Certificate of Insurance and you don't have it with you, you may produce it at a police station within seven days (five days in Northern Ireland).

Question 12.12

Vehicle excise duty is often called 'Road Tax' or 'The Tax Disc'. You must

Mark one answer

☒ keep it with your registration document

☒ display it clearly on your vehicle

☒ keep it concealed safely in your vehicle

☒ carry it on you at all times

Answer

☒ **display it clearly on your vehicle**

It should be displayed on the left hand bottom of the windscreen. This allows it to be easily seen from the kerbside. It must be current, and you can't transfer the disc from vehicle to vehicle.

Question 12.13

For which TWO of these must you show your motorcycle insurance certificate?

Mark two answers

- [ ] When you are taking your motorcycle test
- [ ] When buying or selling a machine
- [ ] When a police officer asks you for it
- [ ] When you are taxing your machine
- [ ] When having an MOT inspection

Answers

✗ When a police officer asks you for it
✗ When you are taxing your machine

You don't have to carry it with you at all times. However, it must be valid and available to present at a police station (within seven days) if requested.

Question 12.14

NI

A police officer asks to see your driving documents. You do not have them with you. You may produce them at a police station within

Mark one answer

- [ ] five days
- [ ] seven days
- [ ] 14 days
- [ ] 21 days

Answer

✗ seven days

You don't have to carry your documents with you. If a police officer asks to see them and you don't have them with you, you may produce them at a police station within seven days (five days in Northern Ireland).

Question 12.15

Before riding anyone else's motorcycle you should make sure that

Mark one answer

- [ ] the machine owner has third party insurance cover
- [ ] your own machine has insurance cover
- [ ] the machine is insured for your use
- [ ] the owner has the insurance documents with them

Answer

✗ the machine is insured for your use

If you borrow a motorcycle you must make sure that you're insured. Find out yourself. Don't take anyone else's word for it.

Question 12.16

Before driving anyone else's motor vehicle you should make sure that

Mark one answer

- ☒ the vehicle owner has third party insurance cover
- ☒ your own vehicle has insurance cover
- ☒ the vehicle is insured for your use
- ☒ the owner has left the insurance documents in the vehicle

Answer

☒ the vehicle is insured for your use

Don't take someone else's word on the matter. New drivers are considered a high risk and this is reflected in high insurance costs. If you're careful and don't have an accident the cost of your insurance will come down, although other factors, such as your occupation and where you live, are also taken into account.

Question 12.17

What is the legal minimum insurance cover you must have to drive on public roads?

Mark one answer

- ☒ Third party, fire and theft
- ☒ Fully comprehensive
- ☒ Third party only
- ☒ Personal injury cover

Answer

☒ Third party only

The minimum insurance requirement by law is third party cover. This covers others involved in an accident, but not damage to your vehicle. Basic third party insurance won't cover theft or fire damage. Check with your insurance company for advice on the best cover for you. Make sure that you read the policy carefully.

Question 12.18

Your car has third party insurance. What does this cover?

Mark three answers

- ☒ Damage to your own car
- ☒ Damage to your car by fire
- ☒ Injury to another person
- ☒ Damage to someone's property
- ☒ Damage to other vehicles
- ☒ Injury to yourself

Answers

☒ Injury to another person
☒ Damage to someone's property
☒ Damage to other vehicles

Third party insurance doesn't cover damage to your own vehicle or injury to yourself. If you have an accident and you damage your vehicle you might have to carry out the repairs at your own expense.

Question 12.19

The cost of your insurance may be reduced if

Mark one answer

- [ ] your car is large and powerful
- [ ] you are using the car for work purposes
- [ ] you have penalty points on your licence
- [ ] you are over 25 years old

Answer

 you are over 25 years old

Provided you haven't had previous accidents or committed any driving offences, your insurance should be less costly as you get beyond the age of 25. This is because statistics show that most accidents are caused by or involve young and/or inexperienced drivers.

Question 12.20

Motor cars and motorcycles must FIRST have an MOT test certificate when they are

Mark one answer

- [ ] one year old
- [ ] three years old
- [ ] five years old
- [ ] seven years old

Answer

 three years old

The vehicle you drive must be in good condition and roadworthy. If it's over three years old it must have a valid MOT test certificate. In Northern Ireland a vehicle first needs an MOT test certificate when it's four years old.

Question 12.21

An MOT certificate is normally valid for

Mark one answer

- [ ] three years after the date it was issued
- [ ] 10,000 miles
- [ ] one year after the date it was issued
- [ ] 30,000 miles

Answer

 one year after the date it was issued

Make a note of the date that your vehicle is due for an MOT. Some garages remind you, but not all of them.

Question 12.22

Your car needs an MOT certificate. If you drive without one this could invalidate your

Mark one answer

- ☒ vehicle service record
- ☒ insurance
- ☒ road tax disc
- ☒ vehicle registration document

NI

Question 12.23

When is it legal to drive a car over three years old without an MOT certificate?

Mark one answer

- ☒ Up to seven days after the old certificate has run out
- ☒ When driving to an MOT centre to arrange an appointment
- ☒ Just after buying a secondhand car with no MOT
- ☒ When driving to an appointment at an MOT centre

Question 12.24

Your vehicle needs a current MOT certificate. You do not have one. Until you do have one you will not be able to renew your

Mark one answer

- ☒ driving licence
- ☒ vehicle insurance
- ☒ road tax disc
- ☒ vehicle registration document

Answer

☒ insurance

You are driving a vehicle which is illegal and could be unsafe. As there is a higher risk of an accident your insurance company would not cover you for any damage incurred.

Answer

☒ When driving to an appointment at an MOT centre

If a car is over three years old it must have a valid MOT certificate if you want to use it on the road. The only time a car is exempt is when it's being driven to an appointment at an MOT testing station. In Northern Ireland the time limit before an MOT test is first needed is four years.

Answer

☒ road tax disc

You'll have to produce your MOT certificate when you renew your road tax disc (road fund licence).

Question 12.25

Which of these vehicles are NOT required to have an MOT certificate?

Mark two answers

- [ ] Police vehicle
- [×] Small trailer
- [ ] Ambulance
- [×] Caravan

Answers

- [×] **Small trailer**
- [×] **Caravan**

Despite not needing an MOT certificate, you should ensure that your trailer is in good order and properly serviced. Tyres, wheel nuts, lights and indicators should be checked regularly.

Question 12.26

Which THREE of the following do you need before you can drive legally?

Mark three answers

- [×] A valid signed driving licence
- [×] A valid tax disc displayed on your vehicle
- [ ] Proof of your identity
- [×] Proper insurance cover
- [ ] Breakdown cover
- [ ] A vehicle handbook

Answers

- [×] **A valid signed driving licence**
- [×] **A valid tax disc displayed on your vehicle**
- [×] **Proper insurance cover**

Make sure that your vehicle's not only safe but legal.

Question 12.27

CBT completion certificates (DL196) issued on or after 01 July 1996 are valid for

Mark one answer

- [ ] two years
- [×] three years
- [ ] five years
- [ ] indefinitely

Answer

- [×] **three years**

In order to complete the CBT course you'll have to demonstrate that you can ride confidently and safely in a variety of road and traffic conditions. Your certificate will enable you to apply for your tests. If you don't pass your tests within its three-year life you'll have to complete the CBT course again.

Question 12.28

When you buy a motorcycle you will need a vehicle registration document from

Mark one answer

☒ any MOT testing station

☒ the person selling the motorcycle

☒ your local council offices

☒ your local trading standards officer

Answer

☒ **the person selling the motorcycle**

You must fill in your details and send it to the Driver and Vehicle Licensing Agency (DVLA) at the address given on the document.

Question 12.29

Which THREE pieces of information are found on a vehicle registration document?

Mark three answers

☒ Registered keeper

☒ Make of the vehicle

☒ Service history details

☒ Date of the MOT

☒ Type of insurance cover

☒ Engine size

Answers

☒ **Registered keeper**

☒ **Make of the vehicle**

☒ **Engine size**

Every vehicle used on the road has a registration document. This is issued by the Driver Vehicle Licensing Agency (DVLA) or the Driver and Vehicle Licensing Northern Ireland (DVLNI) and it keeps a record of the change of ownership. The document states

• date of first registration

• registration number

• previous keeper

• registered keeper

• make of vehicle

• engine size and chassis number

• year of manufacture

• colour.

Question 12.30

You have a duty to contact the licensing authority when

Mark three answers

- [ ] you go abroad on holiday
- [ ] you change your vehicle
- [ ] you change your name
- [ ] your job status is changed
- [ ] your permanent address changes
- [ ] your job involves travelling abroad

Answers

- [x] **you change your vehicle**
- [x] **you change your name**
- [x] **your permanent address changes**

The licensing authority need to keep their records up to date. You will receive a reminder when your road tax is due and they will need your current address for this purpose. Every vehicle in the country is registered so that it's possible to trace it's history.

Question 12.31

You must notify the licensing authority when

Mark three answers

- [ ] your health affects your driving
- [ ] your eyesight does not meet a set standard
- [ ] you intend lending your vehicle
- [ ] your vehicle requires an MOT certificate
- [ ] you change your vehicle

Answers

- [x] **your health affects your driving**
- [x] **your eyesight does not meet a set standard**
- [x] **you change your vehicle**

The Driver and Vehicle Licensing Agency (DVLA) hold the records of all vehicles and drivers in Great Britain. They need to know of any change in circumstances so that they can keep their records up to date. Your health might affect your ability to drive safely. This should not be underestimated, as you and others on the road could be at risk.

Question 12.32

You have just bought a secondhand vehicle. When should you tell the licensing authority of change of ownership?

Mark one answer

- [ ] Immediately
- [ ] After 28 days
- [ ] When an MOT is due
- [ ] Only when you insure it

Answer

- [x] **Immediately**

As soon as you can, fill out the registration document of the vehicle and send it off. The requirements will be written on the document. It is an offence not to notify the licensing agency.

This section looks at what to do in the event of an accident.

The questions will ask you about

- First Aid

- warning devices

- reporting procedures

- safety regulations.

Question 13.1
Which of these items should you carry in your vehicle for use in the event of an accident?

Mark three answers
- [ ] Road map
- [ ] Can of petrol
- [ ] Jump leads
- [ ] Fire extinguisher
- [ ] First Aid kit
- [ ] Warning triangle

Answers
- ❌ **Fire extinguisher**
- ❌ **First Aid kit**
- ❌ **Warning triangle**

This equipment could be invaluable and a small price to pay if it helps prevent or lessen injury.

Question 13.2
At the scene of an accident you should

Mark one answer
- [ ] not put yourself at risk
- [ ] go to those casualties who are screaming
- [ ] pull everybody out of their vehicles
- [ ] leave vehicle engines switched on

Answer
- ❌ **not put yourself at risk**

It's important that those at the scene of an accident do not create a further risk to themselves or other road users. If the accident has occurred on a motorway, traffic will be approaching at speed. Consider this when trying to help casualties or warn other drivers.

Question 13.3
You are the first to arrive at the scene of an accident. Which FOUR of these should you do?

Mark four answers
- [ ] Leave as soon as another motorist arrives
- [ ] Switch off the vehicle engine(s)
- [ ] Move uninjured people away from the vehicle(s)
- [ ] Call the emergency services
- [ ] Warn other traffic

Answers
- ❌ **Switch off the vehicle engine(s)**
- ❌ **Move uninjured people away from the vehicle(s)**
- ❌ **Call the emergency services**
- ❌ **Warn other traffic**

If you're involved in, or arrive at, the scene of an accident there are certain actions you should take. It's important to know what to do and also what NOT to do. You could save someone's life, or endanger it.

Question 13.4

An accident has just happened. An injured person is lying in the busy road. What is the FIRST thing you should do to help?

Mark one answer

- [x] Treat the person for shock
- [x] Warn other traffic
- [x] Place them in the recovery position
- [x] Make sure the injured person is kept warm

Question 13.5

You are the first person to arrive at an accident where people are badly injured. Which THREE should you do?

Mark three answers

- [x] Switch on your own hazard warning lights
- [x] Make sure that someone telephones for an ambulance
- [x] Try and get people who are injured to drink something
- [x] Move the people who are injured clear of their vehicles
- [x] Get people who are not injured clear of the scene

Question 13.6

You arrive at the scene of a motorcycle accident. The rider is injured. When should the helmet be removed?

Mark one answer

- [x] Only when it is essential
- [x] Always straight away
- [x] Only when the motorcyclist asks
- [x] Always, unless they are in shock

Answer

✗ Warn other traffic

You could do this by

- displaying an advance warning signal, if you have one
- switching on hazard warning lights or other lights
- any other means that does not put you at risk.'

Answers

✗ Switch on your own hazard warning lights

✗ Make sure that someone telephones for an ambulance

✗ Get people who are not injured clear of the scene

If you're the first person to arrive at the scene of an accident, further collision and fire are the first concerns. Switching off vehicle engines will reduce the risk of fire. Your hazard warning lights will let approaching traffic know that there's a need for caution.Don't assume someone else has called the emergency services.

Answer

✗ Only when it is essential

If a motorcyclist has been injured in an accident it's important not to remove their helmet unless it is necessary to keep them alive.

Question 13.7

You arrive at a serious motorcycle accident. The motorcyclist is unconscious and bleeding. Your main priorities should be to

Mark three answers

- [ ] try to stop the bleeding
- [ ] make a list of witnesses
- [ ] check the casualty's breathing
- [ ] take the numbers of the vehicles involved
- [ ] sweep up any loose debris
- [ ] check the casualty's airways

Answers

- [X] try to stop the bleeding
- [X] check the casualty's breathing
- [X] check the casualty's airways

At a road accident the danger of further collisions and fire need to be dealt with first. Injuries should be dealt with in the order

- Airway
- Breathing
- Circulation and bleeding.

Question 13.8

You arrive at an accident. A motorcyclist is unconscious. Your FIRST priority is the casualty's

Mark one answer

- [ ] breathing
- [ ] bleeding
- [ ] broken bones
- [ ] bruising

Answer

- [X] breathing

At the scene of an accident you must first make sure there is no danger from further collisions or fire before dealing with any casualties. The first priority when dealing with an unconscious person is to make sure they can breathe. This may involve clearing their airway if they're having difficulty or if some obstruction is obvious.

Question 13.9

At an accident a casualty is unconscious. Which THREE of the following should you check urgently?

Mark three answers

- [ ] Circulation
- [ ] Airway
- [ ] Shock
- [ ] Breathing
- [ ] Broken bones

Answers

- [X] Circulation
- [X] Airway
- [X] Breathing

An unconscious casualty may have difficulty breathing. Check that their tongue has not fallen back, blocking their airway. Do this by tilting the head back slightly.

Question 13.10

In first aid what does ABC stand for?

Mark three answers

- [×] Airway
- [×] Bleeding
- [×] Conscious
- [×] Breathing
- [×] Circulation
- [×] Alert

Answers

- [×] Airway
- [×] Breathing
- [×] Circulation

To check if a casualty is breathing put your face close to their mouth. Look, listen and feel for any sign of breathing.

Question 13.11

You arrive at the scene of an accident. It has just happened and someone is unconscious. Which of the following should be given urgent priority to help them?

Mark three answers

- [×] Clear the airway and keep it open
- [×] Try to get them to drink water
- [×] Check that they are breathing
- [×] Look for any witnesses
- [×] Stop any heavy bleeding
- [×] Take the numbers of vehicles involved

Answers

- [×] Clear the airway and keep it open
- [×] Check that they are breathing
- [×] Stop any heavy bleeding

Stay with the casualty and send someone to ring for an ambulance.

Question 13.12

At an accident someone is unconscious. Your main priorities should be to

Mark three answers

- [×] sweep up the broken glass
- [×] take the names of witnesses
- [×] count the number of vehicles involved
- [×] check the airway is clear
- [×] make sure they are breathing
- [×] stop any heavy bleeding

Answers

- [×] check the airway is clear
- [×] make sure they are breathing
- [×] stop any heavy bleeding

Remember this procedure by saying ABC. Airway – Breathing – Circulation

DSA THEORY TEST for car drivers and motorcyclists

Question 13.13

You have stopped at the scene of an accident to give help. Which THREE things should you do?

Mark three answers

- Keep injured people warm and comfortable
- Keep injured people calm by talking to them reassuringly
- Keep injured people on the move by walking them around
- Give injured people a warm drink
- Make sure that injured people are not left alone

Answers

- ✗ Keep injured people warm and comfortable
- ✗ Keep injured people calm by talking to them reassuringly
- ✗ Make sure that injured people are not left alone

If you stop at the scene of an accident to give help and there are casualties don't

- move injured people, unless further danger is threatened
- give the injured anything to drink.

Question 13.14

You arrive at the scene of an accident. It has just happened and someone is injured. Which of the following should be given urgent priority?

Mark three answers

- Stop any severe bleeding
- Get them a warm drink
- Check that their breathing is OK
- Take numbers of vehicles involved
- Look for witnesses
- Clear their airway and keep it open

Answers

- ✗ Stop any severe bleeding
- ✗ Check that their breathing is OK
- ✗ Clear their airway and keep it open

When you have done this, call the emergency services; they are the experts.

If you feel you are not capable of carrying out first aid, then consider doing some training. It could save a life.

Question 13.15

At an accident a casualty has stopped breathing. You should

Mark two answers

- [ ] remove anything that is blocking the mouth
- [ ] keep the head tilted forwards as far as possible
- [ ] raise the legs to help with circulation
- [ ] try to give the casualty something to drink
- [ ] keep the head tilted back as far as possible

Answers

- [X] **remove anything that is blocking the mouth**
- [X] **keep the head tilted back as far as possible**

These actions will ensure that the casualty has clear airways and in the correct position if mouth to mouth ventilation is required.

Question 13.16

You are at the scene of an accident. Someone is suffering from shock. You should

Mark four answers

- [ ] reassure them constantly
- [ ] offer them a cigarette
- [ ] keep them warm
- [ ] avoid moving them if possible
- [ ] loosen any tight clothing
- [ ] give them a warm drink

Answers

- [X] **reassure them constantly**
- [X] **keep them warm**
- [X] **avoid moving them if possible**
- [X] **loosen any tight clothing**

The effects of trauma may not be immediately obvious. Prompt treatment can help to minimise the effects of shock.

- lay the casualty down
- loosen tight clothing
- call an ambulance
- check their breathing and pulse.

Question 13.17

Which of the following should you NOT do at the scene of an accident?

Mark one answer

- [ ] Warn other traffic by switching on your hazard warning lights
- [ ] Call the emergency services immediately
- [ ] Offer someone a cigarette to calm them down
- [ ] Ask drivers to switch off their engines

Answer

- [X] **Offer someone a cigarette to calm them down**

Keeping casualties or witnesses calm is important, but never offer a cigarette because of the risk of fire. Check for any signs of shock, such as,

- sweating
- clammy skin
- giddiness
- rapid or shallow breathing
- a weak pulse.

Question 13.18

There has been an accident. The driver is suffering from shock. You should

Mark two answers

- [ ] give them a drink
- [ ] reassure them
- [ ] not leave them alone
- [ ] offer them a cigarette
- [ ] ask who caused the accident

Answers

- ☒ **reassure them**
- ☒ **not leave them alone**

They could have an injury that is not immediately obvious. Loosen any tight clothing and check that their breathing is not rapid or slow.

Question 13.19

You are at the scene of an accident. Someone is suffering from shock. You should

Mark three answers

- [ ] offer them a cigarette
- [ ] offer them a warm drink
- [ ] keep them warm
- [ ] loosen any tight clothing
- [ ] reassure them constantly

Answers

- ☒ **keep them warm**
- ☒ **loosen any tight clothing**
- ☒ **reassure them constantly**

People who seem to be unhurt may be suffering from shock. Try to reassure everyone involved at the scene and keep everybody calm.

Question 13.20

You have to treat someone for shock at the scene of an accident. You should

Mark one answer

- [ ] reassure them constantly
- [ ] walk them around to calm them down
- [ ] give them something cold to drink
- [ ] cool them down as soon as possible

Answer

- ☒ **reassure them constantly**

You should lay the casualty down, loosen any tight clothing, whilst reassuring them. If possible, get someone else to call an ambulance to avoid leaving the casualty alone.

Question 13.21

You arrive at the scene of a motorcycle accident. No other vehicle is involved. The rider is unconscious, lying in the middle of the road. The first thing you should do is

Mark one answer

- [ ] move the rider out of the road
- [ ] warn other traffic
- [ ] clear the road of debris
- [ ] give the rider reassurance

Answer

 warn other traffic

The motorcyclist is in an extremely vulnerable position, exposed to further danger from traffic. The traffic needs to slow right down and be aware of the hazard in good time.

Question 13.22

At an accident a small child is not breathing. When giving mouth to mouth you should breathe

Mark one answer

- [ ] sharply
- [ ] gently
- [ ] heavily
- [ ] rapidly

Answer

X gently

With a small child breathe gently into the nose and mouth until you see the chest rise.

Question 13.23

To start mouth to mouth on a casualty you should

Mark three answers

- [ ] tilt their head forward
- [ ] clear the airway
- [ ] turn them on their side
- [ ] tilt their head back
- [ ] pinch the nostrils together
- [ ] put their arms across their chest

Answers

X clear the airway
X tilt their head back
X pinch the nostrils together

Use your finger to check for and move any obvious obstruction in the mouth. It's important to ensure that the airways are clear.

Question 13.24

When you are giving mouth to mouth you should only stop when

Mark one answer

- [ ] you think the casualty is dead
- [ ] the casualty can breathe without help
- [ ] the casualty has turned blue
- [ ] you think the ambulance is coming

Answer

✗ the casualty can breathe without help

Don't give up. Look for signs of recovery and check the casualty's pulse. When the casualty starts to breathe place them in the recovery position.

Question 13.25

You arrive at the scene of an accident. There has been an engine fire and someone's hands and arms have been burnt. You should NOT

Mark one answer

- [ ] douse the burn thoroughly with cool liquid
- [ ] lay the casualty down
- [ ] remove anything sticking to the burn
- [ ] reassure them constantly

Answer

✗ remove anything sticking to the burn

This could cause further damage and infection to the wound. Your first priorities are to cool the burn and check the patient for shock.

Question 13.26

You arrive at an accident where someone is suffering from severe burns. You should

Mark one answer

- [ ] apply lotions to the injury
- [ ] burst any blisters
- [ ] remove anything stuck to the burns
- [ ] douse the burns with cool liquid

Answer

✗ douse the burns with cool liquid

Try to find fluid that is clean, cold and non-toxic. Its coolness will stop the burn and relieve the pain. Keep the wound doused for at least ten minutes. If blisters appear don't attempt to burst them as this could lead to infection.

Question 13.27

You arrive at an accident where someone is suffering from severe burns. You should

Mark one answer

- [ ] burst any blisters
- [ ] douse the burns thoroughly with cool liquid
- [ ] apply lotions to the injury
- [ ] remove anything sticking to the burns

Answer

- [X] **douse the burns thoroughly with cool liquid**

Do this for about ten minutes, making sure that the casualty is comfortable. If any clothing is stuck to the wound, don't try to remove it.

Question 13.28

You arrive at the scene of an accident. A pedestrian has a severe bleeding wound on their leg, although it is not broken. What should you do?.

Mark two answers

- [ ] Dab the wound to stop bleeding
- [ ] Keep both legs flat on the ground
- [ ] Apply firm pressure to the wound
- [ ] Raise the leg to lessen bleeding
- [ ] Fetch them a warm drink

Answers

- [X] **Apply firm pressure to the wound**
- [X] **Raise the leg to lessen bleeding**

As soon as you can, apply a pad to the wound with a bandage or a clean length of cloth. Raising the leg will lessen the flow of blood. Be aware that any restriction of blood circulation for more than a short period of time may result in long-term injury.

Question 13.29

You arrive at the scene of an accident. A passenger is bleeding badly from an arm wound. What should you do?

Mark one answer

- [ ] Apply pressure over the wound and keep the arm down
- [ ] Dab the wound
- [ ] Get them a drink
- [ ] Apply pressure over the wound and raise the arm

Answer

- [X] **Apply pressure over the wound and raise the arm**

If possible, lay the casualty down. Raising the arm above the level of the heart will lessen the flow of blood.

Question 13.30

You arrive at the scene of an accident. A pedestrian is bleeding heavily from a leg wound but the leg is not broken. What should you do?

Mark one answer

- [ ] Dab the wound to stop the bleeding
- [ ] Keep both legs flat on the ground
- [ ] Apply firm pressure to the wound
- [ ] Fetch them a warm drink

Answer

✗ Apply firm pressure to the wound

Apply firm pressure to stop the bleeding. Raising the leg may also help to lessen the blood flow.

Question 13.31

At an accident a casualty is unconscious but still breathing. You should only move them if

Mark one answer

- [ ] an ambulance is on its way
- [ ] bystanders advise you to
- [ ] there is further danger
- [ ] bystanders will help you to

Answer

✗ there is further danger

Moving them could cause further injury. So it's important that this is only done if there is obvious danger to the casualty.

Question 13.32

At an accident you suspect a casualty has back injuries. The area is safe. You should

Mark one answer

- [ ] offer them a drink
- [ ] not move them
- [ ] raise their legs
- [ ] offer them a cigarette

Answer

✗ not move them

Talk to the casualty and keep them calm. If you attempt to move them it could cause further injury. Call an ambulance at the first opportunity.

Question 13.33

At an accident it is important to look after the casualty. When the area is safe, you should

Mark one answer

- get them out of the vehicle
- give them a drink
- give them something to eat
- keep them in the vehicle

Answer

✖ **keep them in the vehicle**

Don't move casualties who are trapped in vehicles unless they are in danger.

Question 13.34

A tanker is involved in an accident. Which sign would show that the tanker is carrying dangerous goods?

Mark one answer

 LONG VEHICLE

Answer

✖

There will be an orange label on the side and rear of the lorry. Look at this carefully and report what it says when you phone the emergency services.

Question 13.35

While driving, a warning light on your vehicle's instrument panel comes on. You should

Mark one answer

- continue if the engine sounds alright
- hope that it is just a temporary electrical fault
- deal with the problem when there is more time
- check out the problem quickly and safely

Answer

✖ **check out the problem quickly and safely**

An illuminated warning light could mean that your car is unsafe to drive. Don't take risks. If you aren't sure about the problem, get a qualified mechanic to check it.

Question 13.36

For which TWO should you use hazard warning lights?

Mark two answers

☒ When you slow down quickly on a motorway because of a hazard ahead

☒ When you have broken down

☒ When you wish to stop on double yellow lines

☒ When you need to park on the pavement

Answers

☒ **When you slow down quickly on a motorway because of a hazard ahead**

☒ **When you have broken down**

Hazard warning lights are fitted to all modern cars and some motorcycles. They should be used to warn other road users of a hazard ahead.

Question 13.37

For which THREE should you use your hazard warning lights?

Mark three answers

☒ When you are parking in a restricted area

☒ When you are temporarily obstructing traffic

☒ To warn following traffic of a hazard ahead

☒ When you have broken down

☒ When only stopping for a short time

Answers

☒ **When you are temporarily obstructing traffic**

☒ **To warn following traffic of a hazard ahead**

☒ **When you have broken down**

Use them on the motorway when you have to slow down suddenly because of a queue of traffic ahead. This is to warn following traffic that you're slowing suddenly and rapidly.

Question 13.38

When are you allowed to use hazard warning lights?

Mark one answer

☒ When stopped and temporarily obstructing traffic

☒ When driving during darkness without headlights

☒ When parked for shopping on double yellow lines

☒ When travelling slowly because you are lost

Answer

☒ **When stopped and temporarily obstructing traffic**

Don't use hazard lights

- to excuse yourself for illegal, dangerous or inconsiderate parking
- when you're moving slowly because you're lost
- when you're moving slowly due to bad weather.

Question 13.39

When should you switch on your hazard warning lights?

Mark one answer

☒ When you cannot avoid causing an obstruction

☒ When you are driving slowly due to bad weather

☒ When you are towing a broken down vehicle

☒ When you are parked on double yellow lines

Answer

☒ **When you cannot avoid causing an obstruction**

This doesn't mean parking to shop or use a bank machine. If you need to stop for these reasons, do so in an authorised parking place.

Question 13.40

You have broken down on a two-way road. You have a warning triangle. You should place the warning triangle at least how far from your vehicle?

Mark one answer

☒ 5 metres (16 feet)

☒ 25 metres 82 feet)

☒ 45 metres (147 feet)

☒ 100 metres (328 feet)

Answer

☒ **45 metres (147 feet)**

Carry an advance warning triangle in your vehicle. They fold flat and don't take up much room. Use it to warn other road users if your vehicle has broken down or if there's been an accident. Place your warning triangle at least 45 metres (147 feet) from your vehicle on a straight, level road

Question 13.41

You are in an accident on a two-way road. You have a warning triangle with you. At what distance before the obstruction should you place the warning triangle?

Mark one answer

☒ 25 metres (82 feet)

☒ 45 metres (147 feet)

☒ 100 metres (328 feet)

☒ 150 metres (492 feet)

Answer

☒ **45 metres (147 feet)**

If there's a bend or hump in the road, place the triangle so that approaching traffic slows down before the bend. You must give traffic enough time to react to the warning.

Use your hazard warning lights as well as a warning triangle, especially in the dark.

Question 13.42

Your motorcycle has broken down on a motorway. How will you know the direction of the nearest emergency telephone?

Mark one answer

- [ ] By walking with the flow of traffic
- [ ] By following an arrow on a marker post
- [ ] By walking against the flow of traffic
- [ ] By remembering where the last phone was

Answer

 By following an arrow on a marker post

If you break down on a motorway you should

- pull onto the hard shoulder and stop as far over to the left as you can
- switch on hazard lights (if they are fitted)
- make your way to the nearest emergency telephone.

Marker posts spaced every 100 metres will direct you to the nearest telephone.

Question 13.43

You have broken down on a two-way road. You have a warning triangle. It should be displayed

Mark one answer

- [ ] on the roof of your vehicle
- [ ] at least 150 metres (492 feet) behind your vehicle
- [ ] at least 45 metres (147 feet) behind your vehicle
- [ ] just behind your vehicle

Answer

 at least 45 metres (147 feet) behind your vehicle

If you need to display a warning triangle make sure that it can be seen clearly by other road users. Place it on the same side of the road and clear of any obstruction.

The police may ask you to produce which three of these documents following an accident?

Mark three answers

☒ Vehicle registration document

☒ Driving licence

☒ Theory test certificate

☒ Insurance certificate

☒ MOT test certificate

☒ Road tax disc

Answers

☒ **Driving licence**

☒ **Insurance certificate**

☒ **MOT test certificate**

The first thing you must do is stop. It is an offence not to do so.

You are involved in an accident with another driver. Someone is injured. Your vehicle is damaged. Which FOUR of the following should you find out?

Mark four answers

☒ Whether the driver owns the other vehicle involved

☒ The other driver's name, address and telephone number

☒ The car make and registration number of the other vehicle

☒ The occupation of the other driver

☒ The details of the other driver's vehicle insurance

☒ Whether the other driver is licensed to drive

Answers

☒ **Whether the driver owns the other vehicle involved**

☒ **The other driver's name, address and telephone number**

☒ **The car make and registration number of the other vehicle**

☒ **The details of the other driver's vehicle insurance**

Try to keep calm and don't rush the proceedings. Take your time. You might be a little shaken by the incident, but try to ensure that you have all the details before you leave the scene.

NI

Question 13.46

You have an accident while driving and someone is injured. You do not produce your insurance certificate at the time. You must report it to the police as soon as possible, or in any case within

Mark one answer

- [×] 24 hours
- [×] 48 hours
- [×] five days
- [×] seven days

Answer

 24 hours

You must also give

- your name and address
- your vehicle owner's address
- the registration number of the vehicle

to the police, or anyone with reasonable grounds for wanting them.

In Northern Ireland accidents have to be reported to the police 'forthwith'.

Question 13.47

At a railway level crossing the red light signal continues to flash after a train has gone by. What should you do?

Mark one answer

- [×] Phone the signal operator
- [×] Alert drivers behind you
- [×] Wait
- [×] Proceed with caution

Answer

 Wait

Don't

- proceed
- phone the signal operator immediately
- zigzag between the gates.

There may be another train coming.

Question 13.48

You break down on a level crossing. The lights have not yet begun to flash. Which THREE things should you do?

Mark three answers

- [×] Telephone the signal operator
- [×] Leave your vehicle and get everyone clear
- [×] Walk down the track and signal the next train
- [×] Move the vehicle if a signal operator tells you to
- [×] Tell drivers behind what has happened

Answers

- [×] **Telephone the signal operator**
- [×] **Leave your vehicle and get everyone clear**
- [×] **Move the vehicle if a signal operator tells you to**

Keep calm. Don't

- walk up the track to warn approaching trains
- try to restart the engine
- try to move the vehicle unless told to do so by the signal operator.

Question 13.49

You have stalled in the middle of a level crossing and cannot restart the engine. The warning bell starts to ring. You should

Mark one answer

☒ get out and clear of the crossing

☒ run down the track to warn the signal operator

☒ carry on trying to restart the engine

☒ push the vehicle clear of the crossing

Answer

☒ **get out and clear of the crossing**

Try not to panic, and stay calm, especially if you have passengers on board. If you can't restart your engine before the warning bells ring, then leave the vehicle.

Question 13.50

Your vehicle has broken down on an automatic railway level crossing. What should you do FIRST?

Mark one answer

☒ Get everyone out of the vehicle and clear of the crossing

☒ Phone the signal operator so that trains can be stopped

☒ Walk along the track to give warning to any approaching trains

☒ Try to push the vehicle clear of the crossing as soon as possible

Answer

☒ **Get everyone out of the vehicle and clear of the crossing**

Ensure that everyone is WELL CLEAR of the crossing. In the event of an accident debris could be scattered in several directions.

Question 13.51

Your tyre bursts while you are driving. Which TWO things should you do?

Mark two answers

☒ Pull on the handbrake

☒ Brake as quickly as possible

☒ Pull up slowly at the side of the road

☒ Hold the steering wheel firmly to keep control

☒ Continue on at a normal speed

Answers

☒ **Pull up slowly at the side of the road**

☒ **Hold the steering wheel firmly to keep control**

A tyre bursting can lead to a loss of control, especially if you're travelling at high speed. The correct procedure can help to stop the vehicle safely.

Question 13.52

Which TWO things should you do when a front tyre bursts?

Mark two answers

☒ Apply the handbrake to stop the vehicle

☒ Brake firmly and quickly

☒ Let the vehicle roll to a stop

☒ Hold the steering wheel lightly

☒ Grip the steering wheel firmly

Answers

☒ **Let the vehicle roll to a stop**

☒ **Grip the steering wheel firmly**

Try not to react by applying the brakes harshly. This could lead to further loss of steering control. Indicate your intention to pull up at the side of the road and roll to a stop.

Question 13.53

You are driving on the motorway and get a puncture. You should

Mark one answer

☒ pull onto the hard shoulder as safely as possible

☒ stop in the lane you are in and change the wheel

☒ pull into the central reservation as safely as possible

☒ stop in any lane but use emergency flashers

Answer

☒ **pull onto the hard shoulder as safely as possible**

The vehicle might swerve and weave. Try not to brake, and hold onto the steering wheel as it might shudder or pull to one side. Try to let your vehicle roll to a stop safely on the hard shoulder.

Question 13.54

Your vehicle has a puncture on a motorway. What should you do?

Mark one answer

☒ Drive slowly to the next service area to get assistance

☒ Pull up on the hard shoulder. Change the wheel as quickly as possible

☒ Pull up on the hard shoulder. Use the emergency phone to get assistance

☒ Switch on your hazard lights. Stop in your lane

Answer

☒ **Pull up on the hard shoulder. Use the emergency phone to get assistance**

Pull up on the hard shoulder and make your way to the nearest emergency telephone and request assistance. It is dangerous to try and change an offside wheel, due to fast traffic passing very close to your vehicle.

Question 13.55

You should use the engine cut-out switch to

Mark one answer

- ☒ stop the engine in an emergency
- ☒ stop the engine on short journeys
- ☒ save wear on the ignition switch
- ☒ start the engine if you lose the key

Answer

❌ **stop the engine in an emergency**

Most motorcycles are fitted with an engine cut-out switch. This is designed to stop the engine in an emergency and so reduce the risk of fire.

Question 13.56

You see a car on the hard shoulder of a motorway with a HELP pennant displayed. This means the driver is most likely to be

Mark one answer

- ☒ a disabled person
- ☒ first aid trained
- ☒ a foreign visitor
- ☒ a rescue patrol person

Answer

❌ **a disabled person**

The driver might not be able to walk the distance to the emergency telephone. Disabled persons can show this sign to alert police controls.

Question 13.57

On the motorway the hard shoulder should be used

Mark one answer

- ☒ to answer a mobile phone
- ☒ when an emergency arises
- ☒ for a short rest when tired
- ☒ to check a road atlas

Answer

❌ **when an emergency arises**

Pull onto the hard shoulder and use the emergency telephone to report your problem. The telephone connects you to police control, who will put you through to an emergency breakdown service. Never cross the carriageway to use the telephone on the other side.

Question 13.58

What TWO safeguards could you take against fire risk to your vehicle?

Mark two answers

- Keep water levels above maximum
- Carry a fire extinguisher
- Avoid driving with a full tank of petrol
- Use unleaded petrol
- Check out any strong smell of petrol
- Use low octane fuel

Answers

- ✖ Carry a fire extinguisher
- ✖ Check out any strong smell of petrol

The fuel in your vehicle can be a dangerous fire hazard. Don't

- use a naked flame near the vehicle if you can smell fuel
- smoke when refuelling your vehicle.

Question 13.59

You have broken down on a motorway. When you use the emergency telephone you will be asked

Mark three answers

- for the number on the telephone that you are using
- for your driving licence details
- for the name of your vehicle insurance company
- for details of yourself and your vehicle
- whether you belong to a motoring organisation

Answers

- ✖ for the number on the telephone that you are using
- ✖ for details of yourself and your vehicle
- ✖ whether you belong to a motoring organisation

Have these details ready before you phone to save time. Be sure to give the correct information. It is safer to always face the traffic when you speak on the telephone.

Question 13.60

You are on the motorway. Luggage falls from your vehicle. What should you do?

Mark one answer

- Stop at the next emergency telephone and contact the police
- Stop on the motorway and put on hazard lights whilst you pick it up
- Reverse back up the motorway to pick it up
- Pull up on the hard shoulder and wave traffic down

Answer

- ✖ Stop at the next emergency telephone and contact the police

Pull over onto the hard shoulder near an emergency telephone and phone for assistance. Don't

- stop on the carriageway
- attempt to retrieve anything.

Question 13.61

You are travelling on a motorway. A bag falls from your motorcycle. There are valuables in the bag. What should you do?

Mark one answer

☒ Go back carefully and collect the bag as quickly as possible

☒ Stop wherever you are and pick up the bag, but only when there is a safe gap

☒ Stop on the hard shoulder and use the emergency telephone to inform the police

☒ Stop on the hard shoulder and then retrieve the bag yourself

Answer

☒ **Stop on the hard shoulder and use the emergency telephone to inform the police**

However important you think retrieving your property may be, DON'T walk onto the motorway. Your bag might be creating a hazard, but not as great a hazard as you would be.

Question 13.62

You are travelling on a motorway. A suitcase falls from your vehicle. There are valuables in the suitcase. What should you do?

Mark one answer

☒ Reverse your vehicle carefully and collect the case as quickly as possible

☒ Stop wherever you are and pick up the case but only when there is a safe gap

☒ Stop on the hard shoulder and use the emergency telephone to inform the police

☒ Stop on the hard shoulder and then retrieve the suitcase yourself

Answer

☒ **Stop on the hard shoulder and use the emergency telephone to inform the police**

Walking onto the carriageway is very dangerous. The traffic is travelling at high speeds and may not have the time or room to change lanes to avoid you. Your property is never as valuable as your life.

Question 13.63

You are driving on a motorway. A large box falls onto the carriageway from a lorry ahead of you. The lorry does not stop. You should

Mark one answer

☒ drive to the next emergency telephone and inform the police

☒ catch up with the lorry and try to get the driver's attention

☒ stop close to the box and switch on your hazard warning lights until the police arrive

☒ pull over to the hard shoulder, then try and remove the box

Answer

☒ **drive to the next emergency telephone and inform the police**

Lorry drivers are sometimes unaware of objects falling from their vehicles. If you see something fall off a lorry onto the motorway watch to see if the driver pulls over. If the lorry doesn't stop you should

• pull over onto the hard shoulder near an emergency telephone

• report the hazard to the police.

Question 13.64

You are driving on a motorway. When can you use hazard warning lights?

Mark two answers

☒ When a vehicle is following too closely

☒ When you slow down quickly because of danger ahead

☒ When you are towing another vehicle

☒ When driving on the hard shoulder

☒ When you have broken down on the hard shoulder

Answers

☒ **When you slow down quickly because of danger ahead**

☒ **When you have broken down on the hard shoulder**

Hazard lights will warn the traffic travelling behind you that your vehicle is a potential hazard. Don't forget to turn them off again when you return to the carriageway or normal speed.

Question 13.65

You are riding on a motorway. The car in front switches on its hazard warning lights whilst moving. This means

Mark one answer

☒ they are going to take the next exit

☒ there is a danger ahead

☒ there is a police car in the left lane

☒ they are trying to change lanes

Answer

☒ **there is a danger ahead**

Hazard lights should only be used when driving if you're on a

• motorway

• dual carriageway subject to the national speed limit

and you need to warn following traffic of a danger ahead.

This section looks at the safety of loads.

The questions will ask you about

- stability
- towing regulations.

Question 14.1

Overloading your vehicle can seriously affect the

Mark two answers

- [ ] gearbox
- [x] steering
- [x] handling
- [ ] battery life
- [ ] journey time

Answers

- [x] steering
- [x] handling

Any load will have an affect on the handling of your vehicle, and this becomes worse if you overload it. Any change in the centre of gravity or weight the vehicle is carrying will affect it's handling on bends.

Question 14.2

Who is responsible for making sure that a vehicle is not overloaded?

Mark one answer

- [x] The driver or rider of the vehicle
- [ ] The owner of the items being carried
- [ ] The person who loaded the vehicle
- [ ] The owner of the vehicle

Answer

- [x] The driver or rider of the vehicle

Your vehicle must not be overloaded. This will affect control and handling characteristics. If your vehicle is overloaded and it causes an accident, you'll be responsible.

Question 14.3

On which TWO occasions might you inflate your tyres to more than the recommended normal pressure?

Mark two answers

- [ ] When the roads are slippery
- [x] When driving fast for a long distance
- [ ] When the tyre tread is worn below 2mm
- [x] When carrying a heavy load
- [ ] When the weather is cold
- [ ] When the vehicle is fitted with anti-lock brakes

Answers

- [x] When driving fast for a long distance
- [x] When carrying a heavy load

Check the vehicle hand book, which should give you guidance on the correct tyre pressure in these circumstances. Travelling at speed for long distances can cause the tyres to become hot, which could damage the side walls.

Question 14.4

Any load that is carried on a luggage rack MUST be

Mark one answer

- ☒ securely fastened when riding
- ☒ carried only when strictly necessary
- ☒ visible when you are riding
- ☒ covered with plastic sheeting

Answer

☒ **securely fastened when riding**

Don't risk losing any luggage off your machine. It could fall into the path of following vehicles and cause an accident. It's an offence to travel with an unsecured load.

Question 14.5

Any load that is carried on a roof rack MUST be

Mark one answer

- ☒ securely fastened when driving
- ☒ carried only when strictly necessary
- ☒ as light as possible
- ☒ covered with plastic sheeting

Answer

☒ **securely fastened when driving**

If you wish to carry items on the roof there are roof boxes available from automotive supply stores. These will help to keep your luggage secure and dry.

Question 14.6

A heavy load on your roof rack will

Mark one answer

- ☒ improve the road holding
- ☒ reduce the stopping distance
- ☒ make the steering lighter
- ☒ reduce stability

Answer

☒ **reduce stability**

Be aware of this when you negotiate bends and corners. Your vehicle and/or load could become unstable. You could lose control.

Question 14.7

Which THREE are suitable restraints for a child under three years?

Mark three answers

- ☒ A child seat
- ☒ An adult holding a child
- ☒ An adult seat belt
- ☒ A lap belt
- ☒ A harness
- ☒ A baby carrier

Answers

- ☒ **A child seat**
- ☒ **A harness**
- ☒ **A baby carrier**

The driver is responsible for ensuring that children under three wear suitable child restraints. If the child is in the front seat, a restraint must be used. If the child is in the rear seat, restraints must be used if available. A harness or booster seat should be appropriate to the child's weight.

Question 14.8

What do child locks in a vehicle do?

Mark one answer

- ☒ Lock the seat belt buckles in place
- ☒ Lock the rear windows in the up position
- ☒ Stop children from opening rear doors
- ☒ Stop the rear seats from tipping forward

Answer

- ☒ **Stop children from opening rear doors**

Child locks are fitted to most modern cars. They prevent the door being opened from the inside.

Question 14.9

Your vehicle is fitted with child safety door locks. You should use these so that children inside the car cannot open

Mark one answer

- ☒ the right-hand doors
- ☒ the left-hand doors
- ☒ the rear doors
- ☒ any of the doors

Answer

- ☒ **the rear doors**

If you're travelling with children in the rear seats, fitting child safety locks is a sensible safety precaution. There will be times when children are eager to get out of the car as it comes to a stop, child safety locks will prevent them until you're sure it's safe for them to do so.

You should load a trailer so that the weight is

Mark one answer

☒ mostly over the nearside wheel

☒ evenly distributed

☒ mainly at the front

☒ mostly at the rear

Answer

☒ **evenly distributed**

If you tow a trailer you need to give some thought to how you load it. The load should be

- evenly distributed
- secured so that it can't move about while you're travelling.

Movement of the load might affect steering and cause danger to other road users.

Question 14.11

You want to tow a trailer with your motorcycle. Which one applies?

Mark one answer

☒ The motorcycle should be attached to a sidecar

☒ The trailer should weigh more than the motorcycle

☒ The trailer should be fitted with brakes

☒ The trailer should not be more than 1 metre (3 feet 3 inches) wide

Answer

☒ **The trailer should not be more than 1 metre (3 feet 3 inches) wide**

To tow a trailer behind a motorcycle you must

- have a full motorcycle licence
- have a motorcycle with an engine larger than 125cc.

Motorcycle trailers must not exceed 1 metre (3 feet 3 inches) wide.

Question 14.12

You are planning to tow a caravan. Which of these will mostly help to aid the vehicle handling?

Mark one answer

☒ A jockey-wheel fitted to the towbar

☒ Power steering fitted to the towing vehicle

☒ Anti-lock brakes fitted to the towing vehicle

☒ A stabiliser fitted to the towbar

Answer

☒ **A stabiliser fitted to the towbar**

It is highly recommended that you take a caravan manoeuvring course. The Camping and Caravanning Club provide a course for those wishing to tow trailers. They also publish literature and a really helpful video. For more information Tel: 01203 694995

Question 14.13

Before towing a caravan you should ensure that heavy items in it are loaded

Mark one answer

as high as possible, mainly over the axle(s)

as low as possible, mainly over the axle(s)

as low as possible, forward of the axle(s)

as high as possible, forward of the axle(s)

Answer

 as low as possible, mainly over the axle(s)

Loading like this will help the caravan to be more stable

Question 14.14

A trailer must stay securely hitched-up to the towing vehicle. What additional safety device can be fitted to the trailer braking system?

Mark one answer

Stabiliser

Jockey wheel

Corner steadies

Breakaway cable

Answer

 Breakaway cable

In the event of a tow bar failure the cable pulls on the caravan brakes, snaps and allows the car to run free of the stopped caravan.

Question 14.15

If a trailer swerves or snakes when you are towing it you should

Mark one answer

ease off the accelerator and reduce your speed

let go of the steering wheel and let it correct itself

brake hard and hold the pedal down

increase your speed as quickly as possible

Answer

 ease off the accelerator and reduce your speed

Strong winds or buffeting from large vehicles might cause a trailer or caravan to snake or swerve. If this happens ease off the accelerator. Don't

• brake harshly

• steer sharply

• increase speed.

Question 14.16

Are passengers allowed to ride in a caravan that is being towed?

Mark one answer

- Yes
- No
- Only if all the seats in the towing vehicle are full
- Only if a stabilizer is fitted

Answer

 No

Riding in a towed caravan is highly dangerous. The safety of the entire unit is dependent on the stability of the trailer. Moving passengers would render the caravan unstable and could cause loss of control.

Question 14.17

You are towing a caravan along a motorway. The caravan begins to swerve from side to side. What should you do?

Mark one answer

- Ease off the accelerator slowly
- Steer sharply from side to side
- Do an emergency stop
- Speed up a little

Answer

✗ **Ease off the accelerator slowly**

Try not to brake or steer heavily, this will only make matters worse and you could lose control all together. Keep calm and regain control by easing off the accelerator.

Question 14.18

If a trailer swerves or snakes when you are towing it you should

Mark one answer

- ease off the throttle and reduce your speed
- let go of the handlebars and let it correct itself
- brake hard and hold the brake on
- increase your speed as quickly as possible

Answer

 ease off the throttle and reduce your speed

Don't be tempted to use the steering to stop swerving or snaking. This won't help the situation. Ease off the throttle and reduce your speed.

Question 14.19

How can you stop a caravan snaking from side to side?

Mark one answer

- ☒ Turn the steering wheel slowly to each side
- ☒ Accelerate to increase your speed
- ☒ Stop as quickly as you can
- ☒ Slow down very gradually

Answer

☒ **Slow down very gradually**

Keep calm and don't brake harshly or you could lose control completely.

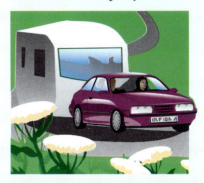

Question 14.20

You are towing a small trailer on a busy three-lane motorway. All the lanes are open. You must

Mark two answers

- ☒ not exceed 60 mph
- ☒ not overtake
- ☒ have a stabiliser fitted
- ☒ use only the left and centre lanes

Answers

☒ **not exceed 60 mph**
☒ **use only the left and centre lanes**

You should be aware of the speed limit for the vehicle that you're driving. Allow the faster-moving traffic to flow. Don't use the right-hand lane.

Question 14.21

You have a side-car fitted to your motorcycle. What effect will it have?

Mark one answer

- ☒ Reduce stability
- ☒ Make steering lighter
- ☒ Increase stopping distance
- ☒ Increase fuel economy

Answer

☒ **Increase stopping distance**

If you want to fit a side-car to your motorcycle

- make sure that your machine is suitable to cope with the extra load
- make sure that the side-car is fixed correctly and properly aligned.

A side-car will affect the handling of your machine. Give yourself time to adjust to the different characteristics.

Question 14.22

When riding with a sidecar attached for the first time you should

Mark two answers

 keep your speed down

 be able to stop more quickly

 accelerate quickly round bends

 approach corners more carefully

Question 14.23

A trailer on a motorcycle must be no wider than

Mark one answer

 1 metre (3 feet 3 inches)

 1/2 metre (1 foot 8 inches)

 1 1/2 metres (4 feet 11 inches)

 2 metres (6 feet 6 inches)

Question 14.24

Before fitting a side-car riders should

Mark one answer

 have the wheels of their bike balanced

 have their bike's engine tuned

 pass the extended bike test

 check that their bike is suitable

Answers

✖ **keep your speed down**

✖ **approach corners more carefully**

A motorcycle with a sidecar will feel very different to ride than a solo motorcycle. Until you get used to the outfit keep your speed down, especially when negotiating corners and bends.

Answer

✖ **1 metre (3 feet 3 inches)**

When you're towing a trailer you must remember that you may not be able to filter through traffic. Don't 'forget' that the trailer is there.

Answer

✖ **check that their bike is suitable**

Make sure that the sidecar is properly fixed and aligned. If your machine was registered on or after 1 August 1981 the sidecar must be fitted on the left side of the machine.

Question 14.25

You want to tow a trailer behind your motorcycle. You should

Mark two answers

- ☒ display a 'long vehicle' sign
- ☒ fit a larger battery
- ☒ have a full motorcycle licence
- ☒ ensure that your engine is more than 125 cc
- ☒ ensure that your machine has shaft drive

Answers

- ☒ **have a full motorcycle licence**
- ☒ **ensure that your engine is more than 125 cc**

When you tow a trailer

- your stopping distance may be increased
- any load on the trailer must be secure
- the trailer must be fitted to the machine correctly
- you must obey the speed limit restrictions that apply to all vehicles with trailers.

Question 14.26

When may a learner motorcyclist carry a pillion passenger?

Mark one answer

- ☒ If the passenger holds a full licence
- ☒ Not at any time
- ☒ If the rider is undergoing training
- ☒ If the passenger is over 21

Answer

- ☒ **Not at any time**

You are not allowed to carry a pillion passenger until you hold a full motorcycle licence. This allows you to gain experience riding solo before carrying a passenger.

Question 14.27

Which THREE must a learner motorcyclist under 21 NOT do?

Mark three answers

- ☒ Ride a motorcycle with an engine capacity greater than 125 cc
- ☒ Pull a trailer
- ☒ Carry a pillion passenger
- ☒ Ride faster than 30 mph
- ☒ Use the right-hand lane on dual carriageways

Answers

- ☒ **Ride a motorcycle with an engine capacity greater than 125 cc**
- ☒ **Pull a trailer**
- ☒ **Carry a pillion passenger**

If you're a learner motorcyclist under 21 you must not ride a motorcycle on the road with an engine capacity over 125 cc.

Question 14.28

Pillion passengers should

Mark one answer

- [ ] have a provisional motorcycle licence
- [ ] be lighter than the rider
- [ ] always wear a helmet
- [ ] signal for the rider

Answer

- [x] **always wear a helmet**

Pillion passengers must

- sit astride the machine facing forward on a proper passenger seat
- wear a safety helmet, which is correctly fastened.

Question 14.29

Pillion passengers should

Mark one answer

- [ ] give the rider directions
- [ ] lean with the rider when going round bends
- [ ] check the road behind for the rider
- [ ] give arm signals for the rider

Answer

- [x] **lean with the rider when going round bends**

Pillion passengers should also keep both feet on the pillion footrests provided.

Question 14.30

When carrying extra weight on a motorcycle, you may need to make adjustments to the

Mark three answers

- [ ] headlight
- [ ] gears
- [ ] suspension
- [ ] tyres
- [ ] footrests

Answers

- [x] **headlight**
- [x] **suspension**
- [x] **tyres**

Extra weight can affect a motorcycle's feel and balance. To help, you can adjust the

- suspension
- tyre pressures.

You may find that extra weight on the back affects the headlight aim, and this should be adjusted to compensate.

Question 14.31

To carry a pillion passenger your bike should be fitted with

Mark two answers

- rear footrests
- an engine of 250 cc or over
- a top box
- a grab handle
- a proper passenger seat

Question 14.32

To obtain the full category 'A' licence through the accelerated or direct access scheme, your motorcycle must be

Mark one answer

- solo with maximum power 25 kW (33 bhp)
- solo with maximum power of 11 kW (14.6 bhp)
- fitted with a sidecar and have minimum power of 35 kW (46.6 bhp)
- solo with minimum power of 35 kW (46.6 bhp)

Answers

- ✘ **rear footrests**
- ✘ **a proper passenger seat**

A pillion passenger should be instructed not to

- give hand signals
- lean away from the rider when cornering
- fidget or move around
- put their feet down to try and support the machine as you stop
- wear long, loose items that might get caught in the rear wheel or drive chain.

Answer

- ✘ **solo with minimum power of 35 kW (46.6 bhp)**

If you want to ride in countries who are members of the European Community you must have a valid driving licence. You will also need to find out what specific rules apply to any country you may be visiting concerning insurance, visas and other motoring regulations.

Conclusion

This book is intended to help you to prepare for the car or motorcycle theory test. If you've prepared properly and fully you won't find your theory test difficult.

Passing your theory test means that you've taken the first step towards safe driving. However, it is only one stage in becoming a safe and competent driver. The knowledge you've acquired should be put into practice on the road. By passing a stringent two-part test, and continuing to apply the knowledge that you've gained on the way, you can make an important contribution to safety on our roads.

When you've passed your driving test you might like to have some additional training, and get a reduction in your insurance costs, by taking part in the 'Pass Plus' scheme. You should ask your driving instructor about it.

You'll never know all the answers. Throughout your driving career there will always be more to learn. Remember, any passengers you carry will be your responsibility. By being reliable, efficient and safe you'll be on your way to becoming a safe driver.

Service standards for theory test candidates

DSA and DVTA are committed to providing the following standards of service for test candidates.

- Ninety five percent of telephone calls will be answered within ten seconds.

- Theory tests will be available during weekdays, evenings and on Saturdays. A test appointment should be available for 95% of test candidates within two weeks.

- Test notification will be issued within five working days of receipt of a correctly completed application form and appropriate fee.

- More time may be needed to make arrangements for candidates with special needs, but a test should be available for 95% of such candidates within four weeks.

- All candidates should be able to obtain a test booking within two months of their preferred date at the centre of their choice.

- A refund of test fees will be issued within three weeks of a valid claim with the supporting information.

- No more than 0.5% of tests will be cancelled by contractors (acting on behalf of DSA and DVTA).

- All letters, including complaints, will be answered within 15 working days.

Complaints guide for theory test candidates

DSA and DVTA aim to give their customers the best possible service. Please tell us

- when we've done well
- when you aren't satisfied.

Your comments can help us to improve the service we offer. If you have any questions about your theory test please contact DSA.

Tel: 0870 01 01 372

Fax: 0870 01 04 372.

Candidates with comments or queries about tests in Northern Ireland please contact DVTA.

Tel: 0645 000 666

Fax: 0870 01 04 372.

If you have any complaints about how your theory test was carried out, or any part of our customer service, please take up the matter with a member of staff if the circumstances allow. You may complete a form, available at theory test centres. Alternatively you can write to the Customer Services Manager at the following address

Customer Services
Driving Theory Test
PO Box 445
Coventry CV1 2ZZ.

If you're dissatisfied with the reply you can write to the Managing Director at the same address.

If you're still not satisfied, you can take up your complaint with

The Chief Executive
Driving Standards Agency
Stanley House
Talbot Street
Nottingham NG1 5GU.

In Northern Ireland

The Chief Executive
Driver & Vehicle Testing Agency
Balmoral Road
Belfast BT12 6QL.

None of this removes your right to take your complaint to your Member of Parliament, who may decide to raise your case personally with the DSA or DVTA Chief Executive, the Minister or the Parliamentary Commissioner for Administration (the Ombudsman). Please refer to our leaflet 'If things go wrong.'

Compensation code for theory test candidates

DSA will normally refund the test fee, or give a free re-booking, in the following cases

- if we cancel your test
- if you cancel and give us at least three clear working days notice
- if you keep the test appointment but the test doesn't take place, or isn't finished, for a reason that isn't your fault.

We'll also repay you the expenses that you incurred on the day of the test because we cancelled your test at short notice. We'll consider reasonable claims for

- travelling to and from the test centre
- any pay or earnings you lost after tax (usually for half a day).

Please write to the address below and send a receipt showing travel costs and/or an employer's letter, which shows what earnings you lost.

DVTA has a different compensation code. If you think you're entitled to compensation write to

Customer Services
Driving Theory Test
PO Box 445
Coventry CV1 2ZZ.

This compensation code doesn't affect your existing legal rights.

Theory Test Centres in Great Britain and Northern Ireland

Scotland

Aberdeen
Ayr
Dumfries
Dundee
Dunfermline
Edinburgh
Elgin
Fort William
Gairloch*
Galashiels
Glasgow NW
Glasgow Central
Greenock
Helmsdale*
Huntly*
Inverness
Isle of Arran*
Isle of Barra*
Isle of Benbecula*
Isle of Islay, Bowmore*
Isle of Mull, Salen*
Isle of Tiree*
Kirkwall
Kyle of Lochalsh*
Lerwick
Motherwell
Oban*
Pitlochry
Portree
Stirling
Stornoway
Stranraer
Tarbert, Argyllshire
Tongue*
Ullapool
Wick

Northern

Barrow
Berwick-Upon-Tweed
Birkenhead
Blackpool
Bolton
Bradford
Carlisle
Chester
Doncaster
Durham
Grimsby
Harrogate
Huddersfield
Hull
Leeds
Liverpool
Manchester
Middlesbrough
Morpeth
Newcastle
Oldham
Preston
Runcorn
Salford
Scarborough
Scunthorpe
Sheffield
Southport
St Helens
Stockport
Sunderland
Wigan
Workington
York

Midlands & Eastern

Birmingham
Boston
Bury St Edmunds
Cambridge
Chesterfield
Coventry
Derby
Dudley
Grantham
Ipswich
Kings Lynn
Leicester
Lincoln
Lowestoft
Luton
Mansfield
Milton Keynes
Northampton
Norwich
Nottingham
Oxford
Peterborough
Reading
Redditch
Shrewsbury
Solihull
Stoke-on-Trent
Stratford Upon Avon
Sutton Coldfield
Wolverhampton
Worcester

Wales & Western

Aberystwyth
Bangor
Barnstaple
Basingstoke
Bath
Bournemouth
Bristol
Builth Wells
Cardiff
Cheltenham
Exeter
Fareham
Gloucester
Haverfordwest
Hereford
Isles of Scilly*
Isle of Wight
Merthyr Tydfil
Newport
Penzance
Plymouth
Portsmouth
Rhyl
Swansea
Salisbury
Southampton
Swindon
Taunton
Torquay
Truro
Weymouth
Yeovil

London & South East

Aldershot
Basildon
Brighton
Canterbury
Chelmsford
Colchester
Crawley
Croydon
Eastbourne
Gillingham
Guildford
Harlow
Hastings
Ilford
Kingston
Sidcup
Slough
Southend
Staines
Stevenage
Uxbridge
Vauxhall
Watford
Wood Green
Worthing

Driving theory test centres in Northern Ireland

Ballymena
Belfast
Londonderry
Newry
Omagh
Portadown

* Denotes a Test Centre restricted to occasional demand. Those which offer a Same Day Results service are shown in bold.

Essential guidance for all types of driving
Driving Standards Agency

The Highway Code

Research has proved conclusively that keeping a copy of The Highway Code in the home significantly improves driver knowledge, and therefore safety, on the road.

The latest Highway Code has been completely revised to include new legislation, with greater emphasis on safe driving and special sections on vulnerable road users such as horse riders, cyclists and the elderly. Plus advice to reflect the changes in lifestyle and technology, with rules dealing with driver fatigue and recommendations about the use of mobile phones.

ISBN 0 11 551977 7   £1.49

Test Yourself Papers for the Driving Theory Test

Five practice papers for the theory test, with questions taken from the official question bank and the correct answers supplied for further reference and revision. Be fully prepared by simulating the theory test at your leisure.

0 11 551984 X   £4.99 (INCL VAT)

The Driving Test

The practical driving test – fully illustrated and written in a clear and easy-to-understand style. Fully updated with the officially recommended syllabus for learning to drive.

ISBN 0 11 552190 9   £6.99

Know Your Traffic Signs

This useful publication illustrates and explains the vast majority of traffic signals, signs and road markings which any road user is likely to encounter. It is the most comprehensive explanation of the signing system available, and is exceptional value for money.

ISBN 0 11 551612 3   £2.50

Printed in The United Kingdom for The Stationery Office J0079338 06/99 C1500 63789

is available from the
and The Stationery Office

The Driving Manual

The essential reference manual for all motorists and instructors, from learners to advanced motorists - updated to include the very latest advice and legislation on good driving, covering subjects as diverse as defensive driving, bends and junctions, manoeuvring, towing and European driving, plus legal information.

0 11 552191 7   £12.99

The Official Motorcycling Manual

The authoritative guide to motorcycling, containing new graphics and photographs and updated to include the very latest information and advice. An essential reference book for motorcyclists who are keen to improve their machine handling and safety skills, including expert guidance on riding in traffic, defensive driving, in bad weather and at night.

0 11 552193 3   £9.99

Audio Mock Theory Test

Devised to help new drivers prepare for the Theory Test with simulated test conditions. Just ring **0930 217 217** The test takes 30 minutes to complete, callers must be 18 or over, and calls are charged at 50p per minute.

Cyberdrive

The website for new drivers - aimed to help you to pass your test and advance your driving skills:

www.cyberdrive.co.uk

Order Form

These titles are available from:

● **The Stationery Office, The Publications Centre, PO Box 276, London SW8 5DT**
Mail or Fax this order form, or telephone.
Telephone orders: 0171 873 9090 quoting ref ACH/TT
Fax orders: 0171 873 8200
General enquiries: 0171 873 0011
Online: www.tso-online.co.uk

Stationery Office publications are also available from:

● **The Stationery Office Bookshops**
(see inside back cover for details)

● **Accredited Agents and all good booksellers and multimedia retailers**

Please send me the following titles:

Title	ISBN	Quantity	Price
The Highway Code	ISBN 0 11 551977 7	....	£1.49
Test Yourself Papers for the Driving Theory Test	ISBN 0 11 551984 X	....	£4.99 (incl VAT)
The Driving Test	ISBN 0 11 552190 9	....	£6.99
Know Your Traffic Signs	ISBN 0 11 551612 3	....	£2.50
The Driving Manual	ISBN 0 11 552191 7	....	£12.99
The Motorcycling Manual	ISBN 0 11 552193 3	....	£9.99
	Handling charge per order		£2.94
	Total enclosed		£.........

PLEASE COMPLETE IN BLOCK CAPITALS

Name...

Address ....

....

.... Postcode................... | ACH/TT |

☐ I enclose a cheque for £.................... payable to: *'The Stationery Office'*

☐ Please charge to my account with The Stationery Office, No:

....

☐ Please debit my Mastercard/Visa/Amex/Connect/Diners card Account No.

Signature... Expiry date ....

☐ Please tick if you do not wish to receive further details on titles from The Stationery Office.
Prices are correct at time of going to press but may be subject to change without notice. Stationery Office Account holders should note that credit card transactions will not appear on their statements. A full listing of terms and conditions of sale can be obtained on request from The Stationery Office Publications Centre, 51 Nine Elms Lane, London SW8 5DR.